# COUNTIES IN
# COURT

# COUNTIES IN COURT

## Jail Overcrowding and Court-Ordered Reform

Wayne N. Welsh

TEMPLE UNIVERSITY PRESS

*Philadelphia*

Temple University Press, Philadelphia 19122
Copyright © 1995 by Temple University. All rights reserved
Published 1995
Printed in the United States of America

⊗ The paper used in this book meets the requirements of the American National
Standard for Information Sciences—Permanence of Paper for Printed Library Materials,
ANSI Z39.48-1984

Text design by Gore Studio, Inc., Nashville

**Library of Congress Cataloging-in-Publication Data**

Welsh, Wayne N., 1957–
Counties in court : jail overcrowding and court-ordered reform /
Wayne N. Welsh.
p.   cm.
Includes bibliographical references and index.
ISBN 1-56639-340-X. — ISBN 1-56639-341-8 (pbk.)
1. Prisons—United States—Overcrowding.   2. Jails—United States—
Overcrowding.   3. Criminal justice, Administration of—United
States.   I. Title.
HV9471.W46   1995
365'.6—dc20                                        94-47139

*To Dea, Hadrian, and Sabina*
*May the Gods and Goddesses always be with you*

# Contents

# Figures and Tables

## Figures

## Tables

# Preface

Heeding the country's alarm over street violence, the Senate over-whelmingly passed a $23 billion anti-crime bill yesterday to put 100,000 more police on city streets, build more prisons and ban the sale of combat-style firearms. . . . On the broad anti-crime measure, Senate Judiciary Committee Chairman Joseph R. Biden Jr. (D., Del.) said, "Crime is the single most pressing issue on the minds of the American people."

**—Carol Skorneck, Associated Press, 1993**

Only deep moral values . . . can hold back . . . the encroaching jungle of crime and disorder . . . and restrain the darker impulses of human nature.

**—Ronald Reagan, speech to the International Association of Chiefs of Police, 1981**

ONCE AGAIN, fear of crime is the hottest political issue around. We stand poised to "get tough" on crime yet again, even though jails and prisons are already filled well beyond capacity. Ten regional state-federal prisons proposed by the Senate in its 1993 crime bill, at a cost of $3 billion, will scarcely dent current overcrowding in state and federal prisons, let alone make room for more. Chronic overcrowding in the nation's city and county jails was not even addressed. Even if new prisons were to fractionally reduce overcrowding, the twentieth century has taught us two lessons well: New prisons fill up almost as soon as they open, and there are always several offenders standing in line to take the place of each one who is temporarily removed from the streets.

As the numbers of men and women incarcerated in local, state, and federal prisons reached record levels in the 1980s, institutions all across the country were being sued for violating prisoners' constitutional rights. Although we often act and talk as if we could simply "lock them all up and throw away the key," the simple and sobering truth is that we may detain or punish only in accordance with minimum standards set by state and federal law. When we advocate severe punishment for all law violators, we forget that half of those detained in city or county jails are technically innocent, awaiting trial. We forget that only a portion of inmates (50 percent or less) in state or federal prisons were convicted of violent offenses (U.S. Department of Justice 1992c, 7). Equally overlooked is evidence that increased incarceration rates rarely correspond to increases in actual crime rates. The dramatic, incremental increases in incarceration rates throughout the 1980s were neither prompted nor accompanied by any comparable increase in crime rates, regardless of which measure of crime is used (see, e.g., National Crime Survey or Uniform Crime Report statistics).

While many problems beside overcrowding have been the subject of lawsuits against jails and prisons (e.g., inadequate and negligent provision of medical care, chronic breakdowns in facility maintenance, failure to provide adequate levels of supervision and safety), overcrowding compounded all other problems of correctional administration. As court decrees required officials to reduce inmate populations by all means necessary, a permanent sense of crisis set in. Officials quickly realized that they could not build enough jail beds in their lifetimes to meet projected needs, even when they resorted to high-interest debit financing through bond issues that further weakened the long-term economic prospects of their communities. Cities and counties across the country have been in the midst of their own economic crises, struggling just to maintain basic services.

The jail crisis spread throughout the criminal justice system and has affected every facet of criminal justice processing: from arrest to charging, from prosecution to sentencing, from probation to incarceration to parole. Criminal justice is primarily a *local* affair, and cities and counties receive the brunt of the workload because the vast majority of criminal defendants are arrested, held, charged, detained, and prosecuted at the city and county levels.

The public and their elected officials express outrage about the use of "early release" to reduce jail and prison populations. In jurisdictions such as Houston, convicted offenders serve approximately one-twelfth of their sentences because of severe overcrowding and court-imposed population caps at the Harris County Jail. The perception is that these early releasees laugh at the system and then continue their interrupted criminal careers without remorse or mercy. The murder of basketball

star Michael Jordan's father by an "early-released" offender in North
Carolina provides at least one vivid example lending credence to these
fears. Could it be that our attempts to "get tough" have actually resulted
in "getting soft," via the burden of overcrowding and court orders? If
so, what is the solution? Do we change our state and federal laws so as
to deny rights to accused and convicted offenders, or must we change
our norms about what constitutes acceptable punishments for different
types of crime? Is it possible to do both, or neither, and with what effects?

At its most fundamental level, this book is about criminal justice
in America. It is about organizational change in local criminal justice
systems as a result of unanticipated and unwanted intervention by the
courts. It is about the interaction of criminal justice agencies and government officials that affect fiscal and policy decisions regarding corrections. It is about public fears of crime and legislative responses. It is
about conditions of confinement in the nation's front-line intake centers for criminal justice. It is about the soaring overcrowding that began
in the late 1970s and has, with little abatement, continued ever since.

The book also probes within the "black box" surrounding the onset,
process, and outcome of social policy litigation and the limits of court-
ordered change. It is about the mobilization of legal action against jails
for unconstitutional conditions of confinement, and the responses of
public officials to legal complaints. It is about bitterly contested lawsuits involving plaintiffs (inmates) and their attorneys (public, private,
and "ideologically committed" attorneys from groups such as the
American Civil Liberties Union), and defendants (sheriffs, jail commanders, county commissioners and supervisors) and their attorneys
(usually permanent employees of the county). It is about judges in state
and federal courts who hear these protracted lawsuits and shape remedial decrees. It is about the critical aspects of local legal and political
environments that shape the onset, process, and outcomes of jail lawsuits. We can understand jail overcrowding, court orders, and responses by county officials only by locating these phenomena within
their proper social and historical contexts.

It is fashionable to be cynical these days. Criminal justice in general,
and corrections in particular, seems to have settled into a permanent
state of crisis. Court orders against jails and prisons abound, crime rates
remain unacceptably high, and long-term solutions to criminal justice
problems seem as elusive as the mythical philosopher's stone. At the
same time, courts have set limits on acceptable conditions of confinement; they have opened an important dialogue that was forced us to

reexamine our willingness and capacity to punish; and they have stimulated more proactive responses by criminal justice and government officials. Inquiries about court intervention are no longer usefully served by normative arguments alone (should the courts intervene, "yea" or "nay"?). We must ask how and why lawsuits against jails begin, proceed, and end; what are the critical factors that dynamically influence litigation onset, process, and outcome; and how much real change is possible. My goal is to systematically address these important questions.

I wish to express my gratitude to my friend and former advisor Henry Pontell for providing a nurturing environment during the time that a large part of the data for this project was collected. I also thank two other colleagues, Matt Leone and Pat Kinkade, who assisted in collecting some of the data.

Thanks to Doris Braendel, Senior Acquisitions Editor for Temple University Press, for her patience and guidance in bringing this book to realization. I especially thank an anonymous reviewer for two rounds of the most detailed and helpful comments I could ask for. Naturally, any errors or omissions are my responsibility alone.

Finally, I thank my wife, Dea, for all her love and support.

# COUNTIES IN
# COURT

# CHAPTER 1

## Introduction

If the public, through its judicial and penal system, finds it necessary to incarcerate a person, basic concepts of decency, as well as reasonable respect for constitutional rights, require that he be provided a bed.

**—Judge William P. Gray, *Stewart v. Gates*, 1978**

Not the least of the Sheriff's problems is the abysmal design of the jail. Architecturally, the jail is a gross case of malpractice in design.

**—Judge James L. Facht, *Hudler v. Duffy*, 1980**

Replacement [of the jail] must occur regardless of the source of funds. . . . The Court's power in this regard is a negative one: it cannot order respondent board of supervisors to appropriate funds. But it can, and will, order the facility closed, if necessary, to eliminate unlawful conditions.

**—Judge Richard A. Bancroft, *Smith v. Dyer*, 1983**

This court will not tolerate the miserable overcrowding in the jail which was existent in March when these hearings began. The responsible executives in the Sheriff's Office, Board of Supervisors, and the County Executive have offered nothing whatever in response to this most pressing problem.

**—Judge Bruce Allen, *Branson v. Winter*, 1982**

O VER THE PAST twenty or so years, courts have found conditions of confinement in many jails and prisons to be in violation of constitutional guarantees such as the Eight Amendment (banning cruel and unusual punishment) and the Fourteenth Amendment (guaranteeing due process rights). Correctional and government officials have been or-

3

dered to make sweeping changes to comply with court directives: to improve medical care and recreation services, to reduce chronic overcrowding, to increase staffing levels and improve training, to make use of various pretrial and postconviction release mechanisms, even to build new facilities—all under the watchful eye of the court.

In 1993, 40 states had at least one state prison under a court order or consent decree to limit population or improve general conditions of confinement; 11 of these states were operating their entire prison system under judicial decree (National Prison Project 1993). Many states (e.g., Alabama, Arkansas, Florida, Georgia, Mississippi, Rhode Island, Texas) have faced judicial scrutiny since the mid-1970s. Jail litigation did not develop as quickly as prison litigation. Prisons were bigger game, and jails received less press coverage. The statutory grounding for litigation, however, was similar, and litigation filed against jails steadily increased after 1980 (Taft 1983). In 1992, 27 precent of the nation's large jails (those with 100 inmates or more) were under court order to reduce overcrowding and/or improve general conditions of confinement (U.S. Department of Justice 1993). Overcrowding, the problem most frequently cited in court orders, severely limits an institution's capacity to provide adequate safety, medical care, food service, recreation, and sanitation.[1]

If we are ever to understand how our cities and counties got into this jail litigation "mess," or if we are ever to find our way out of it, we must more systematically locate problems, causes, and interventions within the broader legal, political, and organizational environments of jails. The problems of jails neither begin nor end at the gates of the institution. As Hans Mattick observed twenty years ago:

> Only a systematic, fundamental, sustained, and cooperative effort on the part of the legislative, judicial, and executive branches of government at all levels, together with an interested and informed public, will enable the jails of the United States to play a constructive role in a rational system of criminal justice. The problems that beset jails will not be "solved" by improvising a piecemeal political patchwork of minor ameliorations. They will not yield to the political opportunism of scapegoating a few jail administrators who are the prisoners of conditions over which they have little control. If we are serious about jail reform, more basic methods and changes are required. (Mattick 1974, 822)

This book attempts to identify some of the major gaps in our current knowledge about court-ordered reform and to define the questions and controversies we need to address. Seven key themes guide my analysis.

1. While most of the research on court-ordered correctional reform has examined state or federal prisons, city-or county-operated jails are distinct from state and federal prisons, and their unique problems require separate analysis.

2. The complex ways in which criminal justice agencies, governments, courts, and litigants interact to shape jail problems and policy responses have rarely been explicit foci of analysis. This gap calls for an explicit interagency approach to court-ordered change.

3. The impact of local environments on jail problems and litigation needs to be systematically analyzed. Unique dimensions of local legal and political environments (e.g., state statutory and regulatory law, local crime rates and punishment practices) dynamically influence the onset, process, and outcomes of litigation.

4. Previous analyses have failed to explain why most jails are not under court order, nor are they able to account for differences across jurisdictions that are under court order. A comparative approach can help identify which contextual factors distinguish cities or counties under court order from those that are not.

5. Legal process variables in jail litigation include level of court, nature of plaintiffs' and defendants' legal representation, and type of defendants. We need to investigate the interactive influence of these variables across a sample of jail reform lawsuits.

6. Impacts of court-ordered jail reform need to be examined empirically rather than speculatively, and different levels of change (at both micro and macro levels) must be considered. What are the intended and unintended outcomes of court-ordered change? How does change in one agency or institution affect entire justice systems?

7. Jail litigation raises questions about the usefulness of law as a means of social reform. What role do civil courts play in reforming jails, and to what degree do courts have the capacity to effect meaningful change in public institutions?

In this book, I develop an integrative model of jail litigation in order to explore the complex legal, organizational, and political factors that shape litigation and its impacts in an ongoing, dynamic manner. The data and analyses presented illustrate the systemic and political nature of jail litigation, and examine how connections between justice agencies, government, and the courts influence jail problems, court-ordered reforms, and outcomes.

## Differences Between Jails and Prisons

The "central evil" of jails is perhaps the fact of local administration (Mattick 1974). Jails are different from prisons. For one thing, they are operated at the municipal or county, rather than state or federal, level. Unlike prisons, they house convicted offenders generally serving sentences of one year or less and also pretrial detainees, typically about 50 percent of the jail's daily population (U.S. Department of Justice 1993). The latter point is particularly important. Any newly charged suspect, legally innocent until proven guilty, begins his or her journey through the justice system by being booked and charged at the local jail. If police form the "front line" of the criminal justice system, then jails are surely the second.

While serious problems in prison administration persist, conditions in local jails are often even more pronounced.

> Once a penal institution becomes part of a state correctional system, it is more likely to receive the attention of professional administrators who may be concerned with the possibility of instituting corrections functions; it is less likely to be a patronage dumping ground; uniform standards may be formulated and enforced; specialization of institutions and initial and in-service training of personnel can be undertaken; economies of scale become possible; transfers of prisoners and personnel between institutions become easier; civil service and merit promotions can be introduced; and, in general, more financial, human, and other resources become available. (Mattick 1974, 778)

The politics and demographics of jails are quite different from those of state or federal prisons, and their unique problems require separate analysis. First of all, jails have a very large turnover relative to prisons. There is a constant flow of inmates in and out of the jail, and the average inmate stays less than three days. Consequently, jails are characterized by a high number of both admissions and discharges. From 1990 to 1991, there were over 20 million admissions and releases from local jails (U.S. Department of Justice 1992a). Further, because jails are usually operated by the county, rather than the state, they face different fiscal pressures than do prisons (Advisory Commission on Intergovernmental Relations 1984). Counties have fewer discretionary funds available than do states; indeed, many counties are faced with strict limits on taxation and spending imposed by acts of state legislatures and the federal government. Further, local politics are often volatile (Welsh et al. 1990). Influential actors—including sheriffs, judges, district attorneys, and county commissioners or supervisors (who are responsible for fiscal allocations)—are locally elected and must keep one eye on their constituents' fears and prejudices.

Research on corrections has largely concentrated upon prisons and ignored jails. A major reason for this deficiency has been the poor record-keeping practices of jails, and the lack of comprehensive jail surveys until the 1970s. Several good overviews of jail problems exist (e.g., Flynn 1983; Goldfarb 1975; Hall 1985, 1987; Mattick 1974). Empirical studies of jail operations (e.g., Abt Associates 1980; Gibbs 1983; Irwin 1985; Jackson 1991; Klofas 1987) or of jail litigation (Champion 1991; Kerle and Ford 1982; Mays and Bernat 1988; Welsh 1990, 1992a, 1992b, 1993a; Welsh and Pontell 1991) have been less common. However, lawsuits over jail conditions have refocused the attention of the courts, the public, policymakers, and researchers alike on the problems of jails (Feeley and Hanson 1986, 1990; Taft 1983). Thus, while the problems of jails are relatively old, constitutional challenges and court intervention are comparatively new.

## A History of the Problem

Jails in the United States have been overcrowded and characterized by poor living conditions virtually since their inception. Recent massive increases in jail populations (from 158,394 in 1978 to 444,584 in 1992) have only magnified such longstanding problems as inadequate medical care, unsanitary living conditions, insufficient food services, exercise, and recreation, vague and discretionary disciplinary procedures, poorly trained and poorly paid staff, inadequate staffing levels, and institutional violence. These problems are not new, nor are they explainable purely by conditions within jails themselves.

Jail problems have been uncovered and compounded in recent years by government budget crises, "get tough" criminal justice policies, and civil lawsuits that have resulted in court orders to reform unconstitutional conditions of confinement. The result has been public and political backlash when jails are forced to relase inmates early or even to deny new admissions because of court-imposed population caps (Babcock 1990; Cuvelier et al. 1992; Dunbaugh 1990). To understand how "jail overcrowding" and court orders against jails have come to be defined as social problems in the United States, we need to locate jails within an interconnected system of criminal justice and county government, and within their historical, social, and cultural context.

The U.S. jail system has its roots in twelfth-century England as a device used by the county (shire) and its sheriff to detain people temporarily pending trial (Advisory Commission on Intergovernmental Relations 1984; Mattick 1974). It was not a place of punishment, but the massive population displacement and increases in crimes brought about by industrialization and urbanization in England led to the passage of many new laws to control the dislocated and disorderly "rabble" (Irwin 1985). The jail became a tool of these policies.

Like their European counterparts, eighteenth-century American jails were used to detain persons pending state trial or some form of state punishment, complete with fee-type compensation for jail keepers. Prior to the American Revolution, incarceration as a form of punishment was rare. Instead, public and corporal punishments were the norm. Colonists' postrevolutionary concern for basic human rights and their fear of unrestrained government power over citizens eventually led to calls for reform.

Following the Declaration of Independence, colonists attempted various criminal code reforms based partly on their own adverse reactions to their earlier European experience, but also influenced by Enlightenment thinkers and the socially conscious, reform-oriented Quakers. Death penalties and corporal punishments were abolished except for the most serious crimes, and fines or periods of imprisonment took their place. At about the same time, the newly created states began to build their own state-run facilities for more serious offenders. It is something of a historical curiosity that jails took charge of less serious offenders and pretrial arrestees, while state prisons took charge of the more serious felons who previously would have been punished corporally or executed. This distinction may have been rooted in both convenience and precedent. Jails were already in existence and were handling a large turnover of minor offenders by the 1820s, and the temporary jailing of debtors, drunks, vagrants, and prostitutes had been common practice in England for many years (Mattick 1974, 784).

Early reformers clearly emphasized rehabilitation, yet they did not suggest that jails or prisons should be pleasant places. In 1867, the Pennsylvania Prison Society noted that its purpose was,

> not to destroy prisons, not to destroy their just terrors, but to have their discipline so regulated that no bad principles in the man incarcerated shall be made worse, and the whole administration of the penal laws so modified and enforced, that no injustice, no extreme of infliction, and no sentiment of maudlin humanity shall make the prison less than a place in which to guarantee society against violence and fraud, and to ensure to the guilty a just punishment for crime, while that punishment is made to minister to the moral improvement of the convicted offender. (Quoted in Atherton 1987, 4)

The negative effects of isolation were not anticipated, nor was the flood of inmates that soon inundated the jail (Allen and Simonsen

1986; Mullen 1985). In fact, the director of Philadelphia's Walnut Street Jail resigned in 1801 in disgust at the horrible conditions that had developed there (Mullen 1985). In 1820, a committee of the Pennsylvania Society of Friends visited the jail and decided that the current building was unfit; prisoners were not being adequately segregated according to age, sex, or offense; overcrowding severely weakened the penal goal of reform; and prisoners were too often idle. Larger and better-planned facilities, rather than abandonment of the "separate" system of confinement, were seen as the solution. State prisons based on the Pennsylvania system were erected in Pittsburgh (Western Penitentiary), Philadelphia (Eastern Penitentiary), and several eastern states (Hawkins and Alpert 1989). Competing models of imprisonment—such as the "congregate" system at Auburn, New York—emerged at about the same time. The idea of incarceration as a social response to crime was becoming firmly entrenched.

As in England, the advent and expansion of the industrial age in America was accompanied by social upheaval, displacement of people from the countryside to the city, and a vastly increased correctional population. Although displacement appears to have followed, rather than preceded, the construction of large prisons in America (Hawkins and Alpert 1989), it is clear that jail and prison capacities rarely kept pace with admissions. By the early nineteenth century, most large cities or counties had erected jails. As industrialization expanded into the West and Midwest, jails proliferated as a means of controlling increasing numbers of unruly persons, thieves, and drifters (Irwin 1985).

Despite two hundred years of periodic reforms, modern jails are criticized for many of the same problems as their ancestors: inadequately trained personnel; official misuse, misjudgment, or mismanagement of capacity; failure to provide for basic human needs while expending maximum fiscal resources; and failure to protect the safety of inmates or the public (Advisory Commission on Intergovernmental Relations 1984). To some, the jail has become an infamous veteran of government institutions: "a millenarian albatross that has remained stubbornly immune to successive attempts toward reform" (Advisory Commission on Intergovernmental Relations 1984, 3).

Chronic deficiencies in jail conditions have included inadequate (or absent) medical care, little or no recreation, poor sanitation (e.g., chronically inadequate and malfunctioning plumbing; rodent and insect infestation), poor food services (inadequate nutritional content, quantities, and delivery of food), and inadequate personal safety (homicides, suicides, gang violence, and sexual assault). Alvin Bronstein, director of the ACLU's National Prison Project, provides a vivid list of such conditions:

> physical brutality, gross medical neglect, the silence rules, racial discrimination, kangaroo courts for disciplinary matters, incredible tortures such as the Tucker telephone (a device used at the Tucker reformatory in Arkansas where live telephone wires were attached to the prisoner's genitals), hot boxes and dark cells (segregation cells with a solid door and no light), chain gangs, bread and water diets and worse, economic exploitation by the convict lease system and otherwise, rigid censorship of mail and reading matter, narrowly restricted visitation rights, along with meaningless and brutally hard work. The list is lengthy and as varied as the depth of human cruelty, about which Auschwitz and Attica have taught us so much. (Bronstein 1980, 20)

Such abuses have been well documented in state prison systems, such as those of Texas (e.g., Martin and Ekland-Olson 1987; Crouch and Marquart 1989), Alabama (Yackle 1989), and Arkansas (Harris and Spiller 1977).

## Litigation as a Means of Jail Reform

*The Prisoner Rights Movement*

Until recent years, the courts followed a "hands-off" policy regarding corrections. Courts refused to hear prisoner rights cases, essentially viewing the inmate as a "slave of the state" who had forfeited his/her rights as a consequence of his/her crime. The courts generally claimed that they lacked jurisdiction over such matters, and deferred to the presumed administrative expertise of prison officials.

Two cases were significant in changing this hands-off policy. The Supreme Court decision in *Monroe v. Pape* (1961), which resurrected the Civil Rights Act of 1871, allowed lawyers to seek damages and injunctions in federal courts for state abuses against individual rights. The first corrections case heard under the Civil Rights Act was *Cooper v. Pate* (1964), concerning allegations of religious discrimination against imprisoned Black Muslims. The scope of the Supreme Court decision was narrow, but it was highly significant in allowing inmates to pursue their constitutional rights in court. The Supreme Court issued an affirmation of prisoner rights in *Wolff v. McDonnell* (1974): "There is no iron curtain drawn between the Constitution and the prisons of this country" (418 U.S. 539 at 555).

Several important decisions have followed (thoroughly reviewed in

Bronstein 1980; Call 1986; Cooper 1988; Jacobs 1980; Palmer 1987; Robbins 1987). Jail litigation on behalf of pretrial prisoners often alleges violations of due process under the Fourth and Fourteenth Amendments, while convicted prisoners often claim violations of the Eighth Amendment, which bans cruel and unusual punishment. This is an important distinction.

*Bell v. Wolfish* (1979) set the precedent for litigation involving pretrial prisoners. The case addressed conditions of confinement in a large New York City jail. The Court ruled that double-bunking was not unconstitutional per se, and that obtrusive security measures like body cavity searches were not unconstitutional where genuine security interests were at stake. *Bell v. Wolfish* established that the constitutional standard for pretrial detainees is whether the conditions they were subjected to constituted punishment or not; due process considerations prevent the state from applying sanctions to those not yet found guilty of any crime.

*Rhodes v. Chapman* (1981) significantly affected litigation involving convicted inmates. The Supreme Court decision confirmed that the Eighth amendment is the standard to be used for such cases. It was the first time the Court interpreted that amendment in the context of jail or prison overcrowding, indicating that: "conditions must not involve the wanton and unnecessary infliction of pain, nor may they be grossly disproportionate to the severity of the crime warranting punishment" (452 U.S. 337 at 339). *Rhodes v. Chapman* thus framed the new standard of constitutionality for convicted offenders. Yet the Court's decision reiterated the need for judges to defer to the expertise of correctional administrators while doing little to clarify what conditions actually violated constitutional guarantees. As a result, the lower courts often take conflicting approaches, with some concentrating on a "totality of conditions" approach prescribed by the Supreme Court, and others focusing on "core conditions" such as medical care, prisoner safety, and sanitation (Gottlieb 1988). The Supreme Court refused to review these standards in subsequent cases, presenting lower courts with a difficult task.

In a more recent ruling, *Wilson v. Seiter* (1991), based heavily on *Estelle v. Gamble* (1976), the Supreme Court ruled that conditions of confinement were not unconstitutional unless deliberate indifference to basic human needs could be demonstrated. It is not yet clear whether this ruling has had a chilling effect on prisoner litigation, although some argue that its issuance led to the immediate dismissal of many prisoners' claims in lower federal courts (Wohl 1992). The *Wilson v.*

*Seiter* ruling certainly increases the burden of proof upon plaintiffs. Some fear that defendants may simply cite the lack of funds to avoid "deliberate indifference" claims, but previous rulings by federal courts (e.g., *Gates v. Collier*, 1974; *Miller v. Carson*, 1975) make such excuses questionable (see also Koren et al. 1988, 17–43).

### Controversies over Judicial Intervention

U.S. courts have become increasingly involved in social policy cases since the 1960s (Cooper 1988; Feeley and Krislov 1985; Horowitz 1977; Neely 1981). Although U.S. courts have traditionally heard a larger variety of policy-related cases than courts in other countries, the involvement of judges was new in at least three ways. First, many completely new areas of adjudication were opened up in housing, welfare, and prisoner rights, largely because of legislative neglect: "The very idea is sometimes to handle a problem unsatisfactorily resolved by another branch of government" (Horowitz 1977, 6). Second, the types of remedies pursued by courts have become more complex, often requiring a whole course of conduct rather than one simple act. Finally, such litigation has tended more toward explicit problem-solving and less toward traditional grievance-answering.

Judicial intervention in corrections has been controversial (Bronstein 1980; Cooper 1988; Frug 1978; Glazer 1975, 1978). The separation of powers (among legislative, executive, and judicial branches) may be violated, and judges may lack the necessary expertise to make reform-oriented changes in corrections. Further, judicial intervention is reactive rather than proactive. Courts narrowly define and respond to the particular issues put before them, not to the range of issues that are intertwined in complex social problems (Millemann 1980). Fact finding in adjudication is said to be ill-adapted to determination of social facts, the recurrent patterns of behavior on which policy is based. Judges function at some distance from the social milieu, and tend to handle social facts either by neglect or by improvisation (Horowitz 1977).

Social policy cases concern polycentric problems (Fuller 1978), and it is difficult to forecast effects and structure solutions. Courts are more likely to prohibit current courses of action than to direct positive reform, and they look to past doctrine to form decisions, so that change in this context is likely to be slow and piecemeal (Horowitz 1977). Courts are also ill-equipped to monitor compliance with their directives, although the growing use of "special masters" for this purpose has achieved significant results in some cases.

In addition to problems raised by the adjudicative process, problems surface with personnel—judges and lawyers (Horowitz 1977). First of all, judges must assume a "generalist" position, filling knowledge gaps with their own "generalized normative axioms." It is difficult for them to process specialized information related to correctional administration, such as prison classification measures. Second, legal reasoning tends to be nonprobabilistic and absolute. Lawyers' tendency to invent hypothetical arguments and articulate all possible contingencies (in the enforcement of the decree, for example) may impose overly complex requirements on legal processes.

On the other hand, there may also be important advantages to having courts, as opposed to legislative or executive branches, deal with policy cases. First, their decisions must be based on evidence and reasoning, while other branches may be less "rational." Moreover, precise steps of procedure for hearing and deciding cases are spelled out in advance, and the judicial process, at least ideally, is less subject to political influences than other branches are.

## Law and Social Change

Courts have arguably become the "final repositories of social trust" (Lieberman 1981) for inmates with no other recourse. Inmates receive little sympathy from the public or their elected officials. As a result, correctional institutions in general, and jails in particular, have long escaped public scrutiny. Bronstein (1980) points out the implications of this apathy.

> Of crucial importance . . . has been the invisibility of these institutions. Prisons are usually far away, physically and emotionally. . . . the community ordinarily has as little interest in the people it sends to prison as most of us have in our garbage—we want it disposed of safely, quickly, and without much mess, but we don't particularly care how. (Bronstein 1980, 7)

Perspectives on law and social change have traditionally been guided by two questions (Handler 1978): To what degree can the legal system be used to change social institutions or structural conditions; and to what degree is law merely a codification of societal practices and attitudes? These competing traditions (law as a change agent versus law as repository of social norms) have influenced much thinking about court-ordered correctional reform. Prisoner litigation can be viewed both as an outgrowth of social change and as an impetus toward it.

The growth of prisoners' rights was indeed facilitated by social and cultural change in the United States. C. Ronald Huff dates "the real trust and momentum which brought about a rapid proliferation of prisoners' rights" to the 1960s (1980, 47). The extension of legal rights to prisoners can be seen as a manifestation of social differentiation and the development of mass society. As societies move from simple to complex, their systems of social control become increasingly formal and codified (Durkheim 1947 [1893]). Informal control mechanisms are unlikely to suffice in more complex societies, and there is a greater need to clarify the rights and responsibilities associated with each social position. Although penology was not widely integrated into formal legal codes prior to the 1970s, "the discovery of prisoners' rights signals the emergence of a more formal model of penal jurisprudence" (Huff 1980, 50). The evolution of an increasingly sophisticated, formal codification of prisoners' rights can be seen as an example of the evolution of law in society.

Continuing in a Durkheimian approach, we might also argue that the predominant social and institutional norms and values in a mass society tend to be extended over time to include previously marginal groups (Huff 1980). Prisoners, like other marginal groups, gained a measure of credibility and influence as civil rights concerns gained attention and precipitated various legal and social actions to gain greater recognition of basic rights (Graham 1970). As a result, the 1960s and early 1970s witnessed increasing public and official attention to the dignity and humanity of the masses (see also Rosenberg 1991) and the extension of legal rights to certain minority groups, including prisoners.

Court-ordered change can also play a causal role, leading to important changes in the use of social control in society—not necessarily the ones intended. Thus, court-imposed population caps may lead to frantic attempts by policymakers to reduce inmate populations in current facilities and mostly unsuccessful plans to raise enough money to construct new facilities. Expanding probation, parole, and "alternatives" to incarceration as means of coping with growing offender populations (Cohen 1979) may make social control more diffuse and pervasive. In California, 2 percent of all residents eighteen years of age or older were under correctional supervision in 1992, with 182,000 in jail or prison, and 380,000 on probation or parole (Petersilia 1992). Moreover, intermediate sanctions adopted as "alternatives" to cope with overcrowding (Byrne, Lurigio, and Petersilia 1992; Morris and Tonry 1990; Petersilia 1987) often become "supplements" to the incarcerative apparatus, rather than effecting needed population reductions (Austin and Krisberg 1982; Busher 1983; Scull 1984).

Litigation can be a double-edged sword. Court rulings may question how jails and prisons are operated or legitimize the widespread use of incarceration (Millemann 1980). Because inmates lack political power, litigation may be the only way to create and implement basic prisoner rights. But how far do the legal rights of individual prisoners extend, and how much broad structural change is implied or driven by court intervention (see Bronstein 1980; Huff 1980)? Unfortunately, litigated change may suggest to many that prisons have become humane, even "country clubs," while in reality such change more often leads to minimal reform and compliance with very basic constitutional standards. The mistaken impression that the courts have vindicated jails and prisons through their very limited demands for reform is what David Rothman (1973) calls the "noble lie": the notion that with some tinkering, prisons can be made humane or rehabilitative.

At the same time, court intervention, coupled with fiscal realities, has led us to reconsider our entire system of criminal sanctions. Strong signals by the courts that overcrowded and inhumane conditions of incarceration will not be tolerated have inevitably limited the effectiveness of simplistic "get tough" programs such as the "war on drugs." Through the unrelenting passage of new and tougher laws sending more people to prison for longer periods of time, the war on drugs in the 1980s contributed to massive expenditures for prison construction, early releases of inmates, a shortage of experienced correctional staff, but no declines in crime (Austin and McVey 1989). It is ironic that the overuse of criminal sanctions and overconfidence in their presumed deterrent effects actually leads to a diminished capacity to punish (Pontell 1984). In fact, the "common knowledge" that crime is increasing, or that our need to punish is increasing, is at best questionable (Clear and Harris 1987). Even the most conservative thinkers have begun to ask whether prison can punish in an effective or humane manner, for which crimes it is suitable, and for which crimes and offenders certain nonincarcerative sanctions are appropriate. And yet, public officials seem reluctant to question the overuse of jails. John Irwin (1985) argues that jails serve a latent function of "controlling the underclass," including drug addicts and the mentally ill. Herbert Packer (1968) argues that overextension of the criminal justice system taxes its credibility and capacity: "Another, more benign but equally illegitimate, covert function is the use of the criminal sanction to perform needed social services that for one reason or another we are not prepared to perform directly and on their own merits" (p. 294).

While much dichotomous thinking in the past contrasted law as a "repository of social norms" with law as a "vehicle of social change," a more sophisticated question with genuine policy implications has gained priority: In which situations can the law be used to effect change, and which contingencies facilitate or impede such attempts at change? This book attempts to shed light on these and other unanswered questions about court-ordered correctional reform.

## Models of Court-Ordered Change

Making sense of the complexities involved in the court-ordered reform of public institutions requires us to synthesize, integrate, and simplify diverse findings. As a result, many authors have formulated models of court-ordered change that attempt to explicate the major contingencies mediating the effects of court-ordered reform. Most commonly, the models express legal outcomes as a result of two key variables: the nature of judicial intervention, and defendants' willingness or ability to comply. Most of these models oversimplify. They inadequately operationalize the predictive variables and the outcomes they hypothesize, and they leave out critical stages of litigation onset, process, and outcome.

In one such model, Robert Wood (1990) suggests that the level of judicial intervention (low, intermediate, or high) should be based on three contingencies: the breadth of constitutional violations (narrow, intermediate, or broad), the competence of the target agency (low, intermediate, or high), and the support within the larger political culture for the court's actions (low, intermediate, or high). According to this model, problems occur when there is a mismatch between level of judicial intervention and the contingencies affecting outcome—for example, when judicial intervention is high, but constitutional violations are narrow, the target agency is competent, and the political community is supportive. Unfortunately, the key variables are not well operationalized, and the assignment of any legal case to any one of the cells in a three-by-three matrix is highly subjective. Thus, "level of judicial intervention" oversimplifies the judicial role by operationalizing "low" intervention as a consent decree, "intermediate" judicial intervention as "bench oversight," and "high" judicial intervention as "receivership." Such examples grossly underestimate the range, flexibility, and dynamic fluctuation of judicial behavior in social reform cases. The model is conceptually useful in diagramming a limited portion of what judges and litigants do, but has limited utility for capturing the complexities of court-ordered reform and generating empirically testable hypotheses.

The model proposed by Erwin Hargrove and John Glidewell (1990) focuses more narrowly on the judicial role. The roles of judges in social policy cases, it is argued, resemble other "impossible jobs" in public management, which are characterized by high conflict, low legitimacy of clients, and low respect for professional authority. The model has face validity and provides a conceptually useful framework for locating social policy cases within their larger social milieu. Unfortunately, the concepts are not easy to operationalize, and the analytical process becomes somewhat subjective. In the example of court-ordered jail reform, one might suggest that conflict is high because of the adversarial nature of legal proceedings, but also because of the diverse constituencies with an interest in correctional policy and expenditures—inmates, the public, correctional officials, various county agencies, county executives, state legislators. The legitimacy of clients (inmates) could be judged as low because of widespread but not unanimous perceptions that criminals are responsible for their behavior and deserve harsh punishment. Finally, the expertise and authority of judges to make decisions that influence or determine correctional policy and administration has been granted grudgingly at best (e.g., Glazer 1978). Given such circumstances, judges face considerable obstacles and frustrations. In response, they may, over time, become increasingly directive in their orders and assertive in their attempts to gain compliance.

Drawing upon work by Donald Horowitz (1977) and others, Gerald Rosenberg (1991) identifies two competing models of the court's ability to influence social policy. The "constraint" model focuses on courts' legalistic nature and limited ability to diagnose complex social problems. The "dynamic model," on the other hand, emphasizes their political autonomy and capacity for formulating incremental change. While his analysis favors the constraint model, Rosenberg attempts to identify factors influencing the level of social change resulting from court intervention in specific areas like desegregation and abortion rights.

Rosenberg suggests that courts have some effect on social conditions, but only when other political and social forces are already moving in that direction. Four conditions influence the effectiveness of court-ordered change: the availability of incentives for compliance with court orders, the availability of sanctions for noncompliance, the relevance of markets to implementing court-ordered reforms, and the degree to which institutional actors are already poised to proceed with reform and can use the courts as "scapegoats" for controversial actions.

As in other models, the concepts proposed in this framework are not easy to operationalize. The analytical process relies upon limited quantitative data and becomes somewhat subjective. For example,

Rosenberg examines the degree to which media coverage of cases like *Brown v. Board of Education* (1954, 1955) heightened public awareness of desegregation. To do so, he counts the number of magazine articles on civil rights issues between 1940 and 1965. The analysis largely ignores court process: "The risk in Rosenberg's approach is treating institutions, including the courts, as little more than black boxes through which some kind of exogenous social energy passes on its way to constituting new political forms" (Simon 1992, 939). The model also fails to emphasize the courts' interaction with legal and political environments, local institutional conditions, and surrounding social conditions to produce diverse micro- and macro-level changes.

All such models, however, despite their limitations, have furthered our understanding of how law influences social change and broadened the questions we ask about court-ordered reform. We are no longer content to debate *whether* judges exercise power in the political realm, or *whether* they should do so or not. Instead, we have begun to seek answers to more complicated, policy-relevant questions: *How* and *why* are legal challenges to institutional conditions mobilized? *How* do litigants and judges exercise power in particular environments? *What* changes (both intended and unintended) occur in institutional (micro) and social (macro) conditions? *How* do different contingencies mediate the effects of judicial intervention? My intention in this book is to develop a framework to support further theory and research in these directions—one that will allow us to consider the dynamic and interactive influence of factors within the legal, political, and organizational environments of jails, and to examine (on many levels) the emerging impacts on institutions and agencies of actions and events at previous stages. The model articulates specific outcomes to be explained at each of five stages of litigation—triggering events, determinations of legal liability, decree formulation, postdecree monitoring and compliance, and impacts—and identifies critical explanatory concepts and contingencies at each stage.

## A Research Model for Court-Ordered Reform

To evaluate court-ordered jail reform and improve policy formulation, we need a more integrated, coherent research plan. I propose a model consisting of five analytical categories: a Trigger Stage, a Liability Stage, a Remedy Stage, a Postdecree Stage, and an Impact Stage (see Figure 1). Based on Cooper's (1988) model of social policy litigation, this is an "open system" model: Input from the environment shapes the onset and transformation of disputes in a dynamic manner. Thus, the five stages continually interact; only a rough chronology is implied. Once key variables at each stage are identified, relationships between them can be further explored within an organized analytical framework.

We can examine hypotheses generated by the model through the use of several research methods, including archival analyses, case studies, interviews, and examination of justice statistics. The model prescribes a comparative approach in which hypotheses are examined across different jurisdictions and legal cases.

In the Trigger Stage, longstanding practices and policies within a particular jurisdiction act in concert with some triggering event (a change in law, a riot, a major legal decision, etc.) to push a conflict across a threshold where legal action is initiated. We need to explicitly consider the environmental inputs into this process, which include official policies and actions regarding the use of punishment and incarceration, and relevant case law and statutes affecting prisoners' access to legal forums. Which variables affect the mobilization of jail lawsuits? What influence do multiple parties exert? How do historical practices influence the probability of litigation? Jurisdictions with high incarcer-

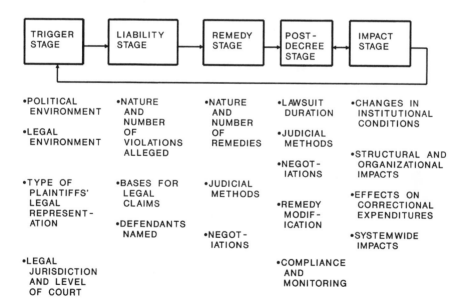

**FIGURE 1** *Research Model of Court-Ordered Jail Reform*

ation rates and low rates of expenditure, for example, are more likely
to face judicial intervention, while states with supportive statutory
laws and state constitutions foster higher rates of prisoner litigation.
Contextual factors (discussed in more detail below) include the type of
plaintiffs' legal counsel and the strategies they adopt, and whether the
lawsuit is filed in state or federal court. The onset of jail litigation and
its eventual form will be at least partly determined by such prelitigation factors, which vary across cases and across jurisdictions.

Development of a case at the Liability Stage is shaped by the interactive efforts of lawyers for plaintiffs and defendants. Each attempts to
create a strong record to shape judicial decisions. In the complaint,
several crucial decisions are made: plaintiffs' lawyers name certain officials as defendants; they allege certain violations of law; and they suggest specific remedies. Because fiscal responsibility for local jails lies
with local government, city or county officials are often named as defendants. The influence of these key actors on jail planning and reform
needs to be examined in a systematic manner. The number of violations
alleged in a case may reflect the complexity of issues in a particular
case, the animosity between litigants, or both. The number and types
of violations alleged depend upon applicable state law, strategies
adopted by plaintiffs' legal counsel, and local jail conditions and punishment practices. The specific issues litigated then play a crucial role
in transforming the initial dispute.

In the Remedy Stage, a liability opinion is issued, eventually leading to a core remedy in the form of one or more decrees. The judge must
consider the nature, scope, and duration of relief available. The nature
of relief provided is affected by the remedies plaintiffs request, the
plans defendants present, what case law and statutes allow, and the
degree to which proposed remedies provide redress of violations. The
means by which judges determine and exercise their policy range at
this stage are crucial to implementation and compliance efforts in the
Postdecree Stage. Remedies may also be influenced by such prior contextual variables as the nature and frequency of alleged violations, the
level of court chosen, and the strategies of plaintiffs' and defendants'
legal counsel. Each of these variables can be investigated across a sample of cases, and hypotheses can be examined through both quantitative and qualitative method.

In the Postdecree Stage, orders are implemented, monitored, and
refined through complex interactions between litigants, judges, and
other stakeholders. Contextual factors from prior stages (e.g., legal

representation, litigant behavior, level of court) influence judicial methods, negotiations, and the duration of a lawsuit. For example, cases involving ideologically committed plaintiff attorneys and government defendants evidence high levels of conflict. Ideologically motivated attorneys fight harder and longer as a result of their commitment and experience, while government officials mount greater resistance as a result of their political power and access to broad county resources. The complexity of a case, as indicated by the number of violations alleged in the complaint, influences lawsuit duration because a greater number of issues must be litigated, requiring more detailed presentation of evidence, testimony, expert witnesses, negotiations, formulation of plans, and monitoring. Cases heard in federal courts may last longer, on average, because of more flexible options available in federal law, and the greater expertise, resources, and persistence of federal judges. This is the stage at which courts may appoint special masters or use contempt orders to encourage compliance—two strategies that have yet to be studied in a systematic manner.

Finally, the Impact Stage focuses attention on criminal justice agencies and systems. To what degree do court-mandated jail reforms alter institutional conditions and service delivery, organizational structures, city or county correctional expenditures, and such systemic features as interagency relationships and local criminal justice processes? These impacts then provide new inputs into an ongoing, dynamic system. For example, if jail population in a specific jurisdiction rises once again to unacceptable levels, courts may reopen dormant lawsuits.

The five-stage model of court-ordered change I present here attempts to advance our understanding of jail problems and organizational reforms by integrating diverse perspectives on the causes, evolution, process, and impacts of litigation against jails. Substantial gaps in our understanding of jail problems and litigation have hindered the development of useful theory and rational policy in this area.

## Data and Methods

This book addresses the onset, process, and outcome of court-ordered jail reform in a systematic manner using several measures and methods, both qualitative and quantitative. I offer five prescriptions to overcome the shortcomings of previous scholarly work: Conduct analyses across different jurisdictions (the comparative approach); integrate qualitative and quantitative research methods (convergent data sources); describe litigation process and outcomes empirically (the empirical approach); specify and test a theoretical model of court inter-vention (the theoretical approach); and consider both intended and unintended effects of change (the open system approach).

On a national level, I use data from the quiennial Census of Jails and the Annual Survey of Jails, both conducted by the Bureau of Justice Statistics in cooperation with the U.S. Bureau of the Census, to illus-trate patterns and trends in jail operations, populations, and litigation, and to examine relationships between model variables across jail juris-dictions.

At the county level, I use comparative data obtained from a study of all jail litigation in California between 1975 and 1989 (see also Welsh 1992a; Welsh and Pontell 1991), when jails in 35 of the 58 counties (60 percent) were under court order. Because California is home to 10 of the 25 largest jail systems in the country (U.S. Department of Justice 1991a), and because its 64,000 inmates constitute the largest jail popu-lation in the United States (U.S. Department of Justice 1991a), it pro-vides a good barometer of jail problems and court orders. Studying all jail cases across a single state avoids potential confounding factors due to differences in state statutory, regulatory, and case law. A comparison of 58 counties far surpasses the limited generalizability of results from single-case studies. Generalizability of *results* to other states awaits fur-ther empirical observation, but I suggest that the *processes* affecting jail litigation onset, process, and outcome are highly similar to those described in the analytical model developed here. Indeed, the model has built upon and extended theoretical relationships and findings sug-gested by diverse but fragmented studies.

I examined three major types of data across California counties. First, statistical data were obtained from state and county agencies to assess differences and changes over time in the legal and political envi-ronments of jails (e.g., arrest rates, incarceration rates) and jail opera-tions (e.g., jail populations, correctional expenditures) across counties. Second, court documents were examined and coded to assess differ-ences in litigation process (e.g., frequency and type of alleged viola-tions) and outcome (e.g., frequency and type of relief granted). Finally, I used the more micro-level "case study" approach typical of research on jail and prison litigation to supplement other data methods. Inter-views with criminal justice and county government personnel in three jurisdictions allowed me to assess organizational climates, interorgani-zational relations, and responses to litigation. The overall methodology is described in more detail in the Appendix.

## Summary

While jail problems are not new, court intervention is relatively recent. Many argue that the capacity of the judiciary to effect meaningful reform in jails is limited, but court intervention spurs diverse adaptations and responses, including reevaluation of the purposes and forms of punishment. As change reverberates throughout local criminal justice systems, court-ordered reform requires adaptations to change by each county agency involved. The micro-level impacts of judicial intervention on correctional systems (e.g., institutional conditions) must be informed by more macro-level, comparative conceptions of the legal, social, and political context in which change occurs. I propose an integrative, comparative model of court-ordered reform that examines critical outcomes, explanatory variables, and contingencies at the Trigger, Liability, Remedy, Postdecree, and Impact stages. Accordingly, the next five chapters discuss major outcomes and influences at each phase of litigation and examine evidence across a sample of legal cases.

# CHAPTER 2

## The Trigger Stage

The experiences of numerous jurisdictions have clearly shown that the problem cannot be solved by simply creating more jail capacity. Officials in communities that have significantly increased the size of their jails have often realized belatedly that if jail overcrowding is to be dealth with effectively on a long-term basis, the problem must be factored into causes and symptoms.

**—Walter Busher,** *Jail Overcrowding*

At this point in time, the ACLU's got a goddamned hunting license, and it's not fair to us.

**—Anonymous county supervisor**

IT IS OFTEN taken for granted that punitive policies of recent years have fostered jail overcrowding, and that liberal Supreme Court rulings under the Warren (1953–1969) and Burger (1969–1986) Courts paved the way for opportunistic lawyers and reform-minded judges to intervene in the affairs of jails and prisons. Rarely is it acknowledged that more than two-thirds of the jails in the United States are *not* under court order, or that jurisdictions vary widely in actual jail conditions, including overcrowding. Such considerations illustrate the dangers of unidimensional analyses and the importance of examining largely neglected environmental factors that shape conditions leading to jail overcrowding and the initiation of jail reform lawsuits.

In the Trigger Stage, a lawsuit emerges from the interaction of unique historical conditions (e.g., practices regarding the arrest, processing, and sentencing of suspected criminal offenders) with some triggering event—an injury, a death, a riot, a major legal decision in the state or federal Supreme Court. Eventually, a conflict is transformed into a legal dispute. We need to consider the specific environmental and contextual inputs into this process. What are the relevant legal and political supports affecting legal mobilization? What influence do multiple parties exert? How do historical punishment and funding practices influence the likelihood of litigation over jail conditions?

Diverse aspects of political and legal environments are involved. The "political environment" in a specific jurisdiction includes official policies and public opinion regarding the use of punishment and incarceration. The "legal environment" includes relevant case law and statutes (both state and federal) affecting prisoners' access to legal forums (Cooper 1988; Huff 1980), as well as contextual factors shaping litigation onset, such as plaintiffs' legal counsel (public, private, or ideologically committed), the strategies they adopt, and the level of court in which the lawsuit is filed. The onset of litigation and its eventual form, therefore, are at least partly determined by prelitigation factors that vary over time, from one case to another, and from one jurisdiction to another.

## The Political Environment

Problems contributing to jail lawsuits often remain undiagnosed, so that judges who order change and government officials who formulate policies often make decisions on the basis of very limited causal theories. Like most social problems, jail overcrowding and related problems are multiply determined, and informed policy choices require a careful analysis of the history, causes, and scope of the problem.

Overcrowding is only one issue that jails get sued over, but it merits special consideration. It is the most frequently litigated issue in jail lawsuits, and has consistently been identified by criminal justice practitioners as one of the most serious problems facing criminal justice systems (Gettinger 1984a; Grieser 1988; U.S. Department of Justice 1988). Overcrowding limits the institution's ability to classify those admitted, house them in a reasonably safe environment, and provide adequate food, legal services, recreation, sanitation, maintenance, and so on. Because of the jail's central role in criminal justice processing (intake of all accused offenders, holding suspects awaiting trial, housing convicted offenders serving short sentences), overcrowding also limits the ability of other justice agencies—police, courts, probation, state prisons—to process their clientele effectively.

In this section, I examine the potential contribution of five broad factors related to jail overcrowding and related litigation: public attitudes; demographic, economic, and social conditions; the organizational climates of jails; law enforcement and punishment policies; and resource distribution and competition among county agencies. The usefulness of these five predictors depends upon three criteria: relative magnitude—the approximate strength of each predictor relative to others, and its predictive power in historical perspective; temporal proximity—the degree to which each predictor precedes and covaries over time with patterns of jail overcrowding and litigation; and uniqueness—the degree to which each stands alone or interacts with other factors to fuel jail overcrowding and jail litigation.

## Public Attitudes and the "Get Tough" Movement

To what degree has the supposed public thirst for punishment contributed to jail overcrowding and court orders? Recent criminal justice reforms at the state and federal levels have included restrictions on or abolition of parole, creation of mandatory minimum sentences (for drug trafficking, for example), determinate sentencing, sentencing enhancements (for use of weapons or violence), and longer sentences.

The recent "get tough" movement can be traced largely to the crisis in authority that confronted the nation in the 1960s and 1970s, the era of the Vietnam conflict and Watergate, of prison riots and rising "crime in the streets" (Cullen, Clark, and Wozniak 1985; Scheingold 1984). Diminished confidence in the nation's leaders created a threat to politicians and an opportunity for those who could convince voters that they were capable of reestablishing the moral order. It became fashionable to be hard-nosed on crime issues.

Yet this recent punitive climate only partially explains the advent and growth of jail litigation. Numerous ideological shifts have shaped correctional policy in the past without sparking legal challenges to jail conditions. "Punitiveness" is cyclical and recurrent, not a unique facet of the 1970s.

As I point out in Chapter 1, before the American Revolution, public and corporal punishments were the norm, while incarceration was rare. Concern for basic human rights and fear of unrestrained government power led to extensive reforms in criminal justice in the late 1700s and early 1800s, including the widespread construction of jails and prisons based upon notions of "moral improvement." Before long, jails and prisons were dramatically overused, and conditions deteriorated.

In the early twentieth century, a progressive reform movement supportive of rehabilitation led to the development of probation, parole, and indeterminate sentencing (Rothman 1980). Such support reflected the interplay between "conscience and convenience" (Rothman 1980). Conscience inspired reformers' belief in the state's ability to transform criminals into productive members of society; administrative convenience made rehabilitative ideals palatable to public officials. The adopted reforms increased official discretion in handling convicted offenders and enhanced the efficiency of processing and control. In particular, indeterminate sentencing allowed officials to alleviate overcrowding in jails and prisons (Sutton 1987).

Crime was neither eradicated nor reduced by progressive reforms, however, and correctional facilities had hardly become humane places of confinement; thus, the Wickersham Commission reported serious, widespread prison crowding in 1931 (Mullen 1985). In addition, administrative demands for secure custody compromised the quality of rehabilitative treatment programs. David Rothman summarizes the outcome: "In the end, when conscience and convenience met, convenience won. When treatment and coercion met, coercion won" (1980,10). Disillusionment, combined with harsh economics and the rising crime rates of the 1920s and 1930s, facilitated a shift toward retributive policies, epitomized by scathing attacks on the probation and parole systems. The legacies of probation, parole, and indeterminate sentencing, however, remained.

Rehabilitative goals were not widely expressed again until the 1960s. The Law Enforcement Assistance Administration (LEAA) spent millions of federal dollars on community corrections programs during the late 1960s and early 1970s (Blackmore 1986). Advocates argued that community-based reintegration, work furlough, and educational programs would be more humane, less expensive, and more effective in reducing recidivism than monolithic correctional institutions. The use of community corrections, while exemplifying rehabilitative ideals, also allowed the state a certain amount of "convenience": alternatives apparently became supplements to, rather than replacements for jails and prisons (Austin and Krisberg 1982; Chan and Ericson 1981; Hylton 1982).

Although reintegration of the offender into the community was to be a primary purpose of community corrections (President's Commission on Law Enforcement and Administration of Justice 1968), the public displayed a marked reluctance to be integrated with ex-criminals. Homeowners strongly resisted proposed community correctional facilities, citing threats to public safety and decreased property values (Blackmore 1986; Smykla 1981). Cynicism spread further when scientific reports came out questioning the value of rehabilitative efforts

(Martinson 1974), even though the overgeneralized conclusions drawn from those reports ("nothing works") have been widely criticized (for reviews see Andrews et al. 1990; Palmer 1992).

An increasingly conservative political climate and rising crime rates marked the late 1970s (Gross 1982; Scheingold 1984). Ronald Reagan was elected president in 1980 partly on a law-and-order platform that placed responsibility for social ills on weak and permissive leadership, and evil individuals who constituted the "crime problem." Out of necessity, however, this conservative ideology has already begun to abate. With jail and prison populations far exceeding available space, and court orders to reduce correctional populations proliferating, the expanded use of alternatives to incarceration has once again become politically feasible and even necessary. A law enforcement offical I interviewed in 1988 was prophetic.

> I think that even Republicans who have never been fans of rehabilitation and tend to be more on the "law-and-order" side of things are coming to realize that we cannot continue to construct jails and prisons fast enough to keep up with the increased penalties that put more people in those institutions. So I think that there will be movement across the political spectrum to support alternatives.

Evidence for this attitudinal shift is found in public opinion surveys. While conservative values have dominated recent political responses to crime, public opinion is less retributive and more complex than is commonly thought. Francis Cullen and his colleagues (1985) found that a majority of Texas residents polled felt that the courts were too easy on criminals (77 percent) and that prison inmates should serve their full sentences (58 percent). However, 79 percent of the same respondents said that rehabilitation was an important function of prison, and 72 percent favored some type of community-based corrections instead of simply "building as many prisons as needed." In surveys of two Ohio cities, Skovron, Scott, and Cullen (1988) found that a majority of respondents (80 percent and 70 percent for the two cities) favored allowing prisoners to earn early release credits through good behavior and to participate in education or work programs while in prison. A large majority (90 percent and 87 percent) also favored the development of local programs to keep nonviolent and first-time offenders active and working in the community. Research using directed discussions among small samples of citizens (focus groups) also supports the diversity of public opinion (Doble 1987).

Perhaps even more important, evidence suggests that policymakers frequently overestimate the punitiveness of the public's attitudes (Gottfredson and Taylor 1987; Komarnicki and Doble 1986). As a result, claims by legislators that they enact tougher laws in response to the "public will" are questionable. There is little doubt that the "get tough" movement has strongly influenced criminal justice policy, but the public has many voices, and many perceive a need for rational change in punishment policies.

Overall, the "get tough" movement provides a significant but only partial explanation of jail overcrowding and jail litigation. Punitive shifts in attitudes are cyclical, even though their temporary effects on correctional populations are significant. Thus, the "relative magnitude" of public attitudes as a predictor of jail overcrowding is moderate. Temporal proximity in this case is high: "Get tough" policies coincide with the rapid growth of jail populations and the onset of jail litigation. The "uniqueness" of public attitudes as a predictor is low: Other factors must be considered to explain the unprecedented rise in jail overcrowding and jail litigation in the 1970s and 1980s.

## Demographic, Economic, and Social Conditions

How much do social structural factors contribute to jail overcrowding? Conflict theorists have suggested that incarceration rates are influenced by the fluctuating needs of dominant elites to maintain social control. High unemployment, for example, may lead to an economically marginalized "surplus population" that threatens dominant interests (Rusche and Kirchheimer 1939). There is some evidence for such views (Carroll and Doubet 1983): For example, incarceration rates have correlated moderately with unemployment in numerous studies (McCarthy 1990). Others have suggested that economic inequality and higher minority composition in specific areas foster more aggressive criminal justice responses and expenditures, which fuel higher rates of imprisonment (Myers and Talarico 1987). The economic decline and isolation of inner cities since 1960 and their devastating effects on poor and minority citizens have been well established (e.g., Adams et al. 1991; Wilson 1987). While available results are not altogether consistent and causal relationships are only partly understood, the evidence indicates that structural factors have some influence on incarceration rates.

Another approach, the demographic perspective, examines how population shifts have contributed to overcrowding (Blumstein 1987, 1988; Blumstein, Cohen, and Miller 1980). According to this view, maturation of the post–World War II baby boom generation led to a large increase in the younger, more crime-prone age groups. The mid-teens are the peak risk years for criminality, but the mid-twenties are the peak risk years for imprisonment because of the greater seriousness of offenses committed by older offenders. According to Alfred Blumstein, (1987, 1988) crime rates began to rise in 1964 (when a large 1947 birth cohort reached the age of 17), but imprisonment rates did not begin to rise until 1972 (when that cohort reached 25). Crime rates began to increase again in 1980, when a large 1961 birth cohort ("echo" boomers) reached 19. Because the 1961 cohort would have passed the peak age for imprisonment by 1990, Blumstein predicted, prison populations would begin to decline once again.

These predictions have not yet been borne out. On the contrary, record increases in jail and prison populations continued each year into 1994. Perhaps fear of crime continues to fuel political campaigns and public misperception even though actual crime rates have stabilized or declined. Although Blumstein noted that the changing age composition of the population intersected with increasingly conservative political agendas and economic stagnation to strain inadequate criminal justice and correctional resources, he appears to have underestimated the lingering contribution of the "get tough" movement and the increasing influence of economic decline.

### Organizational Climate

Also contributing to variation in jail conditions and the probability of court orders are localized management practices, leadership, and climate—that is, how criminal justice actors in jails, courts, probation departments, and other agencies perceive their work roles and settings. Every organization has its own unique "personality." Jail and prison administrators, for example, demonstrate different management styles that influence how personnel are selected and trained, what programs or services are offered, and how prisoners are treated (DiIulio 1987). The organizational climate construct (Forehand and Gilmer 1964) has three principles: Climate distinguishes one organization from others; organizational climates are relatively enduring over time; climate influences the behavior of people working within the organization.

More specifically, *public* social service organizations like jails typically display a "modal climate" that eventually becomes institutionalized. Douglas Bunker and Marion Wijnberg (1985) summarized the characteristics of such organizations: external funding and accountability; bureaucratic centralization and the promulgation of multiple, conflicting, and often changing rules; goal conflict and ambiguity (e.g., unresolved societal conflict about service goals); conflicted delegation (e.g., unresolved bureaucratic versus professional aims; unstructured or overstructured task activity); stressful client–worker interface; and more frequent recognition of employee error than of employee achievement or sound judgment.

These six factors describe traditional jails well, although "new generation jails" (podular/direct-supervision facilities) attempt to address some of them (Zupan 1991). Jails depend heavily upon local and state funding. Their organizational structure is overwhelmingly bureaucratic and rule-ridden (Shover and Einstadter 1988). Correctional workers are ambivalent about their mission, especially following court orders (Harris and Spiller 1977). The interface between guards and inmates is often stressful and conflict-ridden (Shover and Einstadter 1988). Finally, errors receive more administrative attention than sound judgments because errors easily result in inmate lawsuits or public outcry.

Organizational climate is determined by staff characteristics as well as management practices. Poorly trained and poorly paid personnel have traditionally staffed American jails. According to the National Sheriffs' Association (Kerle and Ford 1982,125), jail personnel in 1982 learned their jobs mostly in house and on the job, rather than through standardized, rigorous academy training: the same stunted stage of development that characterized police training twenty years earlier. Jail staff all too frequently consist of the most inexperienced or least promotable of sheriffs' deputies, who are likely to desire a career in law enforcement rather than corrections. Jail management is equally unlikely to be the career goal of county sheriffs entrusted with such responsibilities (Mattick 1974).

Besides influencing jail conditions and court intervention, organizational climate is also susceptible to changes as a result of court intervention—the threat or initiation of lawsuits, court orders, compliance with court orders, resolution of court orders, and prospects of future court involvement. In Texas, for example, court intervention prompted wholesale changes in organizational structure and climate. Prior to litigation, the Texas state prison system was characterized as proud, self-confident, self-sufficient, and insular (Martin and Ekland-Olson 1987). Early in the litigation, the administration's attribution of illegitimacy to court intervention encouraged staff to violate court rulings (Ekland-Olson and Martin 1988). Later in the litigation, court intervention shaped a whole new "bureaucratic-legalistic" order in Texas prison operations (Crouch and Marquart 1989). In other cases, some argue, court orders have impaired the functioning of public institutions by decreasing staff morale and increasing staff turnover and client misbehavior (Glazer 1975, 1978). At least two other broad changes in climate are attributable to court intervention: the creation of independent county departments of corrections with their own recruitment and training procedures, and the improvement of selection, training, and supervision procedures for sheriffs' staff who work in jails. Examples of such changes in climate (and resistance to them) appear in the case studies discussed in Chapters 4 to 6.

We must look to the collective, therefore, as well as to the individual, to explore how the attitudes and behaviors of those who work in correctional institutions contribute to jail conditions and court intervention. The magnitude of jail organizational climate as a predictor of court intervention is difficult to estimate because empirical research on jails is sparse. Case studies of state prisons suggest a strong relationship, but those studies have not attempted quantifiable investigation of either climate or court intervention. As a predictor, climate's usefulness is limited by low temporal proximity and low uniqueness. Its temporal proximity is low because the negative climatic factors implicated in studies of prison litigation are not specifically associated with the peak period of onset and growth in correctional litigation (post-1970). Uniqueness is low because climatic factors offer little explanatory power in isolation from other causal factors. Other factors in the political environment must be considered.

### Law Enforcement and Punishment Policies

*Crime Rates.* To what degree, if any, do increases in crime over the last twenty years explain jail overcrowding? Did crime rates explode without warning, leading to drastic shortfalls in correctional capacities? Although problems with official crime statistics are well known (e.g., Skogan 1975), there is little support for the hypothesis that crime causes overcrowding. In fact, the National Crime Surveys (NCS) show relatively *stable* crime victimization rates in the 1970s, and *declines* in personal theft (15 percent lower), household crimes (18 percent lower), and violent crimes (10 percent lower) between 1981 and 1988 (U.S. Department of Justice 1991b, 1991c). Stabilization or declines in most crime rates continued up to 1991. The Uniform Crime Reports (UCR), based upon crimes reported to police, show increases in reported crime for most categories between 1964 and 1980. From 1980 to 1989, however, total UCR index crimes *decreased* by 3.5 percent. Violent crimes, even when considered separately from the total UCR crimes, increased by only 11.1 percent for this period (U.S. Department of Justice 1992b).

Whether UCR or NCS figures are used, dramatic increases in crime are not substantiated as a cause of jail overcrowding and litigation.

*Incarceration Rates and Prisoner Expenditures.* The number of prisoners under the jurisdiction of state or federal correctional authorities reached a record high of 823,414 in 1991, an increase of 150 percent since 1980 (U.S. Department of Justice 1992c). The number of jail inmates incarcerated by local authorities rose from 158,394 in 1978 to 426,479 in 1991, an increase of 169 percent (U.S. Department of Justice 1992a). These dramatic increases in incarceration rates had nothing to do with increased crime.

The empirical relationship between crime rates and incarceration rates is weak (McCarthy 1990): Periods characterized by high imprisonment rates have not necessarily been characterized by high crime rates (Blumstein 1988). Rather, incarceration rates reflect differences in the laws and legal cultures of different areas, and differences in the application of local policies regarding punishment (Chilton and Nice 1993; Kizziah 1984; Klofas 1987, 1990; Welsh et al. 1990; Welsh and Pontell, 1991). Wherever a particular jurisdiction uses incarceration as a preferred sanction, there are increased demands for correctional space and services.

When high incarceration rates are accompanied by low prisoner expenditures, it becomes more likely that constitutionally acceptable standards of medical care, food, safety, and other conditions will be violated, making prisoner lawsuits more likely. One study, for example, found that states ordered by courts to improve prison conditions were forced to raise expenditures to levels demonstrated by states not under court order (Harriman and Straussman 1983). Inadequate correctional spending may reflect a conservative political climate, a fiscally strapped county, or both, but the net effect is that jail conditions deteriorate and judicial intervention becomes more likely.

*Jail Populations and Capacities.* Similarly, jail populations and capacities reflect official policies at least as much as they reflect actual crime rates (Klofas 1987, 1990; Pontell 1984; Welsh et al. 1990). Jail populations depend partly on admission rates, sentencing policies, and the range of pretrial and postconviction options available (Hall 1985, 1987; Jackson 1991). Overcrowding severely taxes an institution's ability to house its charges safely and provide for basic human needs. The proper classification and segregation of inmates with different security needs and personal characteristics (e.g., gang members) becomes more difficult; security and supervision become less efficient; food services become more irregular or meager; visitation is more restricted; physical plant maintenance suffers; and inmate movement is curtailed (Harris and Spiller 1977; Feeley and Hanson 1990; Yackle 1989).

## Resource Distribution and Competition

Do resource shortages at the local level of government contribute to jail overcrowding and litigation? If so, how and why? Government and correctional officials say that resource shortages have contributed to court orders by limiting new jail construction and the implementation of court-ordered improvements and newly emerging correctional standards, like increased staff levels and improved medical care (Welsh et al. 1990).

Criminal justice expenditures have traditionally been the primary responsibility of local (county and city) governments, and several recent trends have increased that burden. Local governments accounted for 54.6 percent of all justice expenditures in 1988; states for 33.4 percent; and the federal government for only 12.0 percent. Second, from 1985 to 1988 justice expenditures grew faster than any other government function, including education, health, and welfare (U.S. Department of Justice 1990a). Third, increases in correctional expenditures have been by far the most pronounced (64.2 percent). Overall, counties spent 13.7 percent of their total budgets on justice activities in 1988, and 4.6 percent of their total budgets on corrections alone. These trends reflect the increased importance of jail and justice issues on the policy agenda and increased strain on local government budgets, rendering compliance with state and federal standards more difficult.

Policymakers must also share responsibility, however, for historically placing jail needs low on the policy priority list. What happens when counties or states lack the money needed to comply with court orders? The courts have remained steadfast on this issue: Inadequate resources can never be adequate justification for depriving prisoners of their constitutional rights (see *Gates v. Collier*, 1974; *Miller v. Carson*, 1975).

Government organizations also tend to utilize social problems as resources for their own preservation (Selznick 1957), and criminal justice agencies actively adapt to pressures for change in "a sociopolitical jujitsu protective of the institution" (Duffee 1989,110). Domain dissensus, for example, refers to the degree to which an organization's claim to a specific domain is disputed or recognized by other organizations within the environment (Aldrich 1979). Organizations attempt to capture a domain by differentiating themselves from other organizations with similar goals.

The county sheriff, who is responsible for admitting and housing offenders in jail, often receives the bulk of county criminal justice resources. Jail overcrowding and court orders may, in fact, create opportunities for correctional officials to request more resources in order to "get out of the crisis" (see Harris and Spiller 1977; Martin and Ekland-Olson 1987). Other county-funded agencies may attempt to expand their resource base by pointing to the need for specialized offender programs or intermediate sanctions (e.g., electronic surveillance and work release) as means for dealing with jail overcrowding. Courts, similarly strapped for funds and personnel (e.g., prosecutors, public defenders, and judges), may complain that resource shortages lead to large case backlogs, which subvert the administration of justice. Inefficient court processing may also contribute to jail overcrowding and court orders by increasing the length of time pretrial prisoners are held pending trial, and the time it takes to dispose of cases (Hall 1985).

To the degree that agencies with highly related functions compete with differential success for scarce county resources, domain dissensus may lead to an imbalance of resources and a lack of cooperation among the various components of the criminal justice system. Resource shortage or imbalance, in turn, may contribute to inadequate processing of their clientele by some components of the criminal justice system. Resource imbalance favoring law enforcement contributes to more arrests, greater court backlog, system overload (including jail overcrowding), and a "crisis mentality" (Feeley 1983; Pontell 1984; Sherman and Hawkins 1981).

### Summary of Factors in the Political Environment

The preceding review of historical and empirical evidence finds diverse causes of jail overcrowding and court orders. Some (e.g., crime rates) are more myth than cause; some show promise as predictors but lack adequate supporting evidence; others offer apparently strong causal connections to jail conditions and litigation. The evidence, while fragmentary, suggests some preliminary conclusions. The potential usefulness of each predictor can be summarized along three dimensions: its relative magnitude, its temporal proximity to jail overcrowding and court orders, and its uniqueness (see Table 1). Gaps in our current state of knowledge make any synopsis necessarily somewhat subjective. I believe that Table 1 accurately summarizes what we currently know, however, and suggests where we need to look for further understanding.

Public attitudes tell us something relevant about the factors that fuel

**TABLE 1**
ASSESSMENT OF PREDICTORS IN THE POLITICAL ENVIRONMENT

|  | Relative Magnitude | Temporal Proximity | Uniqueness |
|---|---|---|---|
| Public attitudes | Moderate | High | Low |
| Demographic, social, and economic conditions | Unknown | High | Low |
| Organizational climate of jails | Unknown | Low | Low |
| Law enforcement and punishment policies |  |  |  |
|    Crime rates | Low | Low | Low |
|    Incarceration rates | High | High | Moderate |
| Jail populations and capacities | High | High | Moderate |
| Resource shortage and imbalance | Moderate | Moderate | Low |

"get tough" legislation and policies. The hardening of public attitudes in the 1980s illustrates high temporal proximity to jail overcrowding and court orders. However, historical swings in punishment orientation are multifaceted, repetitive, and cyclical (moderate relative magnitude), and public attitudes alone offer only partial explanation at best for current, persistent overcrowding and litigation problems (low uniqueness).

Demographic, social, and economic factors show strong temporal proximity to crowding and court orders on a national level, but their relative magnitude as predictors remains largely unknown because of a shortage of longitudinal data and the instability of predictors. By themselves they cannot explain variation in crowding and court orders across different jurisdictions; their effects require substantial intersection with other forces (low uniqueness).

Organizational climates of jails, as suggested by several case studies, offer potentially strong explanations of variation in jail conditions and the filing of lawsuits over conditions. The relative magnitude of such predictors is potentially very high. However, not much cross-jurisdictional or quantitative evidence is available at this time. On a national level, problems with jail climate have been longstanding and pervasive (low temporal proximity), and such predictors by themselves have not yet explained much unique variation in jail crowding or court orders across different jurisdictions (low uniqueness).

Law enforcement and punishment policies, as indicated by both quantitative and case study evidence, offer the strongest general explanations of jail overcrowding and litigation at this time. For example, evidence suggests a strong, quantifiable relationship between incarceration rates and overcrowding (high relative magnitude), and observable onset and covariation of incarceration rates with patterns of overcrowding and litigation (high temporal proximity). Even without other predictors, incarceration rates offer a substantial explanation of jail crowding and litigation nationally, statewide, and locally (moderate uniqueness). The same is true of corresponding increases in jail population without comparable increases in jail capacities or expenditures. However, the contribution of crime rates to overcrowding and court orders can be largely ruled out: such predictors suffer from low relative magnitude, low temporal proximity, and low uniqueness.

Resource shortages or imbalances at the local level of government offer substantial promise as predictors of crowding and court orders, but empirical evidence is currently scarce. We do find, however, that jurisdictions that suffer resource shortages or imbalances (as when most justice expenditures go toward law enforcement) are more likely to suffer from jail crowding and related litigation problems (moderate relative magnitude), and we saw that trends in county justice expenditures covary in time with the onset and growth of jail litigation (moderate temporal proximity). It is clear that resource shortages and imbalances have not been demonstrably unique causes of overcrowding so far; rather, they seem to exert their most observable effects only when aligned with other predictors discussed above.

Together, these factors trigger and shape jail overcrowding and litigation. We now need to disentangle the contribution of each factor, and examine their interactions. Not only has research on jail overcrowding and litigation so far failed to do so: the search for solutions at the policy level has been surprisingly uninformed by analyses of causal factors at all. Any such explanations must also consider the relative contribution of factors in the legal environment of jails and their jurisdictions.

## The Legal Environment

The analysis above focuses on correlates of jail crowding and court orders, rather than definitive causes. Such patterns often constitute part of the plaintiffs' attempts to establish a historical pattern of abuse or neglect in cases involving jail conditions. While bases for legal claims are examined in more detail in the next chapter, a remaining set of questions for the Trigger Stage concerns how inmates get their cases heard in the courts and which aspects of local and state legal environments hinder or facilitate their efforts.

## Legal Jurisdiction for Filing a Complaint

There are two common statutory bases for initiating lawsuits over jail or prison conditions: habeas corpus and section 1983 of the Civil Rights Act of 1871 (42 USC sec. 1983). In either case, alleged violations of the state and federal constitutions often form the main body of the complaint.

*Habeas Corpus.* Traditionally, habeas corpus limited relief to those petitioners seeking immediate and outright release from custody because of a judgment that was void for lack of subject matter jurisdiction. Today, habeas corpus is available to challenge various degrees of restraints imposed by any authority in violation of the petitioner's constitutional rights. While rules regarding the filing of habeas corpus petitions in federal courts are fairly flexible, state habeas corpus laws vary widely.

Literally, habeas corpus is meant to challenge unlawful custody. The legal usage of habeas corpus, however, is generally much broader.

> Imprisonment should deprive an inmate only of those liberties that the law has prescribed; any further deprivations resulting from unconstitutional prison regulations, practices, and policies constitute an unlawful custody from which release, the traditional habeas remedy, should be available. Release in such cases consists of the elimination of the unconstitutional prison conditions and results in a continued confinement falling within constitutional parameters. (University of Illinois Law Forum, 1980, 202).

These rights have been clearly recognized by the California Supreme Court (*In re Chessman*, 1955) and the state penal code. Section 1473 of the California Penal Code (West 1954 & 1992 Supp.) states: "Every person unlawfully imprisoned or restrained of his liberty, under any pretense whatever, may prosecute a writ of habeas corpus, to inquire into the cause of such imprisonment or restraint." Sections 1483 and 1485 also state, in part, that "the prisoner may be discharged from illegal conditions of restraint, although not from all restraint."

*Section 1983 Litigation.* Section 1983 is the most frequently used and effective device by which prisoners seek judicial redress of grievances, at least in the federal courts (Call 1986). Originally formulated in 1871 to protect the civil rights of previously enslaved black citizens, the Civil Rights Act has been used in more recent times to challenge the legality of actions by various state agencies, including mental institutions, welfare departments, police agencies, and prisons (McCoy 1986). Section 1983 permits a civil action for damages, equitable relief, or both, against persons acting under color of state law who deprive an individual of a federally protected right.

> Every person who, under color of any statute, ordinance, regulation, custom, or usage, of any State or Territory, subjects, or causes to be subjected, any citizen of the United States or other person within the jurisdiction thereof to the deprivation of any rights, privileges, or immunities secured by the constitution and laws, shall be liable to the party injured in an action at law, suit in equity, or other proper proceeding for redress.

Section 1983 is often preferred to habeas corpus petitions for three reasons (Call 1986): exhaustion of state remedies is usually not required (depending upon state law); class actions are easier to maintain and provide a basis for broad, injunctive relief; and the exercise of wide, equitable relief can be justified in a civil suit. However, broad habeas corpus laws in some states (California among them) provide an attractive vehicle for litigation as well (*In re Chessman*, 1955).

## Legal Jurisdiction and Type of Court

How is the decision to file in state or federal court influenced by applicable statutory law? Research on court-ordered correctional reform has overwhelmingly focused on federal rather than local trial courts (e.g., Crouch and Marquart 1989; DiIulio 1990; Martin and Ekland-Olson 1987; Yackle 1989). No studies have examined the extent to which jail lawsuits are based on state, rather than federal, law, or launched in state, rather than federal, courts. Different opportunities and constraints are afforded by each.

The choice of a particular legal forum partly determines the rules of relevance, the cast of actors, costs, delays, norms, and remedies (Felstiner, Abel, and Sarat 1981). Federal courts often have broader powers of relief than state courts (Turner 1973), and such cases often involve higher stakes and more complex issues (Grossman and Sarat 1975). The level of court chosen reflects the interactive influences of local environments and plaintiffs' legal representation.

The sociopolitical environments of local courts tend to limit the initiation of reform litigation in state courts (Galanter 1974, 1975; Kessler 1990). Plaintiff attorneys may perceive that such arenas favor the interests of locally dominant groups (especially local government), and "will exclude from consideration issues which threaten the interests of such groups" (Kessler 1990,126). Mark Kessler describes the resistance encountered by five Legal Services agencies attempting to initiate prison reform litigation in one state. Although skeptical of the ability or willingness of local courts to alter existing inequalities, he suggests that the local legal system "presents a promising arena in which to study relationships between political power, issue agendas, governmental allocations of resources, and the role of law and courts as promoters of change" (Kessler 1990,126). The study's conclusions, while intriguing, are not easily generalizable across different jurisdictions, legal issues, client groups, or public institutions. Ideologically committed attorneys, like those representing the ACLU, are less dependent on local power structures; and plaintiffs' counsel may seek change in local courts more aggressively if enabling case law and statutory law exists.

Trial judges also behave differently in state and federal courts, although attorneys may maneuver to get a case before a particular judge in either. Because judicial persistence becomes important in enforcing compliance (Harris and Spiller 1977), a judge's record in complex civil cases is often informative (Koren et al. 1988). State court judges are less likely to have had previous experience with litigation against jails or other large public institutions than federal judges, whose jurisdiction spans a wider substantive and geographic area. Because most state court judges face periodic reelection, they may be less likely to risk issuing jail reform orders that could be interpreted by the public as "soft on crime." The level of court chosen, therefore, both reflects the influence of the environment and shapes litigation strategies, the crafting of remedies, and attempts to gain compliance.

### Plaintiffs' Legal Representation

Plaintiff attorneys, by virtue of the strategies and mechanisms they employ to launch jail litigation and define legal issues, play a crucial role in jail litigation. Creating a strong record requires skill: an understanding of what appellate courts consider when reviewing cases; knowledge of correctional law; effectiveness in working with expert witnesses; and the ability to guide a case (Cooper 1988). The influence of different types of legal representation on jail litigation has received surprisingly little empirical attention.

Groups like the ACLU have a proactive and ideological commitment toward jail reform. Such frequent litigants may also enjoy competitive advantages (Galanter 1974): greater ability to structure legal transactions, specialized expertise, lower startup costs, informal relations with institutional incumbents, ability to adopt optimal litigation strategies, and bargaining credibility. Private counsel may have less experience with jail reform litigation; they may possess different motivations (e.g., recovery of attorney fees or damages); and they may be limited by their own professional interests and their ties with local business and government elites (Kessler 1990). Public counsel (e.g., legal aid attorneys and public defenders) may lack resources, commitment, or political freedom to challenge local elites. As a result, ideologically committed law firms specializing in prisoner litigation may pursue broader relief with greater vigor than other plaintiff counsel.

## Comparative Analyses of Triggering Factor in Jail Lawsuits
*Law Enforcement and Punishment Policies*

As suggested above, counties can be profitably compared on important dimensions reflecting environmental variation in criminal justice processing. Arrest rates, for example, constitute the raw input into jails, since jails are the front-line intake center for the rest of the criminal justice system (Hall 1985). Arrest rates reflect numerous social forces besides actual crime (see Quinney 1979; Savitz 1982; Skogan 1975) but are useful for examining official responses across jurisdictions and over time. Raw numbers of arrests impact directly upon the criminal justice system's capacity to process defendants. However, it is also useful to examine rates of arrest (e.g., per 10,000 population) to control for the possibility that population size alone is responsible for the volume of arrests.

Incarceration rates reflect, in part, the harshness of local policies, while correlating only weakly with crime rates in numerous studies. They seem to indicate a substantial, independent dimension of local legal cultures (Klofas 1987, 1990; Welsh and Pontell 1991). Jail populations and jail capacities, too, reflect official policies at least as much as they reflect actual crime rates (Klofas 1987, 1990; Pontell 1984; Welsh et al. 1990). In addition to the actual volume of admissions, jail populations will depend partly upon the efficiency of processing mechanisms and pretrial release procedures at the jail, how efficiently and how harshly district attorneys make charging or release decisions, and the range of postconviction alternatives or community programs available (Hall 1985; Jackson 1991). There is some evidence that increases in jail capacity actually drive inmate populations upward (Abt Associates 1980; Blumstein, Cohen, and Miller 1980; Busher 1983; Pontell 1984).

The exact mechanisms by which newly constructed jail beds get filled so quickly are not altogether clear, but a homeostatic relation clearly exists between jail capacity and jail population.

Expenditures per prisoner reflect, in part, policies regarding acceptable conditions of jail confinement. One study has found that states with prisons under court order had typically spent less on their prisoners than states not under court intervention, and were apparently forced to raise expenditures to levels demonstrated by states in the latter category (Harriman and Straussman 1983). States characterized by low rates of prisoner expenditures and high rates of incarceration were especially likely to face court intervention (Chilton and Nice 1993). Little research has examined this relationship with county jails, but available evidence suggests such a connection (Welsh 1992b; Welsh and Pontell 1991).

To examine relationships between environmental factors and the likelihood of jail litigation, I compared 35 California counties under court order to reform jail conditions with 21 counties not under court order.[1] For the years 1976 (prelitigation) and 1986 (mid-litigation), counties under court order had larger jail populations, spent less on jail operations, and filled jails to a greater proportion of their capacity than did counties not under court order (see Table 2). Such conditions, while only partly indicative of local punishment practices, likely predisposed such counties to jail litigation as criminal justice policies hardened and jail populations soared in the 1980s (Welsh et al. 1991). Crime rates in counties under order and not under order did not differ greatly, illustrating once again that crime had little influence on either overcrowding or jail litigation. While causal explanations cannot be firmly supported with cross-sectional data such as these, results in Table 2 also hint that court orders have helped slow the *rate* of growth in incarceration rates and overcrowding (see Feeley and Hanson 1990, 33). Counties under court order also tended to be larger, suggesting that size alone predisposes counties to litigation.

To control for the effects of jail and county size, I further stratified the jail sample. A small sample cannot be stratified into infinite subcategories, but a relatively homogeneous group can be created by dropping counties with the smallest and largest jail populations in 1976 (the first year of data recorded by the California Board of Corrections). All 8 counties with an 1976 average daily population (ADP) of less than 11 were dropped, and all 11 counties with an 1976 ADP of greater than 500 were dropped. Dropping counties at the extremes (for example, Los Angeles, with a 1976 ADP of 8,022, and Mono, with an ADP of 7) re-

**TABLE 2**
**DIMENSIONS OF PUNISHMENT: COUNTIES UNDER OR NOT UNDER COURT ORDER**

| | 1976 | 1986 | Percent Change |
|---|---|---|---|
| Average daily jail population | | | |
| Under order (N = 35) | 607 | 1402 | +131.0% |
| No order (N = 21) | 78 | 184 | +135.9% |
| Incarceration rate[a] | | | |
| Under order (N = 35) | 11.2 | 18.3 | +63.4% |
| No order (N = 21) | 10.5 | 18.5 | +76.2% |
| Overcrowding[b] | | | |
| Under order (N = 35) | 74.7 | 113.7 | +52.2% |
| No order (N = 21) | 57.4 | 108.3 | +88.7% |
| Per prisoner expenditures[c] | | | |
| Under order (N = 35) | $10,066.61 | $10,307.86 | +2.4% |
| No order (N = 21) | $11,049.12 | $12,101.64 | +9.5% |
| Population[d] | | | |
| Under order (N = 35) | 577.92 | 710.04 | +22.9% |
| No order (N = 21) | 74.00 | 92.59 | +25.1% |
| Crime rate[e] | | | |
| Under order (N = 35) | 65.44 | 61.84 | −5.5% |
| No order (N = 21) | 63.54 | 53.64 | −15.6% |

*Sources:* California Board of Corrections, *Jail Inspection Reports,* 1976, 1986 (Sacramento: State of California); California Bureau of Criminal Statistics, *Annual County Profiles,* 1976, 1986 (Sacramento: State of California Department of Justice).
*Note:* $p < .05$
[a]Incarceration rate = average daily jail population/county population × 10,000.
[b]Overcrowding = average daily jail population/state board-rated jail capacity × 100.
[c]Per prisoner expenditures = jail operational expenditures/average daily jail population. Expenditures were converted into constant dollars (1982 = 100; 1976 = 62.0; 1986 = 118.3) using National Deflators (state and local purchases) provided by the California Department of Finance.
[d]Population = county population in thousands.
[e]Crime rate = FBI index crimes per 1,000 population.

sulted in a sample of 16 counties not under order and 23 counties under order. Results are presented in Table 3.

The two constructed samples were now more homogeneous in both jail and county population size. A similar pattern of results was observed, but there was now less difference between counties under order and not under order on measures of overcrowding and prisoner expenditures. Counties under court order now displayed slightly higher crime rates than counties not under order, although both showed decreases between 1976 and 1986. It is still the case, therefore, that crime

## TABLE 3
DIMENSIONS OF PUNISHMENT: COUNTIES UNDER OR NOT UNDER COURT ORDER,
STRATIFIED BY JAIL POPULATION

| | 1976 | 1986 | Percent Change |
|---|---|---|---|
| Average daily jail population | | | |
| Under order (N = 23) | 157 | 353 | +124.8% |
| No order (N = 16) | 100 | 235 | +135.0% |
| Incarceration rate[a] | | | |
| Under order (N = 23) | 11.1 | 17.9 | +61.3% |
| No order (N = 16) | 11.3 | 20.3 | +79.6% |
| Overcrowding[b] | | | |
| Under order (N = 23) | 72.5 | 110.4 | +52.3% |
| No order (N = 16) | 61.5 | 111.0 | +80.5% |
| Per prisoner expenditures[c] | | | |
| Under order (N = 23) | $10,090.70 | $10,441.56 | +3.5% |
| No order (N = 16) | $10,124.24 | $10,841.98 | +7.1% |
| Population[d] | | | |
| Under order (N = 23) | 162.25 | 209.30 | +29.0% |
| No order (N = 16) | 102.79 | 128.08 | +24.6% |
| Crime rate[e] | | | |
| Under order (N = 23) | 60.05 | 57.98 | −3.4% |
| No order (N = 16) | 53.98 | 49.76 | −7.8% |

Sources: California Board of Corrections, *Jail Inspection Reports*, 1976, 1986 (Sacramento: State of California); California Bureau of Criminal Statistics, *Annual County Profiles* 1976, 1986 (Sacramento: State of California Department of Justice).

Note: $p > .05$
[a]Incarceration rate = average daily jail population/county population $\times$ 10,000.
[b]Overcrowding = average daily jail population/state board-rated jail capacity $\times$ 100.
[c]Per prisoner expenditures = jail operational expenditures/average daily jail population. Expenditures were converted into constant dollars (1982 = 100; 1976 = 62.0; 1986 = 118.3) using National Deflators (state and local purchases) provided by the California Department of Finance.
[d]Population = county population in thousands.
[e]Crime rate = FBI Index crimes per 1,000 population.

rates contribute relatively little to the explanation of court orders, and it is likely that court orders restrained growth in overcrowding and incarceration rates. Results suggest increased punitiveness across all counties for the time period under consideration (i.e., higher incarceration rates), but larger counties were more likely to come under court intervention.

The three counties selected for case study differed significantly in their jail populations and rated capacities (Table 4). Santa Clara experi-

## TABLE 4
CHANGES IN AVERAGE DAILY JAIL POPULATION AND BOARD-RATED CAPACITY IN THREE COUNTIES, 1976-1986

| County | Average Daily Jail Population (ADP) | | Percent Change[a] | Board Rated Capacity | | Percent Change[a] |
|---|---|---|---|---|---|---|
| | 1976 | 1986 | | 1976 | 1986 | |
| Contra Costa | 316 | 867 | +174% | 315 | 689 | +119% |
| Orange | 1,173 | 2,862 | +144% | 1,395 | 2,567 | +84% |
| Santa Clara | 958 | 3,111 | +225% | 1,276 | 2,668 | +109% |

Source: California Board of Certifications, *Jail Inspection Reports*, 1976, 1986 (Sacramento: State of California).

[a]Percent change = [(1986 ADP − 1976 ADP) / 1976 ADP] × 100.

enced the greatest growth in jail population from 1976 to 1986 (225 percent), and Orange County the least (144 percent). However, jail capacity lagged behind jail population growth in all three counties. Orange County expanded its jail capacity the least (84 percent), while Contra Costa expanded it the most (119 percent). Santa Clara experienced the greatest shortfall between jail population growth and expansion of capacity (225 percent minus 109 percent = 116 percent).

Each of the counties experienced only modest population increases from 1976 to 1986 but underwent rapid increases in incarceration rates (Table 5). In Orange and Contra Costa, the incarceration rate approximately doubled, while the rate in Santa Clara nearly tripled. Orange County jails spent the least per prisoner in both 1976 to 1986. Contra Costa spent the most, registering a slight increase from 1976 to 1986, while Orange and Santa Clara showed substantial decreases. These results suggest that each county experienced an incarceration boom unrelated to increases in general population, with Contra Costa evidencing much higher expenditures than the other two counties. Contra Costa operates a "direct supervision" jail, which has been designated a "model" by the National Institute of Corrections (Gettinger 1984b; Wener, Frazier, and Farbstein 1987; Zupan 1991). The modular architecture and hands-on management of these "new generation" jails, supporters argue, provide for more effective supervision, movement, and care of inmates than traditional plans (Zupan 1991).

These examples suggest two important points. First, counties under court order vary in dimensions of their political environments both before and after the onset of court orders. Second, not only do counties

## TABLE 5
### County Population, Incarceration Rates, and Per Prisoner Expenditures in Three Counties, 1976–1986

| County | County Population[a] | | | Incarceration Rate per 10,000[b] | | | Per Prisoner Expenditures[c] | | |
|---|---|---|---|---|---|---|---|---|---|
| | 1976 | 1986 | Percent Change | 1976 | 1986 | Percent Change | 1976 | 1986 | Percent Change |
| Contra Costa | 602.1 | 729.8 | +21.2% | 5.2 | 11.9 | +128.8% | $15,242 | $16,399 | +7.6% |
| Orange | 1,752.1 | 2,171.2 | +23.9% | 6.7 | 13.2 | +97.0% | $9,387 | $7,872 | −16.1% |
| Santa Clara | 1,214.8 | 1,403.3 | +15.5% | 7.9 | 22.2 | +181.0% | $16,242 | $10,253 | −36.9% |

Sources: California Board of Corrections, *Jail Inspection Reports*, 1976, 1986 (Sacramento: State of California); California Bureau of Criminal Statistics, *Annual County Profiles*, 1976, 1986 (Sacramento: State of California Department of Justice).

[a]County population in thousands.

[b]Incarceration rate = average daily jail population/county population.

[c]Per prisoner expenditures = jail operating budget/average daily jail population. Excludes capital expenditures on jails. Figures were converted into constant dollars (1982 = 100; 1976 = 62.0; 1986 = 118.3) using the National Deflators (state and local purchases) provided by the California Department of Finance.

under court order differ from counties not under court order; it is important to examine variation across individual counties. How do conditions shape litigation onset, and to what degree can court orders alter them? While cross-sectional data alone are insufficient to make statements about causal relationships, the variations observed in punishment dimensions here raise important questions for quantitative and qualitative examination. These questions are explored further in the case analyses reported in Chapter 3, as well as the analyses of impact reported in Chapter 6.

### Resource Distribution and Competition

The unique distribution of resources among county criminal justice agencies and interagency competition for scarce resources affect jail populations and operations through their influence on the flow of criminal justice processing. By its decisions on resource allocations to each agency, each county creates a unique local environment that influences jail conditions and populations.

Domain dissensus in California counties was measured by the proportion of the county criminal justice budget devoted to jail operations[2] relative to the proportion devoted to such county functions as courts, probation, prosecutor, public defender, and sheriff. First, I compared counties under order with counties not under court order to determine whether patterns of criminal justice expenditures in 1976 and 1986 differed for the two groups (Figure 2).

County sheriffs got the biggest bite of the criminal justice budget regardless of court intervention or year considered, although sheriffs got less in 1986 than they did in 1976. Counties under a court decree spent proportionally less on their sheriffs' budgets than counties not under court order. Counties under court order tended to have jail budgets only slightly higher than counties not under order. Both groups increased their proportional jail expenditures from 1976 to 1986, demonstrating an increased policy priority for jail issues regardless of court intervention. However, if occasional transfers of money are made between the sheriff's law enforcement budget and the sheriff's jail budget, as interview respondents suggested, sheriffs in counties not under order have had substantially more discretionary monies at their disposal. As we shall see later (Chapter 6), jail litigation may fuel bitter budget disputes between county sheriffs and county supervisors.

Court expenditures did not differ for counties under/not under order in 1976, but the two types of counties had grown apart by 1986 (t = $-2.56$, 56 df). Counties not under order decreased their budgetary allocation to courts, while counties under order held court expenditures steady at about 21 percent. The current cross-sectional data do not allow us to determine the causal directionality of this relationship, but there are at least two likely explanations. First, larger counties (which are also likely to be under order) can probably ill afford to cut back on their court budgets and exacerbate already severe case backlogs. Second, in some counties higher expenditures on courts may increase criminal court processing capacity and indirectly contribute to correctional overcrowding and associated problems of jail management. This "punitive climate" hypothesis is somewhat supported by spending patterns on prosecutors, public defenders, and probation.

Prosecutorial budget allocations did not differ for the two groups of counties for 1976, but in 1986 counties under order spent more than did counties not under order (t = $-2.68$, 56 df). Counties under order increased prosecutorial spending from 10.2 to 12.4 percent of the county criminal justice budget, while counties not under order remained constant. Public defenders' share of the pie was always the smallest, for both 1976 and 1986, and for both counties under order and counties not under order. Both types of counties had increased their allocations to the public defender from 1976 to 1986, suggesting increased needs for legal representation of indigents.

COUNTIES NOT UNDER ORDER, 1986

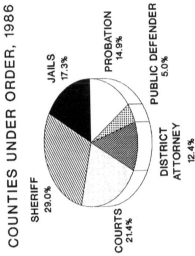

SHERIFF
38.0%

JAILS
16.9%

PROBATION
11.8%

PUBLIC DEFENDER
4.1%

DISTRICT
ATTORNEY
10.8%

COURTS
18.4%

COUNTIES NOT UNDER ORDER, 1976

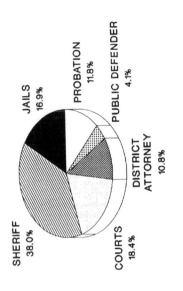

SHERIFF
43.3%

JAILS
11.0%

PROBATION
12.5%

PUBLIC DEFENDER
2.2%

DISTRICT
ATTORNEY
10.0%

COURTS
21.3%

COUNTIES UNDER ORDER, 1986

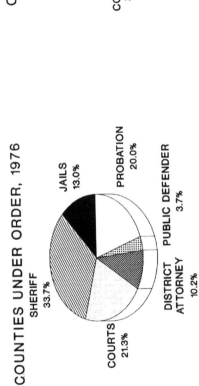

SHERIFF
29.0%

JAILS
17.3%

PROBATION
14.9%

PUBLIC DEFENDER
5.0%

DISTRICT
ATTORNEY
12.4%

COURTS
21.4%

COUNTIES UNDER ORDER, 1976

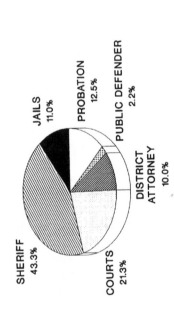

SHERIFF
33.7%

JAILS
13.0%

PROBATION
20.0%

PUBLIC DEFENDER
3.7%

DISTRICT
ATTORNEY
10.2%

COURTS
21.3%

*Counties Under or Not Under Court Order, 1976–1986*

Probation departments' budgetary allocations revealed surprising differences. In both 1976 and 1986, counties under order spent significantly more of their criminal justice budget on probation than did counties not under order (t = −4.11 and −2.80). In counties under order, however, probation received far less of the budgetary pie in 1986 (14.9 percent) than it did in 1976 (20.0 percent). Counties experiencing the greatest jail problems may have had to economize somewhere as jail budgets increased, and perhaps did so at the expense of probation. Such cuts would be ironic. For one thing, probation caseloads far exceed the number of inmates in jail at any one time, and probation caseloads have increased at astronomical rates (Petersilia 1985; Pontell et al. 1989). In addition, the need for probation services is much greater in large counties (those most likely to be under court order). The results suggest conservative shifts in counties under court order: If probation is seen as "soft" punishment, then perhaps greater resources are shifted toward prosecution and the courts. However, the tremendous demand for probation to provide supervision and "intermediate sanctions" as a relief valve for crowded jails has probably contributed to their relative viability even during conservative years (Morris and Tonry 1990; Pontell et al. 1989; Welsh et al. 1990).

As jails have gained a bigger piece of the county budgetary pie, other county justice agencies have competed for scarcer resources. Counties under court order showed trends of increased funding to prosecution and decreased funding to probation, producing changes not only in the budget but also in the processing capability of those agencies. Explicit links to jail overcrowding cannot be proven, but it is clear that resource competition and imbalance among local agencies has intensified since the advent of jail litigation, and that it has done so somewhat differently for those counties under court order.

## *Legal Jurisdiction, Type of Court, and Plaintiffs' Legal Representation*

Plaintiffs in California jail cases were represented by ideologically committed counsel in only a small number of cases examined (N = 8). They were more frequently represented by publicly appointed counsel (N = 11), usually county public defenders, and most frequently by private firms (N = 24). These figures challenge popular conceptions of the ACLU as the primary litigator in inmate lawsuits. Ideologically committed firms choose their cases quite selectively, targeting those institutions with the most grievous violations. Doing so facilitates a long-term litigation plan aimed at establishing legal precedents through several important "test" cases. Ideologically committed firms targeted counties with significantly higher incarceration rates and overcrowding, and somewhat lower prisoner expenditures (Table 6). Such conditions also shape more vigorous litigation strategies by ideologically committed attorneys, affecting the number and nature of legal claims filed in the Liability Stage (see Chapter 3).

Public counsel, usually the county public defender's office, is likely to be appointed when a large number of inmate petitions alleging common violations are presented to a state court judge. Such cases were likely to take place in smaller, more rural counties such as Humboldt and Solano, where other types of legal representation may not be readily available, either because the case does not offer an attractive test case or perhaps because rural locations offer a lower density of skilled or interested private attorneys. No direct measure of differential attorney density was available, but an urbanicity measure was constructed by dividing the litigation sample into "rural" (county population of 200,000 or less) and "urban" groups (greater than 200,000). Ideologically committed attorneys filed 5 of their 8 lawsuits (62.5 per-

TABLE 6

DIMENSIONS OF PUNISHMENT IN COUNTIES UNDER COURT ORDER BY TYPE OF
PLAINTIFFS' LEGAL REPRESENTATION

|  | Ideological (N = 8) | Private (N = 24) | Public (N = 11) | F-value (d.f.) | |
|---|---|---|---|---|---|
| Incarceration rate per 10,000[a] | | | | | |
| 1976 | 12.8 | 10.6 | 10.7 | 0.79 | (2,40) |
| 1986 | 24.9 | 17.3 | 16.6 | 4.33* | (2,40) |
| Overcrowding[b] | | | | | |
| 1976 | 74.7 | 75.6 | 83.0 | 0.39 | (2,40) |
| 1986 | 133.0 | 113.2 | 109.7 | 4.03* | (2,40) |
| Per prisoner expenditures[c] | | | | | |
| 1976 | $9,941.46 | $10,535.10 | $ 9,978.06 | 0.36 | (2,40) |
| 1986 | $7,786.74 | $10,177.66 | $10,168.69 | 2.56 | (2,40) |

*$p < .05$.
[a]Incarceration rate = average daily jail population/county population $\times$ 10,000.
[b]Overcrowding = average daily jail population/state board-rated jail capacity $\times$ 100.
[c]Per prisoner expenditure = jail operational expenditures/average daily jail population. Expenditures were converted into 1980 constant dollars using national deflators (state and local purchases) provided by the California Department of Finance (1982 = 100; 1976 = 62.0; 1986 = 118.3).

cent) in urban areas; private attorneys filed 15 of 24 lawsuits (62.5 percent) in urban areas; in contrast, public defenders represented inmates in urban counties in only 4 of their 11 lawsuits (36.4 percent). While neither the ACLU nor private attorneys were excluded in rural areas, such cases were much more likely to pass to publicly appointed counsel.

Private attorneys may be the most active participants in inmate litigation for several reasons. First, they are more numerous than other types of counsel, especially in large urban areas in the southern (Los Angeles) and northern (San Francisco) parts of the state. Many counties under court order lie in the vicinity of these two metropolises, suggesting a convenient springboard for entrepreneurs. Second, if their practices are reasonably large, diverse, and stable, private attorneys are more able to command the resources needed to engage in prolonged jail litigation and wait two, three, or more years (depending on the length of the Liability Stage) before recouping attorney fees. Third, while damage claims are usually dropped from general-conditions lawsuits in favor of equitable relief, the possibility of recovering attorney fees over an extended period may stimulate the involvement of private attorneys. A private attorney can also garner many "spinoff" cases by gaining access to jail inmates seeking assistance with pending criminal cases, appeals, or individual damage claims. Attorney selection factors have far-reaching consequences for subsequent litigation processes and outcomes.

Different types of legal counsel tended to represent plaintiffs in different types of courts. Of 8 cases filed by ideologically committed attorneys, 6 (75 percent) were filed in federal court. Of the 24 cases filed by private attorneys, only 8 (33 percent) were filed in federal court. All 11 cases (100 percent) in which public counsel participated occurred in state courts. Ideologically committed firms are more familiar with federal law and have greater experience and success litigating broad civil rights issues in the federal courts. The ACLU, for example, is active in jail and prison reform nationwide through the National Prison Project and supplies legal resources (including information, expert witnesses, and financial support) to local branches across the United States. Their greater experience dictates operative beliefs that significant reform is more likely in the federal courts. Major influences on plaintiffs' legal representation are summarized in Table 7.

As discussed earlier, mobilization of jail lawsuits depends upon the specific opportunities afforded by state law. California law, for example, affords favorable opportunities for jail litigation through habeas

**TABLE 7**
PLAINTIFFS' LEGAL REPRESENTATION IN JAIL LAWSUITS AND MAJOR INFLUENCES

| Plaintiffs' Legal Representation | Major Influences |
|---|---|
| Ideological (repeat players) | Incarceration rate (high)<br>Jail overcrowding (high)<br>Prisoner expenditures (low)<br>Urbanicity (urban) |
| Private | Urbanicity (urban)<br>Resource base (stable reserves)<br>Potential for "spin-off" cases (high) |
| Public | Urbanicity (rural)<br>Level of court (state)<br>Number of individual prisoner petitions filed (high) |

corpus petitions. Because only one state is analyzed here, the data are not generalizable to all states, but they illustrate that the legal grounds for litigation in state and federal courts are often quite different.

Of the 43 cases examined, 20 (65 percent) took place in state courts; 14 (33 percent) were filed in federal courts; 1 case (2 percent) was heard by the state Supreme Court (see Table 8).[3] Further investigation identified state habeas corpus laws as the impetus for jail litigation in state courts. Of 28 cases filed in state court, 20 (71 percent) were habeas corpus petitions, 5 (18 percent) were civil rights actions, and 3 (11 percent) were filed under both privisions. While state law thus facilitated the *initiation* of jail litigation in state courts, the local sociopolitical environments of state courts may impose limitations upon *subsequent* litigation activities (see Chapter 4). In general, different prelitigation conditions carry different implications for litigation strategies (Liability Stage), judicial methods and decree formulation (Remedy Stage),

**TABLE 8**
LEVEL OF COURT CHOSEN FOR JAIL LAWSUITS AND MAJOR INFLUENCES

| Level of Court Chosen | Major Influences |
|---|---|
| State | Urbanicity (rural)<br>Plaintiffs' legal representation (private, public)<br>Opportunities afforded by state law (high) |
| Federal | Urbanicity (urban)<br>Plaintiffs' legal representation (ideological) |

and defendants' compliance with court orders (Postdecree Stage). Conditions related to choice of court are further illuminated in Chapters 3 to 5.

## Summary

Environmental conditions prior and concurrent to the onset of jail litigation play an important role in triggering and shaping court intervention in specific jurisdictions. It is crucial to examine trends at the local level where the jail interacts with its environment and with other agencies; national trends may mask important jurisdictional variations.

Five interactive factors in the political environment contributed to jail overcrowding and the filing of jail lawsuits: public attitudes, demographic, social, and economic conditions, the organizational climate of jails, law enforcement and punishment policies, and resource shortages or imbalances. Law enforcement and punishment policies provide the strongest general explanations of jail overcrowding and litigation onset, but we still must seek to disentangle the interactive influence of all five factors to explain variation across jail jurisdictions and lawsuits.

Certain factors in legal environments also influence litigation onset. Applicable state laws regarding habeas corpus in California facilitated the legal mobilization of jail lawsuits. Similarly, legal mobilization was related to different types of courts (state, federal), legal counsel (public, private, ideological), and local political environments, including punishment policies.

At the local level, an increasingly punitive environment was observed across counties between 1976 and 1986, with counties under court order showing higher rates of overcrowding and lower rates of prisoner expenditures. In contrast, crime rates were not related to the likelihood of court orders, suggesting that increased punitiveness contributed much more to court orders than increased crime. However, counties under order also had larger jail populations and county populations. The predisposition of larger counties to court intervention is likely due to a greater volume of criminal justice processing and attendant difficulties in moving cases and housing both pretrial and sentenced prisoners. Evidence suggested that court orders helped slow the rate of change in incarceration rates and overcrowding, although cross-sectional data cannot afford definitive causal statements. Similarly, we examined evidence of resource shortages and imbalances as well as budgetary competition between criminal justice agencies, which may prove especially detrimental in the face of court intervention. In partic-

**TABLE 9**
**MAJOR TRIGGERS OF JAIL LAWSUITS**

POLITICAL ENVIRONMENT
  Jail population (large)
  Incarceration rate (high)
  Overcrowding (high)
  Prisoner expenditures (low)
  Resource imbalance (high)
  Physical condition and design of jail (poor)
  Jail organizational climate (poor)
  Urbanicity (urban)

LEGAL ENVIRONMENT
  Opportunities for prisoner litigation afforded by state law (high)

ular, counties under court order showed evidence of a punitive climate favoring law enforcement, prosecution, and courts, while cutting funds to probation.

Clearly, jail litigation does not occur in a vacuum, and lawsuits spring up neither randomly nor uniformly across jurisdictions. The major "triggers" of jail lawsuits (legal and political) are summarized in Table 9. We now turn to those factors that shape the onset of litigation and transform a dispute into a legal complaint.

# CHAPTER 3

## The Liability Stage

An actual and substantial controversy exists between Plantiffs and
Defendants, in that Plaintiffs complain that Defendants are violating and will continue to violate their most fundamental rights
under the United States Constitution and the laws and statutes of
the United States and California and commit acts and omissions
threatening Plaintiffs' lives and health. Defendants have persisted
in subjecting Plaintiffs to unconstitutional and harmful conditions
despite protests by the Jail's prisoners. Defendants may in the future make minor changes in the jail from time to time in response
to protests but they will do nothing substantial to remedy the unconstitutional and harmful conditions to which they subject Plaintiffs or to change the policies and procedures. Defendants deny that
their actions are illegal or unconstitutional or cause injuries to
Plaintiffs.

**—Complaint, *Stewart v. Gates*, 1975**

$\mathbf{A}$ JAIL LAWSUIT is fashioned by the interactive efforts of lawyers for
plaintiffs and defendants at the Liability Stage. Each attempts to create
a strong record to shape judicial decisions. The legal complaint filed by
plaintiffs is crucial to the initiation of liability proceedings, as plaintiffs
name certain officials as defendants, attempt to establish certain violations of law, and suggest specific remedies to alleviate unconstitutional
conditions. The role of defendants, especially in early stages of litigation, is often reactive, involving denials and a terse response to inmate
complaints. Defendants' counsel becomes more active over time as specific allegations are challenged, evidence is collected, and legal coun-
teroffensives are mounted.

Such dimensions of the legal process are crucial mediators between
the conditions that initially gave rise to a dispute (the Trigger Stage)

and the outcomes that result from court-ordered reform (the Impact Stage). Most fundamentally, dynamics at the Liability Stage influence whether a judicial decision will favor plaintiffs, what type of remedial action will eventually be ordered (the Remedy Stage), and how compliance will be monitored and sanctioned (the Postdecree Stage).

We know little about this crucial stage of jail litigation. Measures of legal claims or court intervention in many studies have been reduced to simple frequency counts (e.g., case filing rates in state or federal courts) or dummy variables (e.g., whether a jurisdiction is under court order or not). Little is known about the complexity of legal process across jail lawsuits, nor how process influences outcomes. Malcolm Feeley and Roger Hanson (1986) summarized our current state of knowledge quite accurately when they stated that "accumulation of descriptive information across a number of sites is essential to ground more advanced work" (p. 35). Our task here is to investigate how cross-jurisdictional variation at the Liability Stage is influenced by previous events at the Trigger Stage, and how processes at the Liability Stage exert influence upon the subsequent stages of a jail lawsuit.

In this chapter, I review the major issues that have formed the substance of complaints in jail and prison lawsuits, as well their legal and historical bases. Comparative analyses examine variation across jail lawsuits on three major dimensions: types of violations alleged, defendants named, and bases for legal claims. Using both quantitative data and case studies, I examine critical events at the Liability Stage of jail lawsuits.

## Constitutional and Statutory Issues

Overcrowding places a burden on all jail services and operations, but it is not the only problem facing jails; indeed, it may not even be the most serious. In general, jails lack many basic services that state-run prisons provide. Because jail inmates face shorter incarceration, and because county funds, staff, and space are limited, most jails lack meaningful work for inmates, treatment programs for substance abuse or mental illness, medical care, educational programs, social services, or counseling programs. Overcrowding magnifies gaps in the jail's ability to safely house, clothe, feed, and supervise prisoners and speeds the physical deterioration of jail facilities (Advisory Commission on Intergovernmental Relations 1984).

The availability of medical services is another serious issue in jail litigation. Legal complaints against jails are rife with tales of life-threatening physical conditions (heart disease, diabetes, epilepsy, drug withdrawal) and serious mental health problems (depression, schizophrenia, suicidal behavior) that were neglected, improperly diagnosed, or untreated. Three examples from two legal complaints illustrate the conditions commonly cited by plaintiffs.

Petitioners complain that they do not receive even minimal medical attention when they are ill. At "sick call," inmates are required to fill out "white cards" stating their complaints. Sometimes these cards are either "lost" or just ignored, for it may take days or weeks before a complaint is addressed by a trained medical service officer. Of course, because of overcrowded conditions, the strain on the medical staff becomes enormous and little time can be spent on individuals.[1]

Both medical care and routine health care at the Jail are, when available at all, inadequate, and usually characterized by a callous disregard for the well-being of prisoners and for the basic tenets of sound medical practice. The standards of medical care at the Jail are well below those generally accepted as adequate in Orange County or the State of California. Defendants do not provide adequate preventive and diagnostic medical services to prisoners upon admission to the Jail. All prisoners already in the Jail are unnecessarily exposed to dangerous medical and/or contagious conditions that new prisoners might possess; and consequently, their lives and health are needlessly impaired. Defendants seize all medicine, drugs and pills, and most eyeglasses from prisoners upon admission to the Jail, even though such medications or devices may be lawfully prescribed and necessary to maintain the prisoner's life and health during chronic illnesses, such as diabetes or epilepsy. As a result of defendants' policies, newly admitted prisoners often suffer seizures and other adverse effects resulting from sudden deprivations of medication. Prisoners who manage to get medication while in the Jail often receive inappropriate and inadequate substitutes for seized prescription medications. Moreover, medication usually is distributed to prisoners at hours convenient to defendants and not to the medical needs of the prisoner.[2]

No psychologist or psychiatrist is available to give routine care to prisoners. Prisoners who are "diagnosed" as having psychological problems by jail officers are "treated" with isolation. Supervision of mentally disturbed prisoners is inadequate, and little or no medical or psychological treatment is provided for them. No attempt is made to transfer mentally ill prisoners to more appropriate facilities.[3]

Legal claims must, of course, be substantiated in court, but evidence strongly supports the existence of chronic deficiencies in jail medical care. Inadequate medical staffing, screening, and care for inmates with serious physical and mental health problems are related to jail deaths and suicides, and contribute to unnecessary suffering (Hayes 1983; Winfree and Wooldredge 1991). Overcrowding, especially in large jail facilities, makes matters worse (Wooldredge and Winfree 1992).

Most experts agree that the prevalence of physical health problems and mental disorder in jail populations is very high in proportion to services commonly available (Jerrell and Komisaruk 1991; Kalinich, Embert, and Senese 1991). A 1972 American Medical Association (AMA) survey found that 66 percent of jails had only first-aid facilities; 17 percent had no internal medical facilities; physicians were available on a regularly scheduled basis in only 38 percent of facilities; physicians were not even available on an on-call basis in half the facilities surveyed. Conditions had improved little six years later, and medical examinations upon admission were still rare unless inmates displayed obvious symptoms or injuries (Advisory Commission on Intergovernmental Relations 1984, 16). Of 3,316 jails surveyed in the quiennial national jail census of 1988 (U.S. Department of Justice 1991a), only 972 (29 percent) reported having a health unit or infirmary; 2,218 (67 percent) had no in-house medical facilities. Most jails still contract for medical services with outside agencies, and the level and type of care available in specific jails vary widely.

Litigation against jails and prisons has involved a large number of statutory and constitutional issues, in which twelve areas are paramount. A brief overview will suffice here (for detailed analyses of correctional case law, see Palmer 1987; Robbins 1987).

1. *Due process rights.* When inmates are brought up on charges of prison rule violations, they retain certain rights of due process, including the right to hear and present evidence at disciplinary hearings (*Wolff v. McDonnell*, 1974).

2. *Overcrowding.* Overcrowding is the problem most frequently resulting in court orders (U.S. Department of Justice 1992a), but standards are difficult to apply (Klofas, Stojkovic, and Kalinich 1992). Should overcrowding be judged in terms of square footage per inmate, capacity of the institution, time allowed outside cells, multiple occupancy, or totality of conditions (*Rhodes v. Chapman*, 1981; *Wilson v. Seiter*, 1991)? So far, the best legal answer is "all of the above."

3. *Censorship.* Inmates surrender many freedoms in prison or jail. Courts have upheld their basic rights to receive and send mail and other publications, but officials retain wide discretion to search or withhold mail when related to legitimate security issues (*Procunier v. Martinez*, 1974; *Wolff v. McDonnell*, 1974).

4. *Access to the courts.* Because of restrictions on their liberty, the state is obligated to ensure that inmates retain reasonable access to the legal system (*Bounds v. Smith*, 1977), including not only attorneys but often legal materials as well. Jail inmates frequently face pending criminal charges and await appeals; they may also petition the courts for changes in their individual conditions of confinement, in order, for example to get dentures or medication.

5. *Religious freedom and racial discrimination.* Inmates' rights to religious expression and freedom from racial discrimination are fairly well established, but prison officials retain wide discretion to ensure security (e.g., *Cooper v. Pate*, 1964). Black Muslims were the first group to succesfully litigate such rights in prison.

6. *Personal hygiene.* Deprivation of personal hygiene (showers, personal care items) does not stand alone as a violation of a fundamental right, but may constitute an Eighth Amendment violation as part of a "totality of conditions" argument (*Balla v. Idaho Board of Corrections*, 1987; *Pugh v. Locke*, 1976; *Rhodes v. Chapman*, 1981).

7. *Inadequate physical plants.* Deprivations constituted by poor sanitation (e.g., pestilence, inadequate or broken plumbing) also come under "totality of conditions" standards (*Balla v. Idaho Board of Corrections*, 1987; *Rhodes v. Chapman*, 1981).

8. *Medical care.* Inmates are assured rights to basic medical care, but legal claims are most likely to be upheld when deliberate indifference to prisoners' suffering (physical or mental) is demonstrated (*Estelle v. Gamble*, 1976).

9. *Educational and recreational programming.* Loss of freedom means that access to educational materials and reasonable indoor and outdoor exercise takes on added importance. It is not clear, however, that any "fundamental rights" exist in this area, and legal standards seem to depend largely upon particular circumstances, judges, and state correctional standards (Collins 1987, Ch. 9).

10. *Physical security and safety of inmates.* The state has an obligation to protect the safety of those committed to its care. Deliberate failure to protect prisoners from assault, injury, or dangerous conditions may constitute an Eighth Amendment violation (e.g., *Smith v. Wade*, 1983).

11. *Visitation.* Deprivation of liberty heightens the importance of contact with the outside world. Again, however, officials exercise wide discretion where legitimate security interests are at stake (*Pell v. Procunier*, 1974; *Stewart v. Gates*, 1978).

12. *Food services.* The quality and quantity of food provided will

always be of concern to those incarcerated by the state, and complaints about insufficient quantity, poor nutritional value, cold food, or insects in food are frequently litigated. There are no established federal rights regarding food services, although violations may form part of a "totality of conditions" ruling. State jail standards are also influential in deciding such issues (*Inmates of Sybil Brand v. County of Los Angeles*, 1982; *Stewart v. Gates*, 1978). Once again, correctional officials retain considerable discretion.

Although the U.S. Constitution is widely used to support inmate legal claims, legal arguments against county jails additionally rely upon state statutes, regulations, and constitutions. These standards vary considerably from state to state but receive careful judicial scrutiny in jail lawsuits. In California, for example, counsel for plaintiffs rely heavily upon the state Minimum Standards for Local Jails (15 CAC sections 1000 et seq.), sections of the state penal code that address jail procedures and policy, and various measures of the California Health and Safety Code and the Fire Code. Evidence suggests that judges hearing jail cases place a heavy emphasis on state statutes and standards in formulating their decisions (e.g., *Inmates of Sybil Brand v. County of Los Angeles*, 1982). When decisions are rendered in state trial courts, a state's interpretation of its own constitution is not easily subject to reversal by the Supreme Court (Herman 1988).

Laws unique to particular states (e.g., habeas corpus) provide crucial opportunities for initiating jail litigation (see Chapter 2). Differential opportunities for formulating and arguing legal claims are also afforded by unique state constitutions and regulatory laws. Such questions have rarely been addressed in a literature dominated by a focus upon federal laws and correctional litigation in federal courts.

The California constitution contains a broad guarantee of due process rights (Article I, sections 11, 21), which is often used to mount claims against mistreatment of pretrial prisoners, and a ban against cruel and unusual punishment (Article I, section 17), which is often used to argue for relief of overcrowding and poor living conditions. Twenty-one of the 43 California lawsuits I studied (49 percent) used these provisions of the state constitution to frame legal claims. The state Minimum Standards for Local Jails were invoked in 25 complaints (58 percent); sections of the state penal code (regarding provision of clothing and food to jail inmates, for example) in 28 cases (65 percent); and sections of the California Health and Safety Code (regarding treatment for addicts, for example) in 7 cases (16 percent). Overall, 36 of 43 complaints (86 percent) resulting in liability decisions cited multiple

**TABLE 10**
MAJOR BASES FOR LEGAL CLAIMS IN CALIFORNIA LAWSUITS

| FEDERAL LAW | BASES FOR LEGAL CLAIMS |
| --- | --- |
| Substantive | Federal Constitution |
| Procedural | Civil Rights Act |
| STATE LAW | BASES FOR LEGAL CLAIMS |
| Substantive | Constitution of the State of California |
| | California Minimum Standards for Local Jails |
| | California Penal Code |
| | California Health and Safety Code |
| | California Fire Code |
| Procedural | State habeas corpus laws |

provisions of state law, usually in addition to provisions of federal law, suggesting the pervasive influence of state legal climates upon jail litigation opportunities and strategies. Major bases for legal claims in federal and state court are summarized in Table 10.

## Legal Complaints in Jail Lawsuits

### Violations Alleged

The specific violations alleged in complaints against correctional facilities have rarely been examined. The number of violations alleged may relect the complexity of issues in a particular case, the litigants' adversarial relationship or both. The number and type of violations alleged depend upon applicable state law, strategies adopted by plaintiffs' legal counsel, and local jail conditions and punishment practices. The legal complaint plays a crucial role in framing and transforming the initial dispute. For example, allegations of inadequate medical care may require the testimony of health officials and documentation such as inmate request slips and medical records. The ability of plaintiffs' attorneys to create a strong record at the Liability Stage influences later negotiations with defendants and the court, the formulation of remedies, and mechanisms for monitoring and sanctioning compliance (Cooper 1988).

I examined variations in complaints across all California counties (35 counties, 43 cases overall) under court order for jail conditions over a 15-year period (1975–1989). The number of violations alleged in complaints ranged from a low of 1 to a high of 28, with an average of 12.8 per case. The most frequent allegations involved overcrowding (violations alleged in 86 percent of cases), recreation (77 percent), hygiene provisions (77 percent), access to courts (77 percent), medical care (74 percent), sanitation (67 percent), food services (65 percent), heating and ventilation (63 percent), visitation (48 percent), lighting (45 percent), inmate safety (45 percent), classification procedures (45 percent), censorship (41 percent), and staffing levels (36 percent). These core issues have constituted the major basis for jail lawsuits in California, and mirror the most frequent issues litigated nationally (U.S. Department of Justice 1992a). While no single issue constitutes a violation of law by itself, such issues often form the basis for arguments that the "totality of conditions" violates state or federal law.

As suggested earlier, state and federal courts present different vehicles for litigation filing and strategies, and are subject to different environmental influences. Although research has been scarce, it should come as no surprise to find that the jail issues litigated in state and federal courts differ. A greater number of total violations were filed in federal (mean = 15.9) than state court lawsuits (mean = 11.3), suggesting a more restrained posture by attorneys acting in state courts. There were also some variations in the types of issues litigated. In federal lawsuits, attorneys for inmates were more likely to file violations over issues of medical care (93 versus 64 percent), visitation (71 versus 36 percent), and staffing levels (57 versus 25 percent). Federal standards in the areas of medical care and visitation rights are well-established (see Palmer 1987, Chs. 3 and 10); staffing ratios were intimately related to inmate safety and Eighth Amendment claims (*Casselman v. Graham*, 1987; *Cherco v. County of Sonoma*, 1980; *Golden v. Taylor*, 1986; *Hedrick v. Grant*, 1976).

The influence of plaintiffs' legal representation, which begins at the Trigger Stage, becomes critical in the Liability Stage. Because different types of legal counsel employ different litigation strategies to achieve different goals (e.g., ideological reform, entrepreneurship, quick resolution), plaintiffs' legal representation significantly influences both the nature and the number (F (2,40) = 13.0, p < .01) of issues raised in complaints. Ideologically committed firms filed the most claims (N = 8, mean = 19.8), followed by private firms (N = 24, mean = 12.9) and public counsel (N = 11, mean = 7.5). Ideological attorneys thus file fewer cases but more charges per case than other attorneys. One explanation is that ideological attorneys use a "shotgun" approach: Alleging the existence of a large number of violations allows the totality of conditions standard to be more fully addressed. It was suggested earlier, however, that ideological attorneys are conscious of the jurisdictions with the most grievous violations and need to establish important test cases in correctional law. As a result, ideological attorneys file many charges to address many perceived deficits, but also to meet their own needs.

Specific jail conditions and issues are also litigated with differing frequencies (Table 11). Ideological attorneys were more likely to allege violations of medical care, visitation privileges, censorship, and inadequate lighting than private or public counsel. The first three issues fit squarely into the civil rights agenda of the ACLU. Such issues have also been clearly defined in federal case law, a subject of intimate familiarity to ideological attorneys. Poor lighting, a less obvious but important problem, was often related to other concerns such as inmate safety and the ability to read and prepare legal materials for one's defense. Differential experience and different goals, therefore, lead to differences in the nature and frequency of issues litigated by different attorneys, and perhaps the type and frequency of relief they obtain.

In sum, the number and type of violations alleged in legal complaints against jails depends on several major factors: state versus federal law as a basis for legal claims, level of court, nature of plaintiffs'

**TABLE 11**
**INFLUENCE OF PLAINTIFFS' LEGAL REPRESENTATION ON TYPES OF**
**VIOLATIONS ALLEGED IN COMPLAINTS**

| Type of Violation Alleged | Type of Legal Representation | | | |
|---|---|---|---|---|
| | *Ideological* (N = 8) | *Private* (N = 24) | *Public* (N = 11) | $\chi^2$ (2 df) |
| Medical care | 8 (100.0%) | 19 (79.2%) | 5 (45.5%) | 7.88* |
| Visitation rights | 7 (87.5%) | 13 (54.2%) | 1 (9.1)% | 12.01* |
| Access to courts | 8 (100.0%) | 19 (79.2%) | 6 (54.5%) | 5.54 |
| Censorship | 6 (75.0%) | 9 (37.5%) | 2 (18.2%) | 6.35* |
| Food services | 6 (75.0%) | 17 (70.8%) | 5 (45.5%) | 2.56 |
| Recreation | 8 (100.0%) | 18 (75.0%) | 7 (63.6%) | 3.52 |
| Personal hygiene | 7 (87.5%) | 20 (83.3%) | 6 (54.5%) | 4.14 |
| Overcrowding | 6 (75.0%) | 20 (83.3%) | 11 (100.0%) | 2.74 |
| Ventilation | 7 (87.5%) | 15 (62.5%) | 5 (45.5%) | 3.51 |
| Lighting | 7 (87.5%) | 12 (50.0%) | 0 (0%) | 15.12* |
| Safety of inmates | 4 (50.0%) | 13 (54.2%) | 2 (18.2%) | 4.09 |
| Sanitation | 6 (75.0%) | 16 (66.7%) | 7 (63.6%) | 0.29 |
| Classification of inmates | 4 (50.0%) | 14 (58.3%) | 2 (18.2%) | 4.94 |
| Staffing levels | 3 (37.5%) | 10 (41.7%) | 2 (18.2%) | 1.86 |

*$p < .05$.

**TABLE 12**
NUMBER AND NATURE OF VIOLATIONS ALLEGED IN COMPLAINTS
AGAINST JAILS: MAJOR INFLUENCES

| NUMBER OF VIOLATIONS ALLEGED | MAJOR INFLUENCES |
|---|---|
| High | Level of court (federal) |
| | Plaintiffs' legal representation (ideological) |
| | Historical jail conditions (poor) |
| Low | Level of court (state) |
| | Plaintiffs' legal representation (public) |

| NATURE OF SPECIFIC VIOLATIONS ALLEGED | MAJOR INFLUENCES |
|---|---|
| Medical care | Level of court (federal) |
| | Bases for legal claims (federal) |
| | Plaintiffs' legal representation (ideological) |
| | Historical jail conditions (poor) |
| Visitation | Level of court (federal) |
| | Bases for legal claims (federal) |
| | Plaintiffs' legal representation (ideological) |
| | Historical jail conditions (poor) |
| Staffing | Level of court (federal) |
| | Bases for legal claims (federal) |
| | Historical jail conditions (poor) |
| Censorship | Plaintiffs' legal representation (ideological) |
| | Historical jail conditions (poor) |
| Lighting | Plaintiffs' legal representation (ideological) |
| | Historical jail conditions (poor) |

legal representation, local punishment conditions, and prisoner expenditures. Variations in violations alleged and major influences are summarized in Table 12.

## Type of Defendants Named

The defendants named by plaintiffs' counsel in complaints are important influences on litigation process. County supervisors, in particular, have considerable political and fiscal resources to resist jail challenges, and significantly influence the manner in which issues are contested and remedies are formulated. Litigation often creates sharp rifts between co-defendants—county supervisors, county executives, sheriffs, and other justice agencies. We expect conflict between defendants and plaintiffs in social reform–oriented civil lawsuits; we often do not look deeply enough at disputes between groups of defendants. In short, defendants act and interact in a variety of ways that shape disputes over jail conditions, and the naming of specific defendants by plaintiffs' counsel is a critically important event in the Liability Stage.

Naming county supervisors as defendants in jail lawsuits has both advantages and disadvantages. Because the county board of supervisors is responsible for personnel and financial allocations to the jail, those officials share a certain amount of liability for unconstitutional jail conditions. When government officials are named as defendants, it is less likely that they can deflect blame for jail problems (Welsh et al. 1990), and more likely that judges will hold them accountable for planning and expenditures crucial to jail reform. However, forced change often inspires resistance by politically powerful government officials (Sieber 1981), possibly escalating conflict and obfuscating attempts to garner compliance. Government defendants have a variety of tools and resources at their disposal to frustrate plaintiffs' efforts: filing numerous interlocutory appeals to buy time, diffusing responsibility among government agents, requesting extensions, filing motions to surpress evidence, and so on.

The sheriff and jail commander, who share responsibility for managing the jail, are frequently named as co-defendants. Each role has its own sphere of political power and authority because of the fragmentation of local government, and each can be distinguished from county supervisors by a more direct legal liability for unconstitutional jail conditions. The sheriff, with statutory responsibility for jail operations, is clearly the favored target for legal complaints over jail conditions. In contrast to county supervisors, it is somewhat "safer" for plaintiffs' counsel to go after the sheriff in jail lawsuits, although in some larger counties elected sheriffs also carry considerable political clout.

Those most frequently named as defendants in California jail lawsuits were the county sheriff (in 91 percent of cases), the county board of supervisors (62 percent), and the jail commander (33 percent). In those lawsuits naming the board of supervisors as defendants ($N = 26$), more violations were filed in the legal complaint (the mean number of violations alleged was 15.3 versus 8.9), suggesting either greater prior neglect of jail problems in these cases or more vigorous attempts by plaintiffs' counsel to hold supervisors accountable for jail improvements (or both). Indeed, *counties* in which supervisors were named as defendants ($N = 23$) showed lower per prisoner expenditures (in constant dollars) in 1986 ($9,177) than other counties under lawsuit ($12,294), and a greater degree of overcrowding (118 percent versus 106 percent of capacity filled) than other counties under lawsuit.

Plaintiffs' legal representation strongly influences whether supervisors are named as defendants. Private attorneys and public counsel are more closely tied to local business and political elites, and are more likely to fear reprisals against their own businesses or careers. Supervisors with strong local political ties receive support from allies—members of the local bar, business owners, officials in various county agencies—who can apply pressure against a private or public attorney who challenges their authority. Indeed, results suggested that legal representation differentially influenced the naming of supervisors as defendants ($\chi^2 = 6.77$, p $< .04$). Ideologically committed attorneys named supervisors as defendants in 7 of their 8 cases (88 percent), private firms did so in 16 of 24 cases (67 percent), while public counsel did so in only 3 of 10 cases (30 percent). Those most closely tied to local political cultures, therefore, are less likely to challenge elites. Ideologically committed firms, in contrast, are less fettered by local environmental constraints, and may target supervisors more frequently because experience suggests the importance of holding government officials accountable for reform.

The level of court also influences whether politically powerful officials are named as defendants. State courts are often perceived as partial to the interests of local elites (Kessler 1990). Although state law in California presents favorable opportunities for filing jail lawsuits and formulating legal claims in state courts, attorneys may be reluctant to challenge county supervisors directly because they anticipate reprisals, prolonged resistance, or inadequate resources to sustain litigation. Results confirmed that state courts had a chilling effect upon the naming of county supervisors as defendants ($\chi^2 = 5.05$, p $< .03$). Twelve of 14 cases filed in the federal courts (86 percent) named supervisors as defendants, while only 14 of 28 cases filed in state courts (50 percent) did so.

Because of the cross-sectional, correlational nature of these data, conclusions must be tentative. It is important to note, however, that one major actor in jail lawsuits—the county supervisor—appears in less than two-thirds of jail lawsuits. Reasons for this observed variation, I suggest, are not random. The naming of county supervisors as defendants by plaintiffs' counsel requires a degree of skill, resources, and autonomy from local legal and political environments that is best provided by repeat players such as ideological attorneys. The dramatic, continuing influence of this defendant group on outcomes at subsequent stages of litigation is examined in Chapters 4 and 5. Major influences on the decision to name specific defendants are summarized in Table 13.

## TABLE 13
### Defendants Named in Complaints Against Jails: Major Influences

| Defendants Named | Major Influences |
|---|---|
| County supervisors | Overcrowding (high) |
| | Prisoner expenditures (low) |
| | Number of violations alleged in complaint (high) |
| | Plaintiffs' legal representation (ideological) |
| | Level of court (federal) |
| Sheriff | Historical jail conditions (poor) |
| Jail commander | Historical jail conditions (poor) |

## Case Studies

The following case studies provide a background and context of the jail litigation in three counties, incorporating major concepts from the Liability Stage.

### Contra Costa

Contra Costa County is located just east of San Francisco. On 25 December 1984, 41 inmates signed and filed a habeas corpus petition complaining of conditions at the main detention facility in Martinez (*Yancey v. Rainey*, 1985). Inmates complained of 10 specific conditions, including overcrowding and inadequacies in access to courts, food service, personal hygiene and sanitation, grievance procedures, heat and ventilation, and recreation. Sheriff Richard K. Rainey was the only respondent named in the petition. In their prayer for relief, inmates asked the court to declare all applicable rights under the state and federal constitutions and requested a restraining order to prevent possible reprisals or disciplinary transfers due to the filing of the petition. On 27 December 1984, Superior Court Judge Richard Arneson appointed the county public defender to represent inmates. The sheriff was represented by county counsel.

In their return to the writ of habeas corpus, county counsel argued that many of the petitioners' claims were frivolous, including overcrowding (45 out of 50 prisoners on the B module, including the petitioner, were housed in single cells). Inmate petitioners argued in turn that the county's response ignored crucial discrepancies between written procedures specifying services and the actual delivery of those services. For example, both plaintiffs and defendants agreed that winter blankets were issued, but plaintiffs argued that these blankets were functionally inadequate. Both parties agreed that the central computer was set to maintain temperatures at 72 degrees, but plaintiffs argued that the temperature in individual cells rarely met that level. Jail policies required a monthly pest inspection, but there was no evidence that it was regularly conducted. Other responses by defendants were vehemently disputed by plaintiffs: For example, the "law clerk" who the county claimed was on duty in the jail was really a part-time library assistant lacking the legal training and resources needed to fill inmate requests for legal materials. Judge Arneson's response (see Chapter 4) was to handle discussions and negotiations informally (in chambers) prior to issuing his only orders in this case.

## Santa Clara

Santa Clara County is located southeast of San Francisco in "Silicon Valley." Santa Clara has faced lawsuits over both the men's (*Branson v. Winter*, 1981) and the women's jails (*Fischer v. Winter*, 1983). The women's case, filed in U.S. District Court on 6 October 1976, centered on overcrowding, which led to scarcities in beds, bedding, clothing, food, showers, space, staff supervision, and other resources. Conditions in women's jails and prisons certainly deserve more separate and careful analysis, since both jail conditions and lawsuits differ in important ways from those affecting men's jails (Daly, Geballe, and Wheeler 1988; Fabian 1980; Resnick and Shaw 1984). In Santa Clara, it was the men's jail case that created the greatest difficulties for litigants and judges, and that case is the main focus in this study.

As the jail population in Santa Clara mushroomed (Chapter 2), so did media coverage and the visibility of jail issues. By the time 18 male inmates filed habeas corpus petitions in the local Superior Court, judges already had their clerks poised to process the petitions. None of the major law firms in the area would take the case; eventually, the local bar-sponsored Public Interest Law Firm agreed to pursue injunctive relief on the inmates' behalf. Note that the level of court was actually chosen by plaintiffs themselves, and the court subsequently appointed legal counsel.

On 28 April 1981, the Public Interest Law Firm of Santa Clara filed an amended complaint alleging 19 violations of inmates' civil rights (42 USC 1983) and constitutional rights at the men's Main Jail in San Jose, including overcrowding, brutality, and deficiencies in medical care, access to courts, food service and preparation, recreation, personal hygiene and sanitation, grievance and disciplinary procedures, use of isolation cells, and written rules of conduct. The sheriff, the jail commander, the county board of supervisors, and the County of Santa Clara were all named as defendants. All defendants were initially represented by county counsel; later, when tensions and conflicts of interest between the sheriff and the board of supervisors intensified, the sheriff retained private legal counsel (see Chapter 5).

The adversarial nature of these proceedings was foreshadowed when plaintiffs' counsel sought and obtained a stipulation and order granting access to the Main Jail to gather information and evidence (11 May 1981). Who would be granted access, in what numbers, where, and to whom was spelled out in minute detail. Numerous conferences between the judge and counsel for defendants and plaintiffs followed, but little progress was made in establishing issues of fact or disposing of the many contested issues in this case. The only facts that were clearly established and admitted to by defendants were that the jail was seriously overcrowded and that conditions had deteriorated in recent years as a result. Defendants argued that the construction of portable housing units and the approval of jail construction plans by the board of supervisors were sufficient to warrant dismissal of the case. Neither the judge nor plaintiffs agreed with that position. Partial, interim orders regarding jail population reductions were issued only four months later (see Chapter 4), but most of the major issues and respective resolutions in this case remained contested for years, and had to be litigated through a formal, lengthy, and bitterly fought trial process.

## Orange

Orange County is located south of Los Angeles County along the California coastline. As in Santa Clara, deteriorating environmental conditions distinguished Orange County's jail (Chapter 2). Between 1976 and 1986, the jail population more than doubled; the incarceration rate doubled; overcrowding worsened; and expenditures per prisoner decreased. The lawsuit was initiated earlier than the one in Santa Clara, however, and the original complaint focused primarily on long-standing staff misconduct and mistreatment of prisoners, rather than overcrowding. While local punishment practices became influential later, allegations of chronic neglect and mistreatment were the major factors mobilizing plaintiffs to seek legal assistance.

A lawsuit filed by the ACLU on 22 October 1975 alleged 19 violations of inmates' civil rights (42 USC 1983) and constitutional rights at the main jail in Santa Ana, including overcrowding, brutality, and inadequacies in medical care, access to courts, recreation, grievance and disciplinary procedures, personal hygiene provisions, and sanitation. The sheriff, the jail commander, and the county board of supervisors were named as defendants. Eleven inmate plaintiffs were named; the lawsuit was certified on 9 February 1976 as a class action on behalf of all pretrial and sentenced prisoners, both male and female.

In the pattern typical of ideological attorneys, the ACLU chose federal court as its arena, based legal claims upon a substantial body of both state and federal law, alleged a high number of violations, and named county supervisors as defendants. While scapegoating is common in these cases (Welsh et al. 1990), some defendants suggested that plaintiffs' counsel, a local attorney contracted by the ACLU, had been given a "hunting licence" by the judge and was making a profitable living from jail litigation. Plaintiffs' counsel, in contrast, insisted that jail litigation was frustrating and financially precarious, and that gross constitutional violations, including brutality and neglect of life-threatening medical conditions, provided all the motivation necessary.

A protracted series of written exchanges between plaintiffs and defendants followed the complaint. Numerous issues of fact and liability were contested, and the initial discovery period of the case lasted several months. On 13 December 1976, Judge William Gray issued a pretrial conference order that outlined all admitted and remaining (contested) issues of fact to be litigated in trial. Admitted facts pertained to the legal status of prisoners, proper defendants, jail populations, dimensions and amenities of housing facilities at the main jail, and written procedures regarding prisoner mail, visits, and exercise. The bulk of the case, 72 contested issues of fact in total, remained to be decided in court through a formal trial process. The remainder of the 43-page pretrial conference order was devoted to laying out the legal issues and cases to be presented by counsel.

On 25 March 1977, plaintiffs and defendants finally entered into a stipulation over the provision of medical and dental care. These were the only issues disposed of prior to the judge's Memorandum to Counsel of 26 January 1978, which ruled on numerous contested issues of fact, dismissing some as unsupported, and substantiating others (e.g., inadequate access to telephones; inadequate posting of rules of conduct; rights of visitation for minor children). Judge Gray also asked defendants for further information and plans on other issues, such as posting of written rules, and announced the court's intention to formulate orders on visitation and other matters. The Liability Stage in this case, therefore, was a complex and lengthy (30 month) process, handled through formal and burdensome legal procedures. As we will see in the next chapter, events and issues raised at the Liability Stage resurfaced and continued to exert influence throughout subsequent stages of the case.

## Summary

Although much of the literature on remedial decrees proceeds swiftly to the remedy-crafting stage (Cooper 1988), the Liability Stage involves an interrelated set of actions that crucially affects legal outcomes and compliance in jail lawsuits.

Differences in legal "claiming" provide one of the most critical earmarks distinguishing jail reform lawsuits from their state or federal prison counterparts. Certain core issues like overcrowding and medical care dominate complaints in jail lawsuits, with provisions of state law frequently providing the basis for legal claims. While state laws vary greatly, they receive careful attention in jail lawsuits in any state, and findings of violations of state law are not easily subject to reversal by the Supreme Court.

Ideological attorneys filed the most alleged violations in jail lawsuits, partly as a result of more grievous jail conditions, but partly as a result of a litigation strategy aimed at establishing important test cases and meeting a "totality of conditions" standard. Ideological attorneys also filed lawsuits more frequently in federal courts, because of greater familiarity with precedents related to federal case law and constitutional law, as well as the broader expertise, autonomy, and powers of the federal judiciary.

County supervisors were most likely to be named as defendants by ideologically committed attorneys, and least likely to be named by public counsel, suggesting that any "chilling" influence on filing jail reform lawsuits in state courts is more strongly related to the naming of specific defendants (county supervisors) by specific legal counsel (public and private attorneys) than to the initiation of litigation per se. Legal complaints naming county supervisors as defendants also evidenced harsher jail conditions, suggesting that more experienced "repeat players" targeted jurisdictions with more deprived conditions and attempted to assign responsibility to key government officials as a means of achieving reform. Public and private counsel, more likely to possess direct or indirect ties to the local political environment, showed greater restraint. The roles played by politically powerful government defendants become critically important as jail cases progress (see Ekland-Olson and Martin 1988; Welsh and Pontell 1991).

Case studies examining critical, related events at the Trigger and Liability Stages support the patterns demonstrated by quantitative results. In all three cases, but particularly in Santa Clara and Orange, increased incarceration rates, overcrowding, and deteriorating jail conditions preceded the initiation of legal complaints. In two cases, inmates were represented by ideologically motivated reform lawyers; in Contra Costa, the least "urban" of the three counties, the county public defender was appointed to represent inmates after a flurry of petitions was launched in state court.

Although only one case was filed in federal court, all three (as expected) utilized provisions of state and federal law to support their legal claims. Characteristic of cases involving ideological attorneys and federal courts, the Orange County case had a large number of alleged violations (19), although it tied with the other case filed by ideological attorneys (Santa Clara) in state rather than federal court. In all three cases, the legal complaint raised serious issues that were contested by defendants. No one admits liability immediately, but the defendants' tone was more adversarial and their denials were more vehement in the Orange and Santa Clara cases, perhaps setting the stage for a more formal, lengthy, and burdensome trial process. Also consistent with the patterns of quantitative results, lawsuits naming county supervisors as defendants were characterized by more grievous jail conditions, plaintiff representation by ideological attorneys, and a greater number of alleged violations in the legal complaint. By contrast, the Contra Costa lawsuit dealt with more limited and less grievous violations. All of these factors increase in relevance as a lawsuit progresses.

In sum, quantitative and qualitative (case study) analyses supported much the same pattern of results. Measurable and observable dynamics at the Trigger and Liability Stages explain a good deal not only about how lawsuits get into court, but about what happens when they get there. The next chapter explores decisions and events at the remedy formulation stage.

# CHAPTER 4

## The Remedy Stage

It is not difficult to recognize and enter orders against extremely bad living conditions or harsh and cruel discipline as being in violation of constitutional rights. But the question of whether less onerous treatment that may be undesirable, or even deplorable, is bad enough to be termed a constitutional deprivation presents some very difficult problems. In undertaking to resolve these matters, this court has tried to limit its interference to situations in which a constitutional right is quite clearly involved. As to these matters, the court intends to make certain that the remedial actions that it directs are accomplished.

**—*Stewart v. Gates*, 1978**

$\mathbf{M}$ANY WHO ANALYZE court-ordered reform attribute primary control over the formulation of remedial decrees to judges. Yet judicial decisions about constitutional violations and appropriate remedies are not constructed independently. Legal outcomes in complex civil litigation, including jail lawsuits, are shaped by a constellation of actors and events, including the specific legal claims and violations alleged by plaintiffs, requests for specific relief, litigation strategies of plaintiffs and defendants, judicial methods for decree formulation, negotiations between litigants and judges, and the continuing influence of forces in the local legal and political environments. In short, remedy formulation is a product of previous factors at the Trigger and Liability Stages and of new events that emerge at the Remedy Stage. The types of remedies specified, moreover, are crucial to an exploration of jail reform litigation. The use of jail population caps to reduce overcrowding, for example, results in such controversial actions as early release, citation release, and the construction of new facilities.

Although the legal complaint frames the issues to be litigated, there is no one-to-one relation between violations alleged by plaintiffs in the complaint and remedies specified in court decrees. New issues often surface during the course of lengthy litigation. Some claims will eventually be upheld; others will not. If a claim is upheld, plaintiffs may ask for specific relief, judges may order defendants to formulate plans to achieve certain standards of performance, or both parties may negotiate extensively in the remedy-crafting stage. This chapter explores variations in the contextual influences on judicial methods, negotiating styles, and the number and type of remedies formulated in jail lawsuits.

## Remedies in Court Orders Against Jails

### The "Original" Decision

Across 43 California jail lawsuits, the number of remedies specified in the original court order or decree ranged from 1 to 27 (the possible range was from 0 to 37 different jail conditions). There was a mean of 8.7 remedies per decision. The most frequent outcome was that no relief at all was granted across the spectrum of jail conditions (mean occurrences of no relief = 31.3 per case). This finding alone suggests a rather conservative stance on the part of the judiciary in general and brings into question perceptions of pervasive "judicial activism." Remedies where the courts ordered only written plans (mean = 1.5 issues per case) or granted less relief than plaintiffs sought in the complaint (mean = 0.5 issues per case) were rare. Remedies where plaintiffs received relief approximately equal to that sought in the complaint were more frequent (mean = 4.6 issues per case). Plaintiffs rarely received greater relief than they sought (mean = 0.2 issues per case), but they sometimes received relief on issues emerging subsequent to the filing of the original complaint (mean = 2.0 issues per case).

### Additional Decisions and Remedies

The courts commonly continued jurisdiction for some time after the initial decision, issuing numerous new and modified orders. We sometimes talk about jail lawsuits as though there were only a single court "decision"—as though all remedies were specified at a single point in time and the case then shifted immediately into the monitoring and compliance phase. Such a view is far removed from reality. Jail lawsuits are extremely complex, expensive, time-consuming, and demanding. Motions are filed; expert witnesses are brought in; conditions are monitored; negotiations are conducted; sanctions for noncompliance with original orders are sought. In reality, there is rarely a single court "decision" in which remedies are specified. There is instead a whole series of decisions in which remedies are gradually crafted, accumulated, and modified. Legal impact studies that omit the time-consuming step of enumerating modifications thus miss a good deal of the real history of a case.

The number of modified orders (issued subsequent to the original decision) in the lawsuits examined ranged from 0 to 143, with a mean of 11.5 modifications per case. In fully 18 cases (41.9 percent), the courts issued 10 or more modified orders, suggesting a high degree of difficulty in gaining compliance from these counties. Santa Clara, for example, had more modifications (143) than original orders (4). Over entire lawsuit histories (original orders plus modified orders), the courts issued an average of 20.2 orders per case. Appellate courts rarely altered orders issued by the trial court (only 10 orders in three cases).

A tally of the number of cases that resulted in any relief on each issue over the entire history of these cases (from the original decision up to and including the most recent modification), independent of whether an issue was alleged in the complaint or not revealed that overcrowding was the most frequent issue remedied (79 percent of all cases had at least one order to reduce overcrowding). Other issues most commonly remedied were, in general, those about which there were the most complaints (see Chapter 3): medical care (58 percent), hygiene (58 percent), recreation (51 percent), sanitation (49 percent), access to courts (49 percent), food service (44 percent), visitation (40 percent), and classification procedures (40 percent). See Table 14.

Some surprising findings emerge when we examine the entire history of a lawsuit, not just the original decision. As new issues emerge during the course of a trial, courts often order remedies for conditions not originally cited by plaintiffs in the legal complaint. Four types of violations showed such unusual patterns of relief. Although each was rarely alleged in original complaints, remedies later came about as a result of negotiations between litigants, the trial judge, or special masters.

Inadequate pretrial release mechanisms such as bail and release on own recognizance (ROR) were alleged in only 5 complaints, but remedies were ordered or crafted in 21 cases. Inadequate postrelease mechanisms (e.g., county parole, work release, early release) were alleged in only 6 original complaints, but remedies were crafted in 25 cases. Allegations of inadequate physical plants (with calls for extensive renovation, closing, or construction of jail facilities) were made in only 5 original complaints, while remedies were granted in 16 cases. Allega-

## TABLE 14
### Relief Granted over the History of a Case

| Issue | Relief Granted | |
|---|---|---|
| | Yes | No |
| Overcrowding | 34 (79%) | 9 (21%) |
| Inadequate medical care | 25 (58%) | 18 (42%) |
| Inadequate personal hygiene provisions | 25 (58%) | 18 (42%) |
| Inadequate postconviction release | 25 (58%) | 18 (42%) |
| Inadequate recreational opportunities | 22 (51%) | 21 (49%) |
| Inadequate pretrial release | 21 (49%) | 22 (51%) |
| Inadequate sanitation | 21 (49%) | 22 (51%) |
| Inadequate access to courts | 21 (49%) | 22 (51%) |
| Inadequate food services | 19 (44%) | 24 (56%) |
| Inadequate visitation rights | 17 (40%) | 26 (60%) |
| Inadequate classification of inmates | 17 (40%) | 26 (60%) |
| Inadequate physical plant | 16 (37%) | 27 (63%) |
| Inadequate ventilation | 14 (33%) | 29 (67%) |
| Inadequate staffing levels | 13 (30%) | 30 (70%) |
| Inadequate telephone availability | 13 (30%) | 30 (70%) |
| Censorship | 13 (30%) | 30 (70%) |
| Inadequate grievance procedures | 13 (30%) | 30 (70%) |
| Inadequate disciplinary procedures | 11 (26%) | 32 (74%) |
| Fire hazards | 10 (23%) | 33 (77%) |
| Failure to ensure safety of inmates | 10 (23%) | 33 (77%) |
| Improper use of holding cells | 10 (23%) | 33 (77%) |
| Inadequate lighting | 9 (21%) | 34 (79%) |
| Inadequate access to attorneys | 9 (21%) | 34 (79%) |
| Failure to post rules or procedures | 8 (19%) | 35 (81%) |
| Inadequate rules or procedures | 7 (16%) | 36 (84%) |
| Inadequate educational opportunities | 7 (16%) | 36 (84%) |
| Inadequate counseling programs | 7 (16%) | 36 (84%) |
| Inadequate work opportunities | 6 (14%) | 37 (86%) |
| Inadequate staff training | 5 (12%) | 38 (88%) |
| Improper use of isolation cells | 4 (9%) | 39 (91%) |
| Inadequate sleep | 4 (9%) | 39 (91%) |
| Excessive institutional noise | 3 (7%) | 40 (93%) |
| Unfair treatment re: race, etc. | 3 (7%) | 40 (93%) |
| Unfair treatment re: religion | 3 (7%) | 40 (93%) |
| Illegal or unfair transfer | 3 (7%) | 40 (93%) |
| Improper use of administrative segregation | 3 (7%) | 40 (93%) |
| Brutality | 1 (2%) | 42 (98%) |

*Note:* This table includes both original and modified orders. It presents the number of cases resulting in any relief on each issue, independent of the depth of orders issued by the court or the original allegations made by plaintiffs in the legal complaint.

tions of inadequate access to institutions were filed by inmate attorneys in no original complaints: Such issues emerged later during the discovery phase. In 9 cases judges later ordered relief granting access to plaintiffs' attorneys. Given the importance of discovery in building a case, such orders crucially affect litigation outcomes. The complexity of responses to litigation, therefore, requires examination past the original decision or decree. Strategies to reduce jail overcrowding, including early release, work release, early parole, and jail expansion, carry critical political, financial, and personal consequences (see Chapters 5 and 6).

### Attrition: Do Plaintiffs Get What They Want?

There was considerable "attrition" between violations alleged and relief granted. In other words, plaintiffs gained relief of any kind on only a subset of violations originally alleged in the legal complaint. For the 14 most frequently alleged violations, relief of any kind was granted in only a fraction of cases. Remedies were issued in only 37 percent of cases in which a lighting violation was alleged in the legal complaint. "Success" rates for other issues cited in complaints were as follows: ventilation (42 percent), inmate safety (42 percent), inadequate food services (52 percent), staffing levels (53 percent), recreation (59 percent), sanitation (61 percent), access to courts (63 percent), medical care (65 percent), visitation rights (65 percent), classification (68 percent), censorship (70 percent), personal hygiene (70 percent), and overcrowding (86 percent).

Attorneys were thus more successful in gaining relief in some "core" areas than in others. Overcrowding allegations were most likely to result in relief, testifying to the centrality of overcrowding to other problems, and perhaps to the existence of measurable (although multiple) standards. In spite of perceptions by some of a "radical judiciary," courts in this study were quite conservative in granting relief on most of the issues raised by plaintiffs in legal complaints.

### Influence of the Level of Court

The nature and number of remedies issued also varies across state and federal courts. In discussing the Trigger and Liability Stages, I suggested that California's laws dealing with habeas corpus and jail operations facilitate the initiation of litigation in state courts, but the political environment of state courts imposes constraints on subsequent litigant and judicial behavior. In Chapter 3, for example, we saw that public and private attorneys were less likely to name county supervisors as defendants in lawsuits filed in state courts. In federal lawsuits, more orders were issued in the original decisions (means = 13.2 versus 6.3) and over the entire life of the case (means = 26.3 versus 17.4) than in state courts. Federal courts were less likely than state courts to deny relief on particular claims (means = 26.6 versus 33.7 issues per case), but equally likely to grant less relief than plaintiffs asked for (means = 0.4 and 0.6 respectively). Federal courts were more likely than state courts to grant relief equal to what was asked for (means = 8.1 versus 2.8). These results suggest a pattern of greater relief in federal courts, but closer scutiny is required.

Of the 14 most frequently alleged violations, federal courts were significantly more likely than state courts to grant relief only on 4 issues: medical care (85 versus 50 percent of cases in which violations were alleged in each court); recreation (83 versus 45 percent); visitation (90 versus 40 percent); and classification (100 versus 50 percent). As suggested earlier, medical care and vision are well-established issues in federal case law, and federal judges have greater acquaintance and experience with such precedents. Recreation and classification have less well-established precedents, but relate to Eighth and Fourteenth Amendment questions regarding the basic services and protections to be afforded to those deprived of their liberty.

### Influence of Defendants

Counties where county supervisors were named as defendants had particularly serious jail overcrowding and underfunding problems (see Chapter 3), but the defendants' greater political power might have made them more able and willing to resist legal challenges (see e.g., Kessler 1990). Results challenge the "political advantage" thesis, however. In lawsuits naming the board of supervisors as defendants (N = 26), more orders were issued in the original decision (means = 10.8 versus 5.1); more modified orders were issued (means = 16.8 versus 3.6); and more total orders were issued over the life of the case (means = 27.6 versus 8.7).

Greater depth of relief was also found for lawsuits naming supervisors as defendants: fewer occasions where no relief was granted in response to original allegations (means = 29.2 versus 34.8), and more occasions where plaintiffs received relief approximately equal to what was sought in the complaint (means = 5.7 versus 2.6). Such results reflect more grievous violations in these cases as well as greater persistence by plaintiffs' counsel. Indeed, orders to reduce overcrowding were more likely in cases where supervisors were named as defendants

(69 percent) than in other cases (25 percent). The same was true of orders to improve staffing (35 versus 0 percent), orders to improve the physical plant of the jail (39 versus 13 percent), and orders to release sentenced inmates (54 versus 25 percent). These issues define a constellation of politically unpopular and expensive policy decisions for which county supervisors are held uniquely accountable.

### Influence of Legal Representation

Given the pervasive influence of legal representation demonstrated in the Trigger and Liability States, we might expect different types of plaintiffs' counsel to obtain different legal outcomes. In fact, plaintiffs' legal counsel did not influence either the breadth (number of orders) or the depth of relief (rated 0–5) received in the *original* decision. Jail lawsuits, however, are extremely complex, expensive, time-consuming, and demanding. Motions are filed; expert witnesses are brought in; conditions are monitored; negotiations are conducted; sanctions for noncompliance are sought. Ideologically committed attorneys obtained the most modifications (mean = 28.8) and total orders (mean = 39.0) over the life of the case, while private counsel obtained more modifications (mean = 8.9) and total orders (mean = 18.5) than public counsel (means = 4.7 and 10.2, respectively). Ideological attorneys are more vigorous than other counsel, not only in pursuing legal claims, but also in shaping remedies and monitoring jail conditions over time. Their greater experience is also related to success in establishing relevant legal bases for claims and substantiating those claims with evidence (see Chapter 3).

To estimate the relative impact of different explanatory variables, the total number of remedies was regressed on total violations alleged in the complaint; supervisors as defendants (1 = Yes, 0 = No); state court (1 = Yes, 0 = No); and representation by ideological attorneys (1 = Yes, 0 = No). The regression equation was significant ($F = 2.92$, $p < .04$), with only "ideological attorneys" and "supervisor defendants" emerging as statistically significant predictors of total remedies. "State court" and "total violations filed" added little predictive power. The greatest number of court orders and the greatest conflict between litigants in jail reform lawsuits may be expected, therefore, when ideological attorneys challenge county supervisors. More adversarial relations and the dedication of greater legal and political resources are suggested by this volatile combination. Major influences on the total number of remedies are summarized in Table 15.

**TABLE 15**
INFLUENCES ON TOTAL NUMBER OF REMEDIES IN JAIL LAWSUITS

| Variation in the Number of Remedies Specified | Major Influences |
|---|---|
| High | Defendants named (supervisors) |
| | Plaintiffs' legal counsel (ideological) |
| | Legal bases for claims (strong) |
| | Evidence for claims (strong) |
| Low | Defendants named (not supervisors) |
| | Plaintiffs' legal counsel (public) |
| | Legal bases for claims (weak) |
| | Evidence for claims (weak) |

## Summary: Influences on the Nature and Number of Remedies

Remedies can be usefully broken down into those specified in the original court decision and those added subsequent to the decision. Their influences are slightly different.

In the original decision, a higher number of remedies specified was related to the number of violations alleged in the original complaint, the level of court (federal), the defendants named in jail lawsuits (county supervisors), and strong legal bases and supporting evidence for claims. As we saw in Chapter 3, a high number of violations alleged in the complaint indicates more grievous jail conditions but also reflects the efforts of particular plaintiff attorneys. Ideologically motivated attorneys tend to target jurisdictions with more serious violations to establish important test cases; they also file more violations and gain more relief. Nor is it purely coincidental that county supervisors are named in lawsuits where more remedies are specified. Again, as noted, lawsuits where supervisors are named as defendants tend to show greater patterns of jail violations. Ideological attorneys, because of their greater experience and autonomy from local political environments, are more likely to name supervisors in such suits. Finally, federal as opposed to state courts granted twice as many remedies to plaintiffs in original court decisions, suggesting federal judges' greater persistence and independence from local political environments. Major influences on the number of remedies in original court decisions are summarized in Table 16.

Over the entire history of a case, however, the influence of federal

**TABLE 16**
INFLUENCES ON NUMBER OF REMEDIES SPECIFIED IN ORIGINAL
COURT DECISIONS IN JAIL LAWSUITS

| Number of Remedies in Original Decision | Major Influences |
| --- | --- |
| High | Level of court (federal) |
| | Defendants named (supervisors) |
| | Number of violations alleged (high) |
| | Legal bases for claims (strong) |
| | Evidence for claims (strong) |
| Low | Level of court (state) |
| | Number of violations alleged (low) |
| | Legal bases for claims (weak) |
| | Evidence for claims (weak) |

judges on the total number of remedies specified diminishes (see Table 15). Total remedies are more strongly influenced, in the long run, by the involvement of ideological counsel and supervisor defendants, reflecting the more serious nature of jail conditions in those cases, as well as the greater resources and persistence of ideological counsel in holding county supervisors ultimately accountable for jail conditions.

The number of remedies specified, of course, provides only a crude indicator of outcomes at the remedy stage. The breadth as well as the different types of remedies specified are also significant.

Across all jail lawsuits, the most common outcome per violation alleged is that no relief whatsoever is granted. The frequency of "no relief" ("attrition" of claims) in the original court decisions is obviously related to the weakness of evidence for some of the claims, although the complex legal evidence offered across cases cannot be reviewed in any detail here. However, the court's disallowment of claims was also related to the filing of jail lawsuits in state courts and the noninvolvement of county supervisors as defendants. It would appear that state judges are more conservative in granting relief overall, even when county supervisors are not named in lawsuits.

In the original court decision, judicial orders to produce written plans addressing jail conditions were relatively common. In such cases, jail conditions are relatively stable, if not ideal. If jail conditions were rapidly deteriorating at the time of the original decision, it is much less likely that defendants would be given the opportunity to formulate their own plans. Providing that defendants have also acknowledged certain deficiencies in jail conditions and expressed a willingness to ameliorate them, judges much prefer to allow defendants a period of time to develop and submit their own plans. Lacking such acknowledgment and willingness, however, much more intrusive measures are likely, including population caps and early release of prisoners.

It was relatively common for plaintiffs to receive relief approximately equal to what they sought in the complaint (e.g., increases in visitation time and recreation time, improvements in food and medical care), generally because prisoner needs were well demonstrated and claims were well substantiated by evidence. In cases where inmate plaintiffs originally filed their own petitions and claims were substantiated but exaggerated, plaintiffs received less relief than requested: For example, the slight overcrowding on the unit where most Contra Costa petitioners were housed clearly did not warrant jail population caps, at least not at that time. The granting of relief greater than that requested was quite rare. Federal judges were the ones likely to issue such orders, and county supervisors were the defendants likely to receive them. Federal judges' autonomy and county supervisors' initial resistance likely account for many such outcomes.

Plaintiffs sometimes received relief on violations not originally alleged in complaints, or relief quite different from what was requested. Considerable time may pass before the original court decision is used (see for example, the Orange County case study in this chapter), time in which jail conditions may worsen, incarceration rates may increase, new evidence (e.g., testimony by expert witnesses) may be introduced, and new solutions may be suggested and negotiated by litigants. Suppose, for example, that defendants acknowledge that overcrowding is a serious problem. Through new evidence or negotiations, it is determined that better pretrial release mechanisms are needed to reduce jail intake, more postconviction release options are needed to reduce jail time served, or a certain number of new jail cells should be constructed. The judge then issues a decree that may be signed by litigants or by the judge alone.[1] A slightly different problem occurs when plaintiffs' counsel is denied adequate access to the jail at some point between filing the complaint and receiving the judge's decision. The judge may make access orders explicit because of previous problems or because he/she anticipates troubles after the court decision is issued. The major influences on remedy breadth are summarized in Table 17.

Finally, judges order different types of remedies. The most common types of reforms ordered in jail lawsuits involved crowding, medical care, hygiene, early release of convicted inmates, recreation, expedited

**TABLE 17**
BREADTH OF REMEDIES SPECIFIED IN ORIGINAL COURT DECISIONS
IN JAIL LAWSUITS

| Breadth of Remedies in Original Decision | Major Influences |
|---|---|
| No relief | Defendants named (not supervisors) <br> Level of court (state) <br> Evidence for claims (weak) |
| Written plans only | Jail conditions (stable) <br> Defendants acknowledgment of deficiencies (high) |
| Less relief than sought by plaintiffs | Evidence for claims (weak) |
| Relief equal to that sought by plaintiffs | Evidence for claims (strong) |
| Greater relief than sought by plaintiffs | Level of court (federal) <br> Defendants named (supervisors) |
| Relief granted on issues not in complaint | Changes in jail conditions (worsening) <br> Changes in punishment patterns <br> New evidence <br> Negotiated solutions to overcrowding <br> Relations between opposing counsel (good) |

release of pretrial inmates, sanitation, access to courts, food service, visitation, and classification procedures. Pretrial and postconviction release are directly related to overcrowding; other issues are exacerbated by severe overcrowding. Serious violations of such conditions have been ruled to violate basic constitutional rights (see Chapter 3) and occasionally, "common standards of decency" (*Rhodes v. Chapman*, 1981; *Stewart v. Gates*, 1978). Together, these remedies have constituted the major impetus for change in California jails.

While all remedies are related to the strength of legal bases for claims and the strength of evidence presented, two constellations of remedies were additionally influenced by the level of court and the type of defendants named (see table 18). In the first constellation, federal judges were most likely to order relief in the areas of medical care, recreation, visitation, and classification. Not only is federal case law well established in these areas, but such issues relate directly to Eighth and Fourteenth Amendment claims extending basic rights and protections to pretrial and sentenced prisoners. In the second constellation, judges held county supervisors uniquely responsible for unpopular

## TABLE 18
### SELECTED TYPES OF REMEDIES SPECIFIED IN COURT ORDERS AND MAJOR INFLUENCES

| Remedies Specified over the History of the Case | Major Influences |
|---|---|
| Medical care | Level of court (federal) <br> Legal bases for claims (strong) <br> Evidence for claims (strong) |
| Recreation | Level of court (federal) <br> Legal bases for claims (strong) <br> Evidence for claims (strong) |
| Visitation | Level of court (federal) <br> Legal bases for claims (strong) <br> Evidence for claims (strong) |
| Classification | Level of court (federal) <br> Legal bases for claims (strong) <br> Evidence for claims (strong) |
| Overcrowding | Defendants named (supervisors) <br> Legal bases for claims (strong) <br> Evidence for claims (strong) |
| Staffing | Defendants named (supervisors) <br> Legal bases for claims (strong) <br> Evidence for claims (strong) |
| Physical plant | Defendants named (supervisors) <br> Changes in jail conditions (worsening) <br> New evidence <br> Negotiated solutions to overcrowding <br> Relations between counsel (good) |
| Early release | Defendants named (supervisors) <br> Changes in jail conditions (worsening) <br> New evidence <br> Negotiated solutions to overcrowding <br> Relations between counsel (good) |
| Pretrial release | Defendants named (supervisors) <br> Changes in jail conditions (worsening) <br> New evidence <br> Negotiated solutions to overcrowding <br> Relations between counsel (good) |
| Attorney access | Changes in jail conditions (worsening) <br> Relations between counsel (poor) |

and expensive reforms: reduced overcrowding, often through jail population caps and early releases of certain nonviolent sentenced offenders; and increased staffing and improvements to the jail's physical plant, which require budget allocations authorized by county supervisors. Such controversial changes are directly and justifiably contingent upon the actions of county supervisors. To understand court-ordered jail reform, we need to account for the dynamic nature of litigation and the complexity of factors that affect legal process and outcomes over the life of a case.

## Case Studies

Lawsuits naming the board of supervisors as defendants evidence considerable conflict. Politically powerful defendants have the resources and resolve to resist legal challenges, but are most likely to be held accountable for specific reforms (e.g., jail funding, staffing) when facing ideologically committed attorneys and federal judges. A side effect of forced accountability, however, may be that supervisors are less able to deflect blame to other county officials or litigants, facilitating a defensive posture that escalates conflict. The diverse roles played by government defendants, inmate attorneys, and judges in the remedy-crafting stage are illustrated by the three case studies.

### Contra Costa

Judge Arneson issued his only orders in the Contra Costa case (*Yancey v. Rainey*, 1985), on 31 March 1985. The sheriff was directed to do everything within his power to reduce overcrowding, but no population cap was set. Minor improvements and closer monitoring of conditions in each of the other nine areas complained of by petitioners were ordered. The sheriff quickly delegated to four jail managers responsibility for seeking and documenting compliance with court orders in four specific areas.

The Director of Support Services was given responsibility for orders related to issuance of blankets, monitoring of temperatures in the jail, cleaning of thermal blankets, ensuring and documenting monthly inspections of sanitary conditions, and ensuring that food met proper state nutritional standards. The three Operations Directors were requested to provide in-service training to staff about inmate grievances, insure compliance with jail policies, and ensure that mail identified as legal mail be delivered expeditiously, and that all other mail be properly posted in accordance with jail policies. The head of the library was directed to hire a law clerk and an assistant law clerk as required by the court's order; the head of the Work Alternative Program was directed to hire a part-time worker for the law library, as specified in the order. Finally, the head of the Bureau of Administrative Services was directed to rewrite jail policies to comply with the orders related to law library staff, and to ensure that all proper documentation showing compliance was collected. What we see in Contra Costa, therefore, is a coordinated and immediate response to the court's orders, with clear responsibilities for compliance delegated by the sheriff to specific individuals responsible for specific areas of jail operations.

A preexisting network of relations among county agencies minimized court intervention and facilitated proactive responses by defendants. A single judge heard all jail writs, and his office was located near the jail. One county official I interviewed stated that the sheriff and the judge often met with county officials when particular jail problems required attention: "I think he [the judge] has the ability to sit down with the sheriff and county administrator in his conferences. You know, the guy brings the writ in, and he has a hearing, and they sit down and he says, "Well, why don't you fix it?"

Are inmate interests adequately represented by such informal processes? Inmates could choose to file legal claims in federal court if they were dissatisfied with this process; so far they have not. Inter- and intra-agency relations thus mediate responses to litigation, beginning at early stages and continuing to influence outcomes in a dynamic and complex manner (see Chapter 6).

Judge Arneson specified that his order would remain in force until 30 June 1986, subject to further review. In fact, the court relinquished jurisdiction on that date, satisfied with the sheriff's response and documentation of compliance. No subsequent orders have been issued.

### Santa Clara

In his first interim order (21 August 1981), Santa Clara County Superior Court Judge David Leahy noted that further review of evidence was necessary to resolve the complex issues in this case, but that overcrowding was the primary problem: "Immediate relief is required on the principal issue of overcrowding to the extent that the Court cannot permit the day in and day out 'bunking' of pretrial detainees on mattresses placed about the floor areas of the jail" (p. 1). He further noted that "the California Constitution places a substantially higher premium on the fundamental liberty interest than does the national charter" (p. 2). Leahy gave the sheriff 30 days to file a plan with the court for reducing the jail population to its rated capacity of 637 persons within 100 days.

In response, the sheriff and the county filed a plan to create 175 additional jail beds by installing temporary trailers and modular units. In October, when plans had not yet been implemented and overcrowding had worsened, Leahy ordered the sheriff to "immediately release all pretrial detainees booked or held at the main jail or North County jail solely on misdemeanor charges, or failure to appear warrants, who in the judgment of Pre-Trial Services do not pose a danger to themselves or others, subject to the approval of a duty judge" (Order of 10 October 1981, p.1).

By 4 December the county had made little progress in reducing its jail population and had discovered that the temporary trailers and modular units would not be ready within the 100-day limit. Plaintiffs contended that reasonable alternatives to incarceration should be used to reduce the jail population to court-ordered limits; defendants claimed that all reasonable alternatives were already being used. While cognizant of the county's need for more time to comply, Leahy sternly proclaimed that

> the intolerable conditions that occur within the main jail from time to time must be dealt with. Separate and apart from the violation of constitutional rights, which results from the failure to provide at least minimally adequate bedding; extreme instances of overcrowding during the pendency of this case have occasionally reached crisis proportions. Such circumstances pose an unacceptable danger of physical violence and injury not only to inmates but also to staff. (Order of 4 December 1981, p. 3)

Leahy extended the date for compliance to 1 July 1982, and raised the population cap to 725 persons. Further interim orders required defendants to make greater use of postconviction release measures (early release). Leahy's apparent strategy was to use jail population caps as leverage to induce county officials to formulate and execute plans to remedy jail problems within a reasonable period of time. Except for the temporary, emergency population-reduction measurers he ordered, Leahy left it up to county officials to formulate their own plans for reducing the jail population and providing constitutionally adequate facilities.

The next move was up to the county, and a surprising development followed. Superior Court Judge William J. Fernandez issued a memorandum (22 February 1982) in response to a request from defendants to prohibit Judge Leahy from further action in the case. Defendants had alleged that Leahy lacked jurisdiction to enforce orders against the county; in particular he had failed to issue a summons to the Santa Clara district attorney (a real party at interest). In the memo, the court and the Department of the Presiding Judge disqualified themselves "from considering in any way the above-referenced case" (p. 1). The court had found itself in the embarrassing position of hearing a motion against one of its own judges, and some strange legal wording was the result. In his 17 February memo, Fernandez wrote: "Ordinarily a court once a judgment or order has been entered has no authority to prohibit itself from having made its order or judgment" (p. 1). He was quick to point out that "such jurisdictional lack and request for prohibition should be reviewable by the appellate courts and not the Superior Court" (p. 2).

Judge Leahy was successfully challenged by the county and disqualified on 3 March 1982. This action set the tone of the defendants' strategy. While acknowledging that problems existed in the jail, county officials would not passively accept the court's dicta about how to run its jail or its justice system, nor would they accept court-imposed deadlines for addressing those problems.

Why the entire Superior Court bench disqualified itself from hearing the case is not clear. The case may simply have been too time-consuming for local judges with other civil and criminal court responsibilities. A desire to stay clear of an escalating political war surely played a role as well. Potential conflicts of interest between local courts and county government had surfaced early in the case, according to one court official I interviewed:

> I think the real philosophy at the time was that we were working so closely with the county government, trying to get our own budgets staffed, and we had so much business with the county, and everybody knew so much about this case that it would really be better if somebody from the outside could handle it—outside the county.

Indeed, three of the judges subsequently appointed by the state Judicial Council were "outsiders" from nearby Alameda County. Yet "outside" judges were not automatically granted credibility. Some perceived them as unfamiliar with local criminal justice needs and problems and saw their immunity from the local electorate as a drawback: "We have to face voters and he doesn't."

Over the next eight years, the case consumed the energies of four judges. As noted earlier, in jail lawsuits a series of decisions accumulate and evolve over time, making the choice of a dividing point between the Remedy Stage and the Postdecree Stage somewhat arbitrary. For the Remedy Stage, I have chosen in this case to describe events leading up to the initial consent decree, which was the first time any comprehensive relief was specified in the case.

The California State Judicial Council appointed Alameda County Superior Court Judge Bruce Allen to take over the *Branson* case after Leahy was disqualified. Judge Allen did not take long to familiarize himself with the details of the case and develop his own judicial role: He issued the first of many orders on 19 March 1982, only 16 days after Leahy was disqualified. Judge Allen specified population caps of 700 at the main jail (effective 24 March) and further reductions to 637 inmates by 3 May, warning that failure to comply would be punishable by contempt. On the same day he appointed a special master to develop information for use by the court in formulating and enforcing orders. Charles D. Ramey, Criminal Division Coordinator of the Superior Court, was selected for this position.

Allen became very active in his handling of the case, issuing several orders that reduced the county's decision-making power regarding the jail. Literally dozens of orders were issued. On 2 April 1982, Judge Allen ordered the county to refrain from selling land adjacent to the Elmwood jail facility, presumably because such land could play a role in future jail expansion plans. On 6 April he ordered the county controller to take the stand and issue a check in the amount of $10,000 to plaintiff counsel to cover contested attorney fees. On 12 May he ordered defendants to replace or repair all defective toilets and all defective lighting fixtures in the jail within nine days. In a series of orders dated 28 May 1982, Allen ordered the sheriff to buy paint and hire qualified plumbers and electricians to make necessary repairs. He ordered the county controller to approve these expenditures and issue checks to pay for the renovations as a "priority expenditure." He later amended these orders to specify that approval of jail expenditures by the county executive was not required; the sheriff should simply bill the county.

On 3 June 1982, Judge Allen ordered the county to maintain the jail population limits set by the court, and added: "You will procure and maintain thereafter such additional housing and staff supporting facilities as required to comply with this order and to have the same ready as needed for inmate housing" (p. 2). In a series of orders beginning 24 June 1982, Allen ordered the county controller to issue the first of a series of checks to pay for jail repairs incurred by the sheriff, and ordered the county treasurer to immediately pay the warrant issued by the controller.

On 2 July 1982, Judge Allen ordered county supervisors to refrain from plans to discharge seven county employees from the jail's Supervised ROR (release on own recognizance) program, claiming that firing them would have an immediate and unacceptable impact on jail overcrowding. On 9 August 1982, he extended the authority of the sheriff to reduce jail populations to court-ordered limits by accelerating the early release of sentenced inmates under provisions of the state penal code (Cal. PC 4024.1). By 16 August the judge was ordering the sheriff to also make greater use of pretrial release measures specified in the state penal code. On 21 October 1982, he ordered the sheriff to maintain a staff of no fewer than 24 deputies on each shift, every day, and specified that the county was not to deduct any extra costs associated with that order from the sheriff's budget or from other jail services.

On 14 October 1982, the county filed the first of many appeals of Judge Allen's orders, setting the stage for a long and bitter battle. The judge continued to hold hearings and issue orders while the appeals were pending, however. By 22 November 1982, he was becoming increasingly frustrated with the county's noncompliance: "This court will not tolerate the miserable overcrowding in the jail which was existent in March when these hearings began. . . . The responsible executives in the Sheriff's Office, Board of Supervisors, and the County Executive have offered nothing whatever in response to this most pressing problem" (Order of 22 November 1982, 4p.). Although the Court of Appeal later vacated several of Judge Allen's orders (mainly in regard to his direction of county expenditures), Allen continued to issue numerous orders directing jail improvements.

Once the case reached the Court of Appeal, an incredible set of circumstances evolved. Shortly after the first notices of appeal were filed, the presiding judge of the appellate court ordered prehearing conferences pursuant to rule 19.5 of the California Rules of Court. These prehearing conferences resulted in a stipulated settlement that treated the habeas corpus proceeding as an action for violation of the petitioner's civil rights (42 USC sec. 1983). The settlement, oddly enough, also provided for the entry of a final judgment that vacated all existing orders in the case. The settlement was approved by the conference judge and filed. The clerk of the appellate court issued a remittitur on 13 February 1983, which directed the clerk of the Superior Court to enter the final judgment and consent decree.

The appellate court recalled the remittitur and stayed the settlement on 2 March 1983,[2] stating that the consent decree had not been approved by a panel of three judges as required by law. The county then filed a motion to confirm the final judgment. On 29 March 1983,[3] the appellate court ruled that the prehearing conference judge did not have the authority to vacate the judgment or orders of the Superior Court, or to order the entry of a new judgment: "a single judge is not a 'court of appeal' " (p. 5). Given that the proposed settlement was now before an appropriate three-judge panel, should it be legally approved?

For various reasons, the answer was no. First of all, the appellate court lacked jurisdiction to approve the settlement: There was absolutely no precedent for excluding from a settlement the original trial court (the Superior Court in this case) and instead negotiating and approving a settlement at the appellate level. Nor was there precedent for vacating all existing orders of the trial court in addition to those that were actually pending appeal. Third, because the case was in effect a class action on behalf of all inmates at the Santa Clara jail, "any compromise or dismissal of the action must be approved by the trial court in order to protect the interests of all members of the class" (p. 8). Fourth, even if the appellate court did have jurisdiction to review the consent decree in the first instance, it "would decline to do so in the absence of a complete review of the proposal by the trial court" (p. 8). Indeed, the judges stated, the consent decree went far beyond the legal matter on appeal (whether the trial court had the authority to order the county to pay the cost of complying with the court's orders), and presented a far-reaching plan to revamp the entire jail system. Such matters, the court added, are best left to the approval of the trial judge who will hear evidence and bear responsibility for enforcing the judgment.

Fifth, and perhaps most surprising, the court stated that "several features of the consent settlement document are beyond the power of the parties to impose and therefore are beyond the power of any court to approve." Specifically, the justices objected to provisions of the proposed settlement that specified four unprecedented and alarming actions: remove jurisdiction from the trial court judge now hearing the case; eliminate the fact-finding function of the Superior Court; require as a condition prior to any order of modification or enforcement by the trial court a hearing before a fact-finding panel whose findings would be "final and binding" on the trial court; and allow each party, on each motion, the right to disqualify the judge assigned. The appellate justices were justifiably incredulous:

> Such provisions, which go both to the heart of the jurisdiction of the trial court and to the very function of a judge as fact finder in habeas corpus,

constitute an improper interference with the trial court's jurisdiction. Accordingly, the motion to confirm the stipulated final judgment and consent decree is denied. The stipulated final judgment and consent decree shall have no force or effect. (P. 9)

The parties may instead, the court directed, seek the trial court's approval of a settlement. The county's motion was thus denied by the appellate court; the settlement agreement was null and void.

Few people I interviewed were both willing and able to discuss these disturbing aspects of the case. One can only speculate about the conference judge's motives for approving this settlement and the plaintiff's counsel's reasons for signing it. It is possible that the judge sought recognition for settling the notorious and difficult *Branson* case, or that he held some allegiance to county officials. It is possible that plaintiffs' counsel reluctantly gave in to the enormous political and other pressures of litigating the case, including pressures within their own organization. Perhaps they felt that this was the best possible deal. What is clear is that the settlement would have constituted an illegal removal of authority from the trial court. The proposed settlement clearly reflected the county officials' interests and their vehement disapproval of Judge Allen; it would not have represented the rights of inmates.

On 30 March 1983, the appellate court handed diminished authority for the case back to Judge Allen but required him to file with the appellate court copies of any orders, accompanied by a concise statement of facts.[4] In somewhat consoling language, the court stated: "This order is not to be construed as an order appointing a referee" (p. 2).

Judge Allen continued undaunted. On 5 April 1983, he criticized the sheriff for bending to pressure by the municipal courts to restrict the release of pretrial suspects. He succinctly summarized the conflict that had developed between himself and the county: "This county has an immediate, severe shortage of jail housing for prisoners. This Court has questioned the cost effectiveness, usefulness and adequacy of the County's plans and the County has questioned the orders of the Court and suggestions of others" (Order TR2, 6 April 1983, p. 2). In response, Allen appointed an expert witness, Warden Raymond K. Procunier, to review and report to the Court on the adequacy of county jail facilities, alternatives, and planning (Order TR2A). On 17 April, Allen appointed two additional experts, an architect and a builder, at county expense (Order TR4).

In a further series of orders beginning the same day, Allen continued to press for the reduction of jail populations. He ordered an additional 20 beds installed at the Park Alameda jail facility, a work furlough center for inmates who work during the day (Order TR6). The probation department was asked to make recommendations for early release sentence modifications (TR7). On 8 April Allen ordered the county to reallocate a 40-bed portable mobile home unit to the women's facility at Elmwood, rather than the men's unit at the same location (TR8). He also ordered the county to establish a reserve fund of $3 million for jail expenditures, to come from extra county revenues (TR9). On 11 April Allen charged that county officials had failed to fill a pressing need for additional medium-security beds at the Elmwood facility, and questioned their cost estimates for compliance. On 12 April (Order TR8A), he ordered the county to stop construction on the 40-bed unit at the men's Elmwood facility.

In its review of defendants' petitions to stay nine of Judge Allen's orders during the preceding months, the appellate court stayed seven in part or in all respects, including Orders TR2A, TR4, TR4A, TR8, TR9, and TR8A (14 April 1983).[5] Again, stays were related to Allen's propensity to bypass the county executive in important decisions that required county expenditures. A remarkable episode of judicial activism ended when Judge Allen resigned on 24 May 1983, citing his health.

Judge Eugene Premo, then the Presiding Judge of Santa Clara County Superior Court, agreed to take the case. The parties finally ratified a consent decree on 7 June 1983, absent the previous language about vacating existing orders and restricting the powers of the trial court. This event marked the first time that substantive issues of confinement were dealt with comprehensively. Judge Premo also appointed Thomas Lonergan, former jail commander in Los Angeles, as compliance officer. The settlement agreement was, in effect, a blueprint to overhaul the entire jail system. Extensive revisions were specified in the compliance officer's duties and authority, the use of existing housing, the construction of new facilities, the design of management information systems, appropriate staffing, medical and food services, maintenance, the law library, visitation, exercise, reading materials, clothing, supplies and personal hygiene, alternatives to incarceration, additional funds for jail facilities, fire safety, mail, telephone use, reports, decree enforcement and fairness hearings, and payment of attorneys' fees. As we shall see in the next chapter, however, noncompliance remained a serious problem for a long time after the consent decree was signed.

*Orange*

Legal outcomes were slow to develop in Orange County, and resistance by county officials was subtle. No orders were issued for three years, as extensive discovery, testimony, review, and stalled negotiations followed the legal complaint. U.S. District Court Judge William P. Gray, in his Memorandum of Decision (3 May 1978), articulated his judicial philosophy in hearing this case:

> I have tried to be mindful of two well established principles. On the one hand, this court has the obligation to protect the constitutional rights of prisoners to due process and equal protection of the laws, and to be free from cruel and unusual punishment. On the other hand, courts must be careful to refrain from imposing upon jail administrators their personal views as to how penal institutions should be operated and the conditions under which inmates should live. (P. 2).

Judge Gray declared that he would limit his interference to situations in which a constitutional right was quite clearly involved. Once such violations were established, he warned, "The Court intends to make certain that the remedial actions that it directs are accomplished" (p. 2). Judicial conservatism, therefore, was to be tempered with persistence in this case.

In the decision, Judge Gray also explained his thinking about jail overcrowding. A reading of legal cases and other authorities had not convinced him that some specific number of square feet must be accorded an inmate in order to square with constitutional requirements. "Here," Gray added, "the jail is of modern construction, the cell areas are reasonably well lighted and ventilated, and the inmates have several daily breaks in the time spent in their cells. The question here concerned is whether or not the area in which an inmate spends his time is reasonably habitable, as opposed to being cramped and dingy" (p. 8).

His order of 3 May 1978 called for increased availability of telephones, visits by minor children, access to magazines and newspapers through the mail, a minimum of fifteen minutes to eat meals, a minimum of eight hours of sleep prior to court appearances, rights of inmates to be present during "shakedowns" of their cells, restrictions on the use of administrative segregation cells, and posting of written rules of conduct. Most significantly, however, overcrowding had become more serious since the original complaint three years earlier. Judge Gray was displeased by some of the conditions he saw at the jail (*Stewart v. Gates*, 1978):

I noticed several instances in which an inmate was sleeping on his assigned mattress that had been placed directly on the concrete floor of a cell, immediately adjacent to the toilet, because all of the bunks were allotted to other prisoners. If the public, through its judicial and penal system, finds it necessary to incarcerate a person, basic concepts of decency, as well as reasonable respect for constitutional rights, require that he be provided a bed. (450 F. Supp. at 588)

Accordingly, Judge Gray ordered that every prisoner detained more than one night was to be given a bed. In response, county officials commissioned a study that projected jail population needs up to the year 2001, promising that a new jail capable of meeting those needs was being planned. Six years later, overcrowding had worsened considerably, no jail was built, and the lawsuit entered a more active phase (see Chapter 5).

## Negotiations and Judicial Methods at the Remedy Stage

### Negotiations at the Remedy Stage

Defendants differ in their manner and degree of participation in negotiating remedies. Negotiations, of course, are influenced by prior events, actions, and conditions, as well as contextual factors that emerge (perhaps for the first time) at the Remedy Stage. Defendants' participation in remedy formulation is related to six factors: leadership by key actors, seriousness of jail conditions, previous success at negotiations, the quality of relations among county officials, the complexity of problems and solutions, and the degree to which multiple actors are needed to reach a consensus decision.

In Contra Costa, all six factors were observed. Officials praised the leadership of the state court judge and the sheriff in bringing key county officials together to discuss solutions to jail problems. The judge had an office across the street from this jail and was familiar with jail conditions and jail personnel. Prior to issuing his only orders in this case, the judge brought county officials together several times to discuss problems and possible solutions. While the judge's order left discretion to the sheriff, the sheriff immediately implemented a coordinated plan to address all issues defined by the order. This participatory style of negotiation was greatly aided by the fact that county officials knew each other and the judge quite well and communicated regularly on a formal and an informal basis; moreover, relatively few key officials were required to reach consensus compared with larger urban counties. In addition, jail problems in Contra Costa were somewhat less urgent than in the other two cases, partly because a new jail had opened four years prior to the court orders. The problems and solutions were relatively straightforward, and officials had previously negotiated on numerous issues in addition to the county jail case.

In the other two cases, in contrast, defendants' participation in negotiations was limited prior to the initial court decisions. In Santa Clara, the seriousness of the overcrowding problem hampered the negotiation process. Judge Leahy emphasized early in the case the importance of addressing an overcrowding problem that was reaching "crisis proportions." After plans offered by defendants failed to materialize in time (e.g., plans to use temporary trailers), Leahy began ordering more controversial population-reduction methods, including the expanded release of pretrial prisoners and the early release of some sentenced prisoners. As evidenced by their successful motion to disqualify Judge Leahy a short time later, defendants appeared more motivated to litigate than to negotiate for most of the first three years of the case preceding the settlement agreement (see Chapter 5). Negotiations in Santa Clara were tense in the early stages of remedy formulation (under Judge Leahy), absent in the middle stages (under Judge Allen), and totally one-sided in later stages (just prior to Judge Allen's resignation), leading up to the aborted settlement engineered in appellate court. While Santa Clara faced some of the same difficulties as many large counties (complex problems and solutions, multiple actors needed for consensus), poor relations among county officials (particularly between the sheriff and the county supervisors) contributed to its early inability or unwillingness to negotiate (see Chapter 5).

In Orange, three years of discovery, testimony, review, and stalled negotiations passed between the filing of the original complaint in 1975 and the court decision in 1978. By the time Judge Gray issued his 1976 pretrial conference order summarizing facts contested (72) and facts uncontested (7), it was clear that the complexity of jail problems would seriously hamper negotiations. Although defendants and plaintiffs were able to negotiate one stipulated agreement in 1977 (over provision of medical and dental care), most issues remained contested until Judge Gray ruled on these in his Memorandum to Counsel of 26 January 1978. By the time Judge Gray issued his decision of 3 May 1978, jail conditions had worsened considerably, further complicating potential negotiations. As in other large counties, negotiations were limited by the fact that many actors were needed for consensus on jail decisions, and relations between county officials deteriorated as the case dragged on (see Chapter 5). Negotiations, of course, do not stop at the Remedy

**TABLE 19**
PARTICIPATION BY DEFENDANTS IN NEGOTIATIONS AT THE
REMEDY STAGE OF JAIL LAWSUITS

| Participation by Defendants in Negotiations | Major Influences |
|---|---|
| High | Leadership by key actors (strong) |
| | Seriousness of jail conditions (low) |
| | Previous success at negotiating during Trigger and Liability Stages (good) |
| | Relations among county officials (good) |
| | Complexity of problems and solutions (low) |
| | Multiple actors needed for consensus (low) |
| Low | Seriousness of jail conditions (high) |
| | Previous success at negotiating during Trigger and Liability Stages (poor) |
| | Relations among county officials (poor) |
| | Complexity of problems and solutions (high) |
| | Multiple actors needed for consensus (high) |
| | Stage of litigation (early in Remedy Stage) |

Stage, and the next chapter explores negotiations following the original court decision in more detail. Major influences on defendants' participation in negotiations are summarized in Table 19.

*Judicial Methods at the Remedy Stage*

Judicial methods for collecting information, conducting negotiations, and formulating remedies were contingent upon at least five factors: the point in time examined (early versus later in the Remedy Stage), judicial experience and expertise, defendants' acceptance of judicial authority, need for more evidence, and changes in jail conditions preceding remedy formulation.

In Contra Costa to a large degree and Orange to a lesser degree, judges in the early stages of remedy formulation attempted to facilitate discussions between plaintiffs and defendants, dispose of contested issues, and encourage defendants to develop written plans to address jail problems. This style can be characterized as that of the "Conscientious Monitor." In Contra Costa, defendants' acceptance of judicial authority expedited this strategy. Judge Arneson was also very familiar with jail conditions and with complaints by prisoners; in fact, he had heard every petition filed by prisoners in Contra Costa for some years. His experience and expertise in jail issues were considerable. In Orange, Judge Gray was patient in hearing and reviewing evidence for 30 months prior to his original court decision, and his experience in hearing complex civil lawsuits and reputation for being tough but fair were well-known. While defendants would later challenge his authority through the appeals process (unsuccessfully), their acceptance of his authority in the early stages of remedy formulation and throughout the rest of the case was relatively high. Judge Gray made it clear very early that he would limit the court's authority to clear constitutional violations, but he also intended to fully enforce necessary orders. The lengthy period preceding the court decision in Orange was strongly related to the court's need for further information and evidence to rule on contested issues and determine the facts of a very complex case.

In Santa Clara, judicial authority was challenged by defendants almost from the outset, as witnessed first by the county's successful disqualification of Judge Leahy, and later by its repeated appeals of Judge Allen's orders. Attempts to encourage defendants to develop and submit plans to address jail problems met with little success, although it could be argued that Leahy and Allen showed little patience with the defendants. Although each judge had extensive experience on the bench in state courts, neither had experience presiding over such a complex civil lawsuit against public officials. Greater experience in such cases might have fostered the more patient but firm style displayed by Judge Gray. As jail conditions took dramatic downturns, and as county officials increased their resistance to judicial authority, Leahy to a small degree and Allen to a great degree took on the role of "Intervenor." They became less willing to wait for defendants to develop and submit plans to address jail problems, and increased their own intervention in the affairs of county justice and government.

Leahy first issued population caps to pressure county officials to develop their own plans to address jail problems. In this regard, he initially played the role of Conscientious Monitor. When county plans failed, he began instituting more unpopular mechanisms such as expanded pretrial releases and early releases of sentenced offenders. After Leahy's disqualification, the entire Superior Court bench disqualified itself from hearing the case. While the volatility of local politics at this time probably necessitated such a move, the authority granted to "outside" judges by defendants was probably no better, and more likely a lot worse.

Among many other "interventions," Judge Allen ordered the county to refrain from selling land that could be used for jail expansion, the

**TABLE 20**
INFLUENCES ON JUDICIAL METHODS AT THE REMEDY STAGE

| *Judicial Methods Used in Remedy Formulation* | *Major Influences* |
|---|---|
| Conscientious Monitor | Point in time (early in Remedy Stage) |
| | Judicial experience, expertise (high) |
| | Defendants' acceptance of judicial authority (high) |
| | Need for more information (high) |
| Intervenor | Point in time (later in Remedy Stage) |
| | Judicial experience, expertise (low) |
| | Defendants' acceptance of judicial authority (low) |
| | Changes in jail conditions (worse) |

county controller to take the stand and issue a check to plaintiff counsel for attorney fees, the sheriff to make jail repairs and bill the county, and county supervisors to refrain from discharging seven county employees responsible for running a pretrial release program. Judge Allen became increasingly frustrated with the county's inability or unwillingness to develop cost-effective, useful, and adequate jail plans, while the county became increasingly deaf to the suggestions of the court and others. Whether any other judicial style would have fared better given the particular events and conditions in the case at that time it is difficult to say. In the next chapter, I further examine judicial methods at the critical Postdecree Stage. Major influences on judicial methods at the Remedy Stage are summarized in Table 20.

## Summary

Even after a liability opinion is issued, the remedy-crafting stage in jail lawsuits is often slow and arduous, involving lengthy negotiations, moves, and countermoves between opposing counsel and judges. The nature of remedies issued is shaped by prior litigation activities and environmental influences at the Trigger and Liability Stages, as well as emerging dynamics at the Remedy Stage (e.g., the adversarial roles played by ideological attorneys and county supervisors, different judicial methods for crafting remedies and involving litigants, different approaches to negotiation by plaintiffs and defendants). Analyses of case studies and comparative data indicated that jail lawsuits vary along important contextual dimensions that influence the remedy-crafting process and the subsequent progression of litigation.

In this chapter, we observed considerable variation in the number, breadth, and type of remedies specified in court decrees, and we examined major causal influences on those outcomes. Examination of total remedies specified in jail reform lawsuits led to two important conclusions: there is no single decision in jail lawsuits, but a multitude of additional orders and modified orders issued over time; and judicial orders are generally quite conservative rather than "radical," as evidenced by a high rate of attrition between legal complaints and remedies.

Examination of contextual factors from the earlier stages revealed three important influences on the breadth and depth of remedies. First, federal courts provided greater relief on average than state courts, although federal courts were more likely to grant relief on certain issues only (medical care, for example), and both state and federal courts granted much less relief than sought by plaintiffs. Second, ideologically committed attorneys obtained greater relief in court than either private or public counsel, possibly because of their greater resources and experience, freedom from local political constraints, and familiarity with constitutional law. Local environments can thus be favorable in some ways and limiting in others, depending on characteristics of the particular litigants and their legal representation. Third, lawsuits naming the board of supervisors as defendants evidenced considerable conflict. Politically powerful defendants have the resources and resolve to resist legal challenges, but were most likely to be held accountable for specific reforms (e.g., jail funding, staffing) when facing ideologically committed attorneys and federal judges. A side effect of forced accountability, however, may be that supervisors are less able to deflect blame to others, facilitating a defensive posture that may escalate conflict.

The three case studies illustrated similar variation in remedy formulation and examined influences on judicial methods and negotiations between plaintiffs, defendants, and judges. In Contra Costa, litigants reached peaceful resolution in a short period of time. Informal discussions out of court between litigants and the judge efficiently guided defendants' responses, although it is not entirely clear that this process served inmates' best interests. Negotiations were aided by strong leadership on the parts of the sheriff and the judge, as well as a preexisting network of relations between county officials. The sheriff's response to court orders was a swift and coordinated plan to ensure compliance. In Santa Clara, the political waters were turbulent from the outset: No private attorneys in the county would take the case; county defendants successfully disqualified the first judge to hear it; the entire Superior Court bench disqualified itself; and county officials' influence may even have extended to the state Court of Appeal. The first three trial judges to hear the case varied greatly in their methods. Leahy used population caps to apply leverage; Allen intervened in the delicate areas of county finances and executive decisions; later, Judge Premo would attempt a more managerial approach (Chapter 5). In Orange, Judge Gray tempered judicial conservatism with patience and persistence. He avoided confrontations with county officials, carefully outlining the court's role in the case. He was meticulous in grounding his legal analyses in federal case law. It would soon become clear that his patience had limits, however, and that indefinite stalling by the county would not be tolerated.

Through quantitative and qualitative investigation of variations in the breadth and depth of orders, as well as examination of interactions between defendants, plaintiffs, judges, and dimensions of the local legal and political environment, I have described several critical factors that vary across jail lawsuits at the Remedy Stage and resurface after the decree. The original court order or consent decree is rarely the end of a jail case. The next chapter examines relationships between court-ordered remedies and outcomes at the Postdecree Stage: negotiations, modifications, and judicial strategies to monitor and gain compliance.

# CHAPTER 5

## The Postdecree Stage

The experience of this and other courts has demonstrated that it is not enough to make an order, no matter how detailed and explicit. Unless somebody checks the order against the defendants' performance, they do not perform. When someone watches them, they squirm, but they comply, or get out of the way for someone else to do so.

**—Judge Don J. Young, *Jones v. Wittenberg*, 1976**

There is a vast opportunity in the interaction of these governmental units for tasks to go unaccomplished, for responsibility to be ignored, for excuses to be offered instead of accomplished goals.

**—Judge Eugene M. Premo, *Branson v. Winter,*
Memorandum of Decision and Order, 1 February 1984**

THE INITIAL COURT decree rarely spells the end of a jail lawsuit. The Postdecree Stage involves a lengthy and often difficult process of decree implementation, monitoring, evaluation, and remedy refinement. Many additional orders and modifications are likely to be issued over time. The question of appropriate length of judicial supervision becomes salient, as compliance is difficult to define, obtain, and sustain. Lawsuit duration depends partly on what has come before and partly on new issues that emerge during the course of litigation and monitoring—if overcrowding becomes worse, for example, or if key actors in the litigation change. Plaintiffs' and defendants' counsel offer competing strategies and plans, and vigorous negotiations follow. Judicial methods of gaining compliance vary widely, as do the roles played by the respective plaintiffs and defendants.

This chapter examines why some jail reform lawsuits last longer than others, how judges and litigants negotiate, how remedies are modified, and how compliance is achieved, as well as contextual factors that shape responses to remedial decrees at the Postdecree Stage.

## Comparative Analyses

*Lawsuit Duration*

How long should judicial decrees stay in effect? Prior to 1976, courts generally retained jurisdiction over the implementation of a decree until the illegal conduct and its effects had been eliminated. However, following *Pasadena City Board of Education v. Spangler* (1976), the onset of good-faith implementation of an approved plan was all that was required to relinquish jurisdiction. Judges still retain considerable discretion in such determinations, however, and compliance is rarely a simple matter.

Jail lawsuits in California lasted a long time: 54.8 months on average. Only 10 cases (23 percent) lasted a year or less; 6 (14 percent) lasted one to two years; 8 (19 percent) lasted two to four years; 19 (44 percent) lasted more than four years. The longevity of jail lawsuits testifies to the presence of polycentric problems not easily susceptible to reform by judicial decree (Fuller 1978).

A protracted lawsuit is systematically influenced by numerous factors. Contextual factors influencing lawsuit duration and compliance with court decrees include type of legal counsel and strategies, type of defendants and responses, complexity of legal issues, and judicial behavior in both state and federal courts.

Cases involving ideologically motivated plaintiff attorneys and government defendants, as suggested in earlier chapters, often evidence high levels of conflict. Jail lawsuits involving ideological attorneys lasted much longer (mean = 81.1 months) than cases involving private firms (mean = 58.7 months) and public firms (mean = 27.1 months). The involvement of county supervisors led to lawsuits that lasted nearly three times as long as other cases (mean duration = 71.8 versus 24.8 months).

The number of legal claims and remedies is also influential. In a complex case, as indicated by the number of violations alleged in the complaint, a greater number of issues must be litigated, requiring more detailed presentation of evidence, testimony, expert witnesses, negotiations, formulation of plans, and monitoring. A high number of legal claims indicates complexity, antagonism between litigants, or both, while a larger number of remedies requires greater expenditures of time and efforts to achieve compliance. Statistical analyses supported the relationship between issue complexity and lawsuit duration. Lawsuit duration correlated significantly with total violations alleged ($r = .35$) and with total orders over the life of the case ($r = .41$).

Cases heard in the state and federal courts differed in duration, partly because of differences in judicial experience, methods, and sensitivity to local environmental concerns, and partly because of differences in applicable laws and remedies. Federal court litigation lasted, on average, more than twice as long as Superior Court litigation (means = 84.7 versus 38.5 months), suggesting greater judicial persistence, resources, and independence from local political environments. Courts tire of periodic review, and "cases requiring repeated intervention quickly wear out their welcome in court" (Horowitz 1977, 266). Federal judges have less crowded court dockets than state court judges, and more experience with broad civil rights issues.

To estimate their relative strength as predictors of lawsuit duration, the following contextual variables were entered into a multiple regression equation: total violations alleged, total remedies, supervisors as defendants (1 = yes, 0 = no), federal court (1 = yes, 0 = no), and ideological attorneys (1 = yes, 0 = no). The resulting equation was statistically significant ($F [5,36] = 4.39$, $p < .01$), with total orders, federal court, and supervisors as defendants emerging as statistically significant predictors. When all variables entered the equation simultaneously, the number of alleged violations and representation by ideological attorneys had little influence.

Judicial persistence in the federal courts may spell longer periods of monitoring and greater reluctance to relinquish jurisdiction in the face of incomplete compliance. Defendant resistance is another major reason for judicial persistence. County supervisors often mount considerable resistance throughout the litigation process, becoming only marginally more likely to comply as time passes. As a result, the type of court and judicial methods acquire renewed importance in the Postdecree Stage.

## Compliance and Monitoring

Appointing a special master allows a judge to monitor compliance in a complex civil lawsuit in a flexible way. Special masters have increasingly been used as the "eyes and ears" of the court. Their duties include gathering information on jail conditions and procedures, monitoring compliance, and in some cases informally mediating disputes and negotiations between litigants (Brakel 1979; Feeley and Hanson

1990; Montgomery 1980; Nathan 1979; Sturm 1985; Yale Law Journal 1979).

The appointment of a special master is influenced by the type of defendant, issue complexity, and level of court. Government defendants frequently resist attempts by plaintiffs' attorneys to monitor or gain compliance, creating a need for a nonpartisan third party to do so. Issue complexity, as reflected by the number and type of remedies issued, magnifies the judicial need for nonpartisan monitoring. Special masters are most needed in lengthy, contested cases where compliance is most difficult. Rule 53 of the Federal Rules of Civil Procedure provides for the use of special masters (Kaufman 1958; Nathan 1979); provisions in state law, if any, are often vague or derivative (Feeley and Hanson 1990). Federal court judges, therefore, are likely to use special masters more frequently and sagaciously.

Special masters were appointed in 12 of the 43 jail cases examined (29 percent). These cases were characterized by more original orders (means = 12.3 and 7.1), more modifications (means = 27.4 and 5.5), and more orders over the history of the case (means = 39.8 and 12.6). Cases involving special masters, in contrast to other cases, were also more likely to involve orders to reduce overcrowding (83 versus 40 percent), raise staffing levels (50 versus 10 percent), improve pretrial release procedures (58 versus 27 percent), and release sentenced inmates early (75 versus 30 percent). The intrusive nature of such remedies demands labor-intensive observation and consultation, which can best be provided by a skilled special master. In addition, cases involving special masters were more likely to involve the board of supervisors as defendants (83 versus 53 percent) and were more likely to have occurred in federal courts (50 versus 27 percent). There is little doubt that judges needed help to monitor these complex cases. Cases involving special masters lasted nearly twice as long as other cases (means = 79.1 versus 43.8 months).

Sometimes, though, harsher medicine is called for. A civil contempt citation, involving fines or even jail sentences, may be used when defendants fail to meet clearly set standards for performance. Contempt orders, or even the threat of contempt, may be used as a method of last resort to signal the court's resolve to enforce its orders, but they may also unintentionally intensify conflict between defendants, plaintiffs, judges, and communities. Two of the case studies described in this chapter suggest such effects.

The use of contempt is related to the level of court and the type of remedies issued. Federal judges are more likely than state court judges

| County | Level of Court | Allegations (No.) | Original Orders (No.) | Modified Orders (No.) | Lawsuit Duration Mos. | Finding of Civil Contempt | Use of Special Master |
|---|---|---|---|---|---|---|---|
| Alameda | Super. | 10 | 12 | 3 | 39 | no | no |
| Butte | Super. | 18 | 20 | 12 | 56 | no | yes |
| Contra Costa | Super. | 7 | 8 | 0 | 18 | no | no |
| Fresno | Super. | 17 | 8 | 37 | 60 | no | yes |
| Humboldt | Super. | 12 | 13 | 19 | 23 | no | yes |
| Imperial | Fed. | 18 | 11 | 10 | 33 | no | no |
| Kern | Fed. | 7 | 6 | 0 | 16 | no | yes |
| Lakes | Cal. Sup. Ct. | 13 | 11 | 1 | 92 | no | yes |
| Los Angeles (3) | | | | | | | |
|   Dillard | Fed. | 22 | 3 | 19 | 117 | no | no |
|   Sybil Brand | Super. | 28 | 3 | 0 | 59 | no | no |
|   Rutherford | Fed. | 24 | 10 | 15 | 144 | no | no |
| Madera (2) | | | | | | | |
|   Muehlberg | Super. | 7 | 3 | 0 | 1 | no | no |
|   Sparks | Super. | 1 | 3 | 1 | 10 | no | no |
| Marin | Super. | 4 | 3 | 11 | 80 | no | no |
| Mendocino | Super. | 7 | 1 | 0 | 3 | no | no |
| Merced | Super. | 6 | 6 | 0 | 83 | no | no |
| Napa | Super. | 18 | 3 | 1 | 30 | no | no |
| Nevada | Super. | 7 | 2 | 5 | 14 | no | no |
| Orange | Fed. | 19 | 12 | 17 | 152 | yes | yes |
| Placer (2) | | | | | | | |
|   Parsons | Super. | 12 | 6 | 0 | 37 | no | no |
|   Offield | Super. | 10 | 8 | 0 | 21 | no | no |
| Riverside (3) | | | | | | | |
|   Inmates | Super. | 12 | 11 | 14 | 43 | no | yes |
|   Indio | Super. | 14 | 5 | 0 | 2 | no | no |
|   Doss | Super. | 8 | 8 | 4 | 70 | no | no |
| Sacramento | Fed. | 22 | 27 | 8 | 106 | no | yes |
| San Bernardino | Fed. | 14 | 13 | 2 | 19 | no | no |
| San Diego | Super. | 21 | 9 | 14 | 114 | no | no |
| San Francisco | Fed. | 13 | 17 | 22 | 120 | no | yes |
| San Joaquin | Super. | 5 | 3 | 0 | 7 | no | yes |
| Santa Barbara (2) | | | | | | | |
|   Miller | Super. | 10 | 7 | 0 | 9 | no | no |
|   Jahnshahi | Super. | 13 | 3 | 10 | 53 | no | no |
| Santa Clara (2) | | | | | | | |
|   Branson | Super. | 19 | 4 | 143 | 101 | yes | yes |
|   Fischer | Fed. | 10 | 9 | 40 | 155 | yes | yes |
| Santa Cruz | Fed. | 12 | 6 | 0 | 162 | no | no |

*(Continued)*

**TABLE 21 (continued)**
MAJOR DIMENSIONS OF LITIGATION IN CALIFORNIA COUNTIES, 1975–1989

| County | Level of Court | Alleg- ations (No.) | Original Orders (No.) | Modified Orders (No.) | Lawsuit Duration Mos. | Finding of Civil Contempt | Use of Special Master |
|---|---|---|---|---|---|---|---|
| Siskiyou | Fed. | 18 | 11 | 30 | 12 | no | no |
| Solano | Super. | 5 | 2 | 23 | 48 | no | no |
| Sonoma | Fed. | 6 | 18 | 17 | 110 | yes | yes |
| Tehama | Super. | 8 | 5 | 3 | 26 | no | no |
| Trinity | Super. | 14 | 6 | 0 | 5 | no | no |
| Tulare | Super. | 20 | 13 | 12 | 65 | no | no |
| Ventura | Super. | 1 | 1 | 0 | 1 | no | no |
| Yolo | Fed. | 22 | 26 | 0 | 6 | no | no |
| Yuba | Fed. | 15 | 19 | 3 | 34 | no | no |
| TOTAL | | 549.0 | 375.0 | 496.0 | 2,356.0 | | |
| MEAN | | 12.8 | 8.7 | 11.5 | 54.8 | | |
| MEDIAN | | 12.0 | 8.0 | 3.0 | 39.0 | | |

*Note:* "Super." = Superior Court of California; "Fed." = U.S. District Court; "Cal. Sup. Ct." = California Supreme Court. Parenthetical numbers following county names indicate number of cases.

to use contempt because of their greater autonomy from local government and their greater familiarity with federal rules for civil contempt. To the degree that public officials are granted the discretion to decide the means by which they will comply with certain goals set by the court (e.g., specified population reductions by a specific date), rather than having the court specify the means of compliance (e.g., directions to perform highly specific tasks such as building a certain number of jail cells), compliance is more likely and contempt is less likely. More complex issues and resistance by defendants increase the difficulty in meeting court directives.

Since only four counties in the sample were ever found in contempt of court, there was no basis for forming comparison groups. These four cases (Sonoma, Orange, and two Santa Clara lawsuits) were particularly troublesome, resulting in an average of 65 total orders each and lasting an average of 129 months. Each case involved orders to reduce overcrowding; three out of four occurred in federal court; three involved ideological counsel; all four involved the board of supervisors as defendants. Once again, we see that legal outcomes are shaped by contextual factors in an interactive, dynamic manner, and gaining compliance in such cases is extremely problematic.

Table 21 (see pp. 106–107) provides a snapshot of major outcomes of litigation at the Postdecree Stage in California counties, as well as the level of court the lawsuit was filed in, the number of violations alleged in the complaint, and the use of contempt orders and special masters to monitor compliance. Such summary dimensions of litigation, in conjunction with measures of constructs from the other four stages of litigation (see Fig. 1), provide a foundation for more advanced comparative analyses and theories of social policy litigation.

## Case Studies

Fewer orders were issued in Contra Costa (8) than in the other two counties; the lawsuit lasted a much shorter time (18 months); and neither contempt orders nor special masters were used to gain compliance. In contrast, lawsuits lasted much longer in Orange (152 months) and Santa Clara (101 months), included more total orders, and involved the use of contempt orders and special masters. We expect differences in litigation outcomes in each case simply because of variation in the complexity of legal issues. However, lengthy lawsuits and the use of contempt or special masters also reflect failed attempts at settlement that preceded and ran concurrently with court hearings (Horowitz 1977).

As noted in Chapter 4, noncompliance was never an issue in Contra Costa; court orders and negotiations were handled informally in the judge's chambers, and the court relinquished jurisdiction after only one year. In contrast, the Postdecree Stage constituted the most active and complex part of the lawsuits in Orange and Santa Clara.

### Santa Clara

On 7 March 1984, Superior Court Presiding Judge Eugene Premo inherited the jail case after Judge Allen's departure. The entire Superior Court bench had previously disqualified itself from hearing the case (see Chapter 3), and no other judge wanted the case because of its enormous time demands and controversial reputation. Presiding Judge Premo had a less crowded caseload than the other judges, and perhaps felt some responsibility to take the case; maybe he sought recognition as the judge who finally settled *Branson*. Why he took the case is not clear, but the events that followed must have led him to question his choice many times.

Judge Premo had apparently learned from his predecessor's efforts and complaints the need for timely information about the current state of jail conditions, the contribution of other justice system agencies to the overcrowding situation, and the feasibility of various reform plans presented by the county. In addition to its extensive provisions for reforming substantive jail conditions, the consent decree of 7 June 1983 addressed the court's information needs directly by requiring the county to submit a written plan for extensive upgrading of its jail management information system, with particular attention to jail classification and population management. The plan was required to include a computerized database for all jail facilities.

The consent decree marked the introduction of "Compliance Officer" Thomas Lonergan to the case. Lonergan's duties resembled those of a special master, although litigants took great pains to avoid use of that term because of its perceived pejorative quality. Lonergan's extensive powers and duties included monitoring every aspect of the consent decree, reporting to the court, and advising it on the enforcement and modification of the terms of the agreement. He was granted unlimited access to jail facilities, documents, and records, as well as entry to any meetings of county supervisors, county officials, and the sheriff related to the agreement.

That agreement clearly called for new jail facilities and the reduction of jail populations to previous court-imposed limits (Chapter 4). The parties agreed to add more mobile housing, complete and start up the Mountain View Work Furlough Center by 31 December 1983, construct 96 additional modular units for maximum-security prisoners at the county's Elmwood jail facility, provide at least three additional "reserve sites" capable of housing 120 inmates, and submit a comprehensive plan for housing inmates pending completion of the planned new jail (the approximate date specified was 1987).

Several "alternatives" to incarceration were spelled out. As previously ordered, the sheriff would continue to release inmates pursuant to PC 853.6 (cite-and-release of pretrial defendants on their own recognizance) and PC 4024.1 (work release programs). The agreement also specified continued use of the county's Public Works Program (work release for sentenced inmates to perform public services such as cleaning parks and roadways), and the county was required to provide sufficient probation services. Interestingly, this section of the agreement included a concession to the district attorney, reflecting the learning experience of litigants and judges in this case. Provision "E" (p. 21) specified that early release of sentenced inmates was to be used only as a last resort, and only after all alternatives had been maximized or exhausted. Recall that early release orders dated back to Judge Leahy, who was disqualified at the county's request for failing to issue a summons to the district attorney. Such participation would have allowed the district attorney to voice in court that office's concerns and recommendations about early release orders. The agreement noted: "If the trial court orders the early release of any sentenced inmate which is not in compliance with statutory or binding case law, the record shall reflect such release was done over the objection of the Santa Clara County District Attorney's Office, as the representative of the People" (p. 21).

Several unusual features of the agreement further reflect the experience of plaintiffs and judges. First, in a section entitled "Additional Funds for Jail Facilities," the county executive and the board of supervisors agreed to hold a special election to vote upon a measure to obtain funds for constructing and operating jail facilities. While many counties have used these bond financing schemes to raise short-term capital (often accompanied by high long-term interest rates), such policy decisions are normally the exclusive and unchallenged realm of elected officials; it is unusual to find them specified in a consent decree. In contrast to the Allen era, however, defendants agreed to such provisions without being ordered to do so. Perhaps Judge Allen's earlier "radical" efforts at ordering expenditures lowered the perceived threat of these subsequent, milder provisions.

Anticipating further compliance problems, plaintiffs sought and received strict reporting requirements for the county. The county was required to file its first report within 60 days and subsequent reports every three months. Semiannual inspections of the jail were also required. These inspections, led by the compliance officer, would include a qualified sanitarian, dietitian, and public health nurse. Further, plaintiff counsel was granted reasonable access to all facilities and records.

The lack of funds to make required improvements was explicitly dismissed as a potential excuse for noncompliance. The county agreed to "appropriate and expend sufficient funds to meet all the terms of this Agreement completely and in a timely manner" (p. 25). The excuses so often voiced during Judge Allen's tenure, therefore, were to be excluded by this agreement. Further, the county agreed to set aside $250,000 from the sheriff's budget to ensure compliance by the sheriff's department. Should that department fail to comply with any provision of the agreement, the court could authorize the compliance officer to access and use the fund to purchase required goods or services. Such an agreement, once again, provided a stark contrast to Judge Allen's previous orders, which granted the sheriff carte blanche to purchase services and bill the county.

Most significantly, however, the parties explicitly waived their right to challenge Judge Premo pursuant to Code of Civil Procedure (CCP) section 170.6. The previous disqualification of Judge Leahy was likely the stimulus for this section of the agreement. In addition, the parties agreed that all pending appeals but one (Order 9c, specifying credit for time served) would be withdrawn, and that no decision issued by the appellate court was to affect the terms of the agreement. Again, such provisions are significant: Earlier in the case, the county had been continually running to the Court of Appeal to challenge orders.

By 5 August 1983, disturbing patterns of noncompliance had begun to emerge, and Tom Lonergan served notice that his term as compliance officer was not to be a passive one. In his Recommendation #2 (5 August 1983), Lonergan found that inmates in one unit had been unduly punished without benefit of a hearing or finding of guilt over fires set in the jail that morning. In response to the fires, staff had removed all mattresses and telephones from the unit. Lonergan noted that such mass punishment violated terms of the consent decree; he recommended that all mattresses be returned by 4:00 p.m. unless findings of guilt were entered by a disciplinary board following California jail standards. Under terms of the consent decree, Lonergan also called a meeting of jail officials to discuss the failure to post consent decrees in living units and deputy sheriffs' ignorance of the terms of the agreement.

Recommendation #3 (29 August 1983) criticized inmate classification and the current management information system. Adequate classification was essential to inmate safety, and required an adequate information system and adequate staffing, but Lonergan felt that the county had already begun to renege on its agreement to provide necessary staffing for the classification function: "Absent the immediate allocation of the staff recommended in this report it is the recommendation of the Compliance Officer that the Settlement Agreement be terminated or that the Court order the allocation of classification personnel sufficient to provide for the safety of persons confined within the jail" (p. 2). He recommended a thorough study of staffing patterns within the jail, measured against the workload required for different tasks, and observed that staff attitudes toward compliance were uncooperative and covertly hostile.

No recommendations of the Compliance Officer that have been given to Watch Commanders during inspections have been complied with. These include: sanitation; maintenance; disciplinary procedures; and administrative segregation. The only times compliance has been gained has been when the Chief or Captain has been personally notified. The Compliance Officer has learned that staff, and some supervisors, often discuss the Compliance Officer and Settlement Agreement requirements in a joking manner and feel the jail has now been returned to them following the slowdown. Only direct and immediate action as recommended in this report can offset this trend. Effective immediately, the Compliance Officer is requesting office space inside the jail with the facility command staff to emphasize the importance of the Agreement.

Noncompliance with jail population limits was described in Recommendation #4 (23 August 1983). The county had exceeded the 140-inmate limit at the Elmwood medium-security unit and had failed to activate the reserve jail site as specified in the agreement. Lonergan recommended that the court issue an order prohibiting similar acts under penalty of contempt. Filthy living conditions described in Recommendation #5 (garbage on the floors, ceilings, and bars; toilets and showers in disrepair) had been brought to the attention of the sheriff's department for the third time without response. Lonergan recommended that watch commanders be required to conduct daily inspections and submit reports, paying for any repairs from the $250,000 fund provided under the agreement.

Conditions in administrative segregation cells were targeted in Recommendation #6. Proper disciplinary procedures regarding administrative segregation were not being followed, and poor sanitation, inadequate meals, and inadequate lighting were noted. Lonergan applied to the court for an ex parte order requiring the sheriff to establish disciplinary procedures and appeals regarding the use of administrative segregation, and recommended immediate repairs and cleanup in those units. Finally, in Recommendation #7, he chastised county officials for not informing him of meetings held by county officials to discuss terms of the settlement agreement, as clearly specified in Appendix B, Order of Reference #4. Judge Premo followed Lonergan's recommendations almost to the letter, issuing an ex parte order on 6 October 1983.

More orders in response to Lonergan's recommendations followed. One provided the requested staffing for classification purposes (28 December 1983); a more extensive order (15 provisions) specified the use of reserve sites, the remodeling of existing warehouses for minimum-security housing, the construction of a new 40-bed modular housing unit, and the addition of 12 mobile housing units to ease overcrowding (4 January 1984). Premo also granted Lonergan the discretion to order renovations to provide for additional reserve sites, and granted his request for office space within the building. Premo ordered the sheriff to have the classification database system fully operable by 16 December, with the sheriff and undersheriff to be held "personally liable and subject to monetary sanctions" (p. 3). Premo also required plans for improved staffing and written classification procedures.

Premo took stock of the case and the settlement agreement in his Memorandum of Decision and Order dated 1 February 1984. Noting that "the settlement is intended to end the time-consuming, expensive, and at times rancorous litigation which this case has historically experienced" (p. 2), he suggested that the settlement agreement provided a fair structure for operating a constitutionally mandated jail system, but it lacked an adequate enforcement provision. He approved Lonergan's request for more extensive powers regarding decree monitoring, enforcement, and discretion to mediate between litigants and recommend solutions.

Premo noted the pattern of noncompliance that had so far characterized defendants' responses: "[T]he implementation of the Settlement's provisions has been slow and plodding, and the efforts expended, in many cases, were done so in a begrudging manner" (p. 4). He noted resistance by county officials to planned change: "[C]ertain individuals and departments involved in the daily chores of county government seem to function more comfortably in a crisis management environment, and are much less enthusiastic about a planned, efficient and effective government operation which recognizes the responsibility to render government service in a cost effective and constitutionally mandated manner" (p. 4). Poor interagency coordination within the criminal justice system was a major problem:

> The Sheriff's Department, as the primary supervisor of the present jail system, is heavily dependent on the County for support services such as plant maintenance, health care, data processing support, etc. There is a vast opportunity in the interaction of these governmental units for tasks to go unaccomplished, for responsibility to be ignored, for excuses to be offered instead of accomplished goals. (P. 5)

In particular, Premo criticized the sheriff's apparent tendency to "fill all available housing to maximum levels" (p. 6). Relief provisions, alternatives, and new capacity were never enough to maintain population limits set by the court. It seemed, Premo suggested, that the sheriff operated under a form of "Murphy's Law":

> A housing crisis will present itself. . . . The crisis will result in the opening of a new facility, or the addition of extra bunks crowding an existing facility. The crisis will abate. The population flow will return to normal, but the expansion facility/extra beds will remain filled, and another increment in the steady increase in jail population will become permanent. (P. 7)

Food service, health care, and physical plant maintenance had, according to Premo, actually deteriorated since the time of the inspections and reports specified in the settlement. Officials had made only temporary efforts to comply and had not accepted jail maintenance and sanitation as a routine priority. Once again he criticized the county's jail information services and stressed their importance in developing a constitutional jail system: "It has become painfully obvious that the Sheriff's inability to marshall the current information regarding his prisoners has a direct bearing on the entire criminal courts operation. The housing and transportation of in-custody criminal defendants is a crucial aspect of the orderly and speedy administration of justice mandated for the criminal courts of this county" (p. 11). Unfortunately, "data processing and management of information in a modern technological sense in the operation of the criminal justice system has heretofore been non-existent" (p. 13). Premo's comments clearly spelt out the systemic intertwining of the jail with other criminal justice operations in the county and hinted at the need for enhanced interagency coordination to solve jail problems.

Problems continued, however. In his report of 14 February 1984, Lonergan complained of unacceptable sanitation levels, a kitchen in disrepair, and food service practices that violated health codes. Deputies allegedly dealt with an inmate going through heroin withdrawal by removing his bed rather than by notifying medical personnel. Lonergan continued to issue notices of noncompliance regarding classification and housing (27 February 1984).

Serious conflict was developing between Lonergan and the defendants. In his notice of noncompliance #11 (27 February 1984), he accused the sheriff of lying about receiving authorization to open the reserve site at Barracks 3. In fact, Lonergan claimed that he had not learned of such a move until the following day, and denied that he had granted the sheriff permission to do so. In his recommendations, Lonergan suggested that the court begin employing its power to issue contempt orders to deal with noncompliance.

On 7 March Premo ordered the county board of supervisors to appear for a contempt hearing, pending fines of $2,000 each, regarding their failure to provide 96 beds by the end of February as specified in the settlement agreement. The county filed a motion to quash the orders to show cause. In the interim, Premo issued an order requiring immediate improvements in food service and medical care (23 March 1984). He ruled on the motion to quash in his order of 2 April, acknowledging that inadequate notice of the basis for the hearing was supplied, but insisting that the court had the jurisdiction to issue such an order and that the county had been informed according to accepted procedures through its representative, the county counsel.

Following an evidentiary hearing, Premo issued findings and orders on 2 April 1984. He noted that the county's compliance to date had not been satisfactory: "Issues of public safety and constitutional standards of human incarceration continue to be only marginally satisfied" (p. 2). Further, "the Sheriff of Santa Clara County has failed to perform satisfactorily several covenants in the agreement" (p. 2). Premo ordered the county to commence negotiations to hire a private contractor to provide food service to all jail facilities: "This order is based on a long-term and continuing difficulty experienced by the Sheriff's department in the basic responsibility of feeding prisoners in the jail system" (p. 2). He continued to press for improvements to the information system, requiring the county and the sheriff to submit a jointly executed written report specifying plans for the creation of a centrally located office capable of gathering, storing, and disseminating pertinent criminal justice information to all justice system components, including the sheriff. Other orders required the county to further investigate alternatives to incarceration "to compensate for its failure to timely deliver beds on line as required by present and future jail population requirements" (p. 6). Again, Premo threatened the board of supervisors with contempt, this time carrying fines of $5,000 individually and $25,000 for the county.

Over the next few months, additional staff were allocated to jail classification services, although the system experienced extensive implementation problems. Conflict continued to rise in other areas. In his notice of 10 July 1984, Lonergan complained that the county was attempting to intimidate employees who supplied him with information. He asked Premo to restrain the county from requiring employees to furnish information about conversations or interactions with the compliance officer. Lonergan angrily noted that county counsel had asserted client–attorney privilege (a common event in trial litigation, but rare in the stages of a settlement agreement) to refuse to answer questions about information supplied to defendants. This claim, if upheld, would have required county officials to appear in person at every meeting to give testimony concerning their knowledge of the orders and recommendations: "This cumbersome practice in effect undermines both the spirit and letter of the Settlement Agreement, and if required should trigger a termination of the Agreement, and a return to formal litigation where such a privilege is usually asserted" (p. 4).

By November, the situation looked increasingly bleak. In his findings and orders (7 November 1984), Premo noted that the inmate population had risen 20 percent in the last six months. Surprisingly, the use of alternative sanctions declined during the same period. A 200-bed facility proposed by the county and ordered by the court in March had not yet been started. The county had used up all its reserve jail space and was unable to comply with terms of the agreement regarding reserve sites. Overcrowding had seriously undermined the effectiveness of the new classification system. So far that year, 256 misdemeanant prisoners and eight pretrial felony suspects had escaped. Defendants had not yet implemented a timely and effective maintenance program, or provided adequate staffing levels and security equipment. Orders were issued in each area including provisions that required the county to proceed with jail construction plans. Emergency housing and barracks were also employed, giving the image of a system held together with band-aids and chewing gum. In the meantime, Lonergan was given more responsibility to raise population levels for up to five days at any of the county jail facilities. On 21 February, Premo ordered increased use of the Public Works Program to reduce jail overcrowding.

In his letter of 24 June 1985, Lonergan complained of proactive interference by the county, not just noncompliance, with the terms of the agreement. In fact, he acquired information suggesting that the county had appointed a special committee to investigate his own activities. Lonergan recommended that Premo terminate the agreement once and for all:

> The County's dissatisfaction, and unwillingness to operate within the confines of the Settlement Agreement process are clear evidence that the Agreement is effectively over. The adversarial and litigious posture now assumed by the county, as well as the clearly deleterious and damaging effect of their present course of action to the continued operation of the Settlement Agreement within concerned departments makes continuation impossible. (P. 1)

The hopelessness of settlement now seemed confirmed for Lonergan:

> The above facts clearly substantiate cause to terminate the Settlement Agreement and assign Branson for trial. Three different judges, and two compliance officers have been unable to secure adequate remedy and compliance—SETTLEMENT WITH SANTA CLARA COUNTY IS, BASED ON THE RECORD, INAPPROPRIATE. (Original emphasis, p. 3)

By 18 October, the county had asked Lonergan to put all his requests for information or action (e.g., raising population limits, releasing inmates early) in writing. Lonergan relented on his request for decree termination, at least temporarily, noting the continued need for court involvement and monitoring in this case.

On 29 December 1985, Judge Premo issued his final memorandum. He noted, once again, that a comprehensive jail management information system is "the cornerstone of effectively and legally housing and managing an ever increasing jail population" (p. 3). Expressing concern that the county had still not provided 200 promised jail beds, he dismissed its claim that the settlement agreement did not "require" interim single celling. He recommended that litigants seek expert opinion in the case and take advantage of free consulting provided by the National Institute of Corrections (NIC). Premo directed the compliance officer to arrange for such a study and file a report with the court. Finally, he directed that all further reports and pleadings in the case were to be filed in the department of the presiding judge until 1 January 1986, or "when this matter is assigned to a different trial department, whichever occurs first" (p. 5). Judge Premo, in effect, was saying goodbye to *Branson v. Winter.*

Judge Premo resigned from the case a short time later. He had from the beginning suggested that he would exclude himself from presiding over another trial in this case. Indeed, the memorandum in which the Superior Court excluded itself from hearing the case (see Chapter 4) suggests that Premo lacked either the interest or the authority to usher the case into a new trial stage.

The state Judicial Council appointed retired Alameda County Superior Court Judge Spurgeon Avakian to take over. In his first order (dated 27 February 1986), Avakian emphasized the primacy of the overcrowding issue and allowed the county to suspend normal bidding procedures to facilitate jail repairs, planning, and construction. On 12 March he ordered the county to agree by 14 March upon preliminary plans for a 200-bed single-cell facility to be constructed at Elmwood. Plans were to be approved 31 March, and the building was to be completed within

10 months after that. In his notice of 17 March 1986, Compliance Officer Lonergan noted that the county was still in violation of the agreement regarding the use of reserve sites (some were to be taken off-line, others were to be put on-line). In particular, the old World War II Quonset huts being used as temporary overflow barracks lacked adequate toilet facilities, suffered sewer seepage, and needed numerous repairs. Poor sanitation, overcrowding, inadequate air circulation, and violence continued, and the single cells needed for adequate classification were lacking. Lonergan recommended fining the county $10 per day per inmate housed in temporary barracks longer than the previously stipulated five days, population caps at each facility not covered in the previous agreement, and an additional 300 medium-security beds. Lonergan further noted (10 April 1986) that "mishousing and misclassification is occurring on a widespread basis within the system, and a clear and present danger to confined persons and staff exists within the facility [Main Jail]" (p. 1).

Following evidentiary hearings, Judge Avakian issued numerous new orders and modifications of previous orders regarding the release of pretrial inmates (8 April 1986, 7 May 1986) and the early release of sentenced inmates (3 June 1986). He soon extended population caps to all county jail facilities (3 June 1986).

The county's response to this new judge, the fourth in the series, was unsurprising. On 17 June 1986, Avakian cited its "disturbing record of noncompliance" (p. 1): "The Supervisors have apparently failed to realize that the Settlement Agreement is a contract which establishes the County's legal obligations; instead, they react to each stage of necessary action as if their obligation is yet to be defined through a process of litigation" (pp. 1–2). Further: "In a number of situations the County's actions have been such that, were it a private contracting party, it would have been subject to a claim for punitive damages for breach of the implied covenant of dealing in good faith" (p. 2). Avakian noted as an example the county's noncompliance for half a year regarding grievous health and sanitary violations at Elmwood.

Perhaps most important, Avakian was incensed that the county had backed down from its 1985 agreement to add 200 single cells at Elmwood, mainly because of additional costs, and built a dormitory facility instead, without any notice to the court, compliance officer, or counsel for plaintiffs. In December, shortly before he resigned, Judge Premo had issued an additional order for 200 single cells, which had again been contested. Instead of ordering new construction, Avakian addressed the pressing need for single cells (the jail offered only nine single cells for a population of 2,900 inmates) by ordering a conversion of existing space, to be directed by the compliance officer. Any delay would result in fines of $1,000 per day times the number of beds to be converted.

Compliance Officer Lonergan must have been guardedly pleased: Sanctions had finally been ordered, but would Avakian be the first judge in the case actually to enforce them? By 7 July Lonergan was once again writing lengthy notices of noncompliance to the court, and he continued to emphasize the importance of getting other criminal justice actors—police, district attorney, probation—to share responsibility for devising solutions to the overcrowding problem.

The county continued to resist Lonergan's directions and asked Judge Avakian to modify his recommendations. Avakian, however, directed defendants to consult with Lonergan *before* making further motions to the court. After receiving continued motions and complaints regarding Lonergan's powers, Avakian defended his compliance officer in his memorandum of 18 August 1986: "The best way to eliminate initiatives by the Compliance Officer is for the County to take the initiative itself in actions which bring it into compliance with its obligations" (p. 3). When an inmate claimed misclassification and harm suffered as a result of the compliance officer's plans, Avakian ordered the sheriff to make the necessary conversions upon consideration of Lonergan's recommendations.

Judge Avakian noted that the sheriff had requested 108 single cells from the county in August, considerably less than the original 200 specified (8 January 1987). The county had been directed to complete whatever construction was required as expeditiously as possible, on the basis of "urgency and high priority." County officials had submitted no plan whatsoever by 26 December, prompting Judge Avakian to issue an order to show cause re: contempt of court. Avakian made it clear that further inaction on the matter was not justified by pending contempt hearings: "The Court will not permit the County to use a remedial procedure designed to enforce compliance as a vehicle to justify non-compliance" (p. 3). Avakian asked defendants to note that if indeed a contempt finding was justified, the fines threatened in the orders of June 17 and 28 would be levied retroactive to those dates and would continue to accumulate on a daily basis. Prior to the contempt hearing, Avakian issued a continuance order informing the supervisors that they could purge the contempt by demonstrating that they individually had responded to the issues in a responsible manner. Avakian's message seemed clear: Compliance was his goal, not political embarrassment or fines for the board of supervisors.

On 16 March 1987, Judge Avakian found the county in contempt of court for once again failing to build 96 new jail cells on time and for disciplining an employee (the public defender) who had, at Lonergan's request, suggested alternative sanctions to reduce crowding. All but one member of the board of supervisors were fined $1,000 each and were sentenced to serve five days in their own jail. Avakian had made it clear, however, that supervisors still had the opportunity to purge the contempt by admitting their error in criticizing a county employee, upholding the compliance officer's access to county employees, and signing an agreement to build at least 96 single cells by 1 December 1987. Avakian extended a stay of execution on the contempt order until 16 April and then again until 30 April to give the county time to file appeals or perhaps comply. County officials appealed.

The county now argued that the court had violated the separation of powers doctrine by requiring it to build 96 single cells immediately, even though in officials' best judgment it was more cost-effective and consistent with the county master jail plan to comply by adding 400 single cells to the new jail under construction (targeted for January 1988 opening). Such decisions, the county argued, are *executive* decisions. Further, it argued, neither the settlement agreement nor the constitution *requires* single cells. In addition, the contempt orders should be voided because they were based on insufficiently specific orders. Also, the county claimed, the court had inappropriately delegated judicial power (the power to determine single cell requirements) to the sheriff, a real party at interest in the case. Respondents contended that petitioners had waived any separation of powers argument when they entered into the consent agreement. The requirement for single cells was clear and specific, they argued; all parties understood what had been imposed.

The Court of Appeal agreed with the county that Judge Avakian had improperly delegated powers to the sheriff and that the orders forming the basis for contempt were insufficiently specific (*Wilson v. Superior Court*, 1987). Avakian must have been disappointed by the Court's findings: "Patently the June and July orders required action by the supervisors, the duly constituted legislative branch of county government. It is well established as a matter of constitutional doctrine, basic to our form of government, that the judicial branch cannot directly and prospectively require a specific legislative act" (240 Cal. Rptr. 137). On the issue of firing the public defender, the court found that the county officials had exercised legitimate authority and had purged themselves of contempt by guaranteeing the compliance officer's access to county employees. The contempt was annulled by the Court of Appeal on 17 September 1987 (*Wilson v. Superior Court,* 1987), and Judge Avakian resigned from the case shortly afterward.

Alameda County Superior Court Judge Henry Ramsey took over on 24 September 1987. Construction of the new central jail was progressing, and the county was preparing to transfer control of the jail from the sheriff to a newly created County Department of Correction. After prevailing in a separate court battle with the sheriff and deputy sheriffs' association (*Beck v. County of Santa Clara, Winter v. County of Santa Clara,* 1988), the county transferred control to a new Director of Corrections, the new jail opened in early 1989, and Judge Ramsey relinquished jurisdiction on 18 September 1989.

The influence of judicial methods and the roles played by government defendants, plaintiffs' counsel, and the special master can be clearly seen in the Santa Clara case. *Branson v. Winter* (1981) was unique in that five judges heard the case over its eight-year life. The first was disqualified on a procedural issue; the second, fourth, and fifth were state court judges appointed by the California Judicial Council; the third judge accepted the case while serving as presiding judge of the Superior Court. Throughout the case, judges ordered defendants to reduce jail populations by expanding pretrial release criteria, instituting early release for nonviolent sentenced inmates, expanding alternatives to incarceration, and building new jail beds. Judges varied, however, in their persistence and use of sanctions to gain compliance. One interview respondent stressed the importance of the judge:

> [W]here something is going to go to trial, and you are going to get a judgment, and then you are going to go away—like Judge Allen used to say, you pay the man for a load of fish, you get your fish, and that's the end of it. Then it doesn't matter what kind of judge you get . . . but on a case where the trial doesn't matter, it is the enforcement proceedings after that, that go on into the second generation—that is where it is important.

Judges acted within a volatile political environment dominated by a powerful board of supervisors—"all big egos," according to one respondent. "They have their own political axes to grind." The board was defiant, another respondent suggested: "They don't want to settle, they want to *win.*" Remarks from the bench by Judge Allen (6 January 1983) support such an interpretation: "This court finds that the County Executive and the Board of Supervisors are not cooperating in the implementation of orders of this court, and are intentionally and grossly exaggerating the cost of compliance, and are manipulating county

funds for the purpose of frustrating the orders of this court in this case"
(p. 1).

Judge Allen had issued bold orders to government officials on several occasions, frequently ordering the county to pay for jail maintenance and repairs and restricting the ability of county executives to
make decisions regarding jail planning without first consulting the
court. Appeals were continually launched in response to such judicial
methods, and some orders (staffing, early release of inmates, jail expansion, maintenance, and funding) resulted in appellate modifications
(see Chapter 4).

The county may have intended to wage a "war of attrition," as one
respondent suggested. Judges and witnesses had a limited lifespan; the
county could more easily replace the people it lost. It is difficult to
confirm or estimate the wisdom or price, in attorney fees and court
costs, of an attrition strategy, but the duration of the lawsuit (101
months) and impaired relations among local government, county justice agencies, and legal counsel may be traced to this pattern of resistance. In fact, the county sheriff, eventually perceiving his interests to
be in conflict with those of county supervisors, had dismissed county
counsel and hired his own independent counsel. A long-simmering
feud over the sheriff's spending practices had preceded the litigation,
perhaps making the sheriff a convenient scapegoat for jail problems.
One official jokingly proposed a "body count" of all those whose careers were damaged or ruined by the *Branson* litigation.

## Orange

Despite Judge Gray's 1978 order that all inmates were to be provided a
bed, and despite assurances by county officials that plans for a new
jail were in the works, overcrowding worsened and progress stalled in
Orange County. Gray slightly modified his order regarding bed space
on 11 October 1978, permitting defendants to house inmates for one
night only without a bunk but with full bedding if security interests or
a sudden and unusual intake of prisoners required it.

An uneventful appeal by defendants led to the U.S. Court of Appeals (Ninth Circuit) remanding the case back to Judge Gray. The justices merely asked Gray to reconsider his decision in light of the
Supreme Court decision in *Bell v. Wolfish* (1979) and the appellate decision in *Spain v. Procunier* (1979). Each had discussed in some detail
constitutional conditions of incarceration for pretrial prisoners. In an
unpublished decision (No. 78-2861, 9 April 1980), the justices also encouraged settlement under the auspices of the federal court, commend-

ing Judge Gray for "the sensitive and conscientious treatment given by the district court to each of the separate issues presented by the suit."

Following the return of the case to Judge Gray, a brief order clarifying inmates' rights under the judgment was issued (19 August 1980). Gray ordered that inmates retain access to all materials lawfully transmitted through the U.S. postal system, subject only to reasonable withholding for contraband and security purposes. If the reading material was judged a threat to security interests, the inmate was to be so notified in writing. Gray deleted paragraph 8 of the judgment, which would have permitted inmates to be present during any "cell shakedown" conducted by jail staff.

With plans for a new jail stalled, overcrowding got worse. In a motion for contempt filed on 21 November 1984, the ACLU alleged that more than 400 inmates were still sleeping on the floor, in direct violation of the court's order. Further, plaintiffs argued, jail staff made no distinction between pretrial and sentenced inmates when deciding which ones were to sleep on the floor or how long they were required to do so. Citing *Martino v. Carey* (1983), plaintiffs argued that "a court is required to stop 'punishment' of pretrial detainees to any extent, whereas the question as to convicted prisoners is whether a given quantum of misery exceeds constitutional standards" (p. 1006). Plaintiffs also asked Judge Gray to appoint a special master or expert to formulate and advise the court of strategies to alleviate overcrowding and monitor compliance with the judgment. Plaintiffs' counsel made a convincing argument for the use of a special master, citing a statement by District Judge Don J. Young in *Jones v. Wittenberg* (1976):

> There is an ancient saying, "Quis custodiet ipso [*sic*] custodes?" "Who is guarding the guards?" which is peculiarly applicable to this kind of litigation. The answer to the question is, "Nobody." The experience of this and other courts has demonstrated that it is not enough to make an order, no matter how detailed and explicit. Unless somebody checks the order against the defendants' performance, they do not perform. When someone watches them, they squirm, but they comply, or get out of the way for someone else to do so. Thus, rather than using the classical, simple, and entirely appropriate remedy of sending the defendants to jail with the keys in their pockets, this Court will undertake to monitor the defendants' future performance in its order. (P. 6)

The defendants' six years of inaction following the judgment in the Orange County case seemed to confirm Judge Young's observations.

Plaintiffs counsel argued that the sheriff and his staff lacked the expertise needed to run the jail: "The staff and commander of the Orange County jail and the sheriff are simply not trained penologists and are not equipped, trained, or inclined to formulate and put in practice policies which would bring them at once into compliance with this court's order" (p. 7). Indeed, this charge against jail keepers has persisted for many years (Mattick 1974).

In his declaration accompanying the motion, lead attorney Richard P. Herman observed that he had been involved in litigating several dozen cases regarding conditions at the Orange County jail since 1977, including the infamous "dog food case," where the jail was found to have served ground-up leftovers to female inmates on a regular basis. During that time, he suggested, jail staff and officials had demonstrated a flagrant disregard for constitutional principles, and a general ignorance of the judgment in *Stewart v. Gates* (1978). Unchecked crowding exposed inmates to "endemic respiratory disease, excessive stress, physical and psychological deprivation and punishment, and excessive inmate-to-inmate and guard-to-inmate violence" (p. 11). Defendants had been placed on notice that they were in violation of the court's orders six months before the contempt motion was filed, Herman noted, but no response was received, and no attempt at compliance was made.

On 20 March 1985, Judge Gray found the sheriff and the board of supervisors in contempt of court for intentionally violating his orders. The defendants were fined $50,000 plus $10 per day for each inmate who slept on the floor more than one night. The fine would be used to hire a special master to monitor compliance with the court's orders, and Judge Gray appointed retired prison warden Lawrence Grossman to serve that role, with 24-hour access to the jail and all its records. In his order of 10 July 1985, the judge granted the county's request to reduce its lump fine to $25,830 because of costs expended to comply with court orders.

While commending defendants for steps taken to reduce crowding, he noted that they were still in substantial noncompliance with the court's orders dating back seven years. Judge Gray placed a population cap on the main jail on 15 August 1985, specifying reductions to 1,500 inmates by 1 December 1985 (later extended to 15 January 1986), and 1,400 inmates by 31 March 1986 (later extended to 1 May 1986). He also prohibited the sheriff from receiving into the county jail any inmate for whom he could not provide a bed within 24 hours.

On 4 March 1986, Gray issued another order to show cause regarding contempt. The order was based on a report from special master

Lawrence Grossman citing three occasions when the jail population exceeded the population caps by 23, 37, and 20 inmates respectively, and one occasion on which an inmate was not provided a bed within the one-day time limit. Considering the flagrant violations of population caps reported in Santa Clara, one might perceive contempt findings in this instance as harsh medicine for such minor violations. As Judge Avakian pointed out in *Branson v. Winter,* however, the purpose of contempt is to gain compliance. It appears that Judge Gray wanted to send a message that further inaction would not be tolerated.

The sheriff made a case to Judge Gray, supported by the special master, that temporary fluctuations in the jail population, especially on weekends and holidays, made it impossible to maintain the population limit of 1,400 set by the court. Again, Judge Gray was accommodating. In his memorandum of 6 May 1986, he modified the population caps to permit 1,400 inmates on weekdays, rising to a maximum of 1,450 between Friday at 4:00 p.m. and Monday at 8:00 p.m.; and a maximum of 1,500 on three-day weekends.

Following a request by plaintiffs for several modifications to previous orders, Judge Gray updated defendants' compliance efforts in his memorandum of 27 May 1986. He found that defendants were in compliance with the order to publish and post written rules of conduct. Holding cells, however, were still severely overcrowded, and there were still not enough places for inmates to sit. Because suspects were kept in holding areas for a short time, and because the sheriff had promised to install additional benches, the judge simply directed the special master to monitor and report on these conditions. Gray modified his order on telephone availability by extending privileges to inmates in administrative segregation and medical isolation cells. As for complaints that deputies were unnecessarily opening prisoners' legal mail, Judge Gray accepted the sheriff's explanation that the envelopes had been inadvertently exposed to the letter-opening machine. He responded to plaintiffs' complaint about access to legal materials by noting that the present system, whereby inmates could receive up to five law volumes at one time, was adequate for cases not requiring the assistance of an attorney. He recommended, however, that the sheriff assess and update the availability of materials in the jail's law library.

Population limits were further refined in Gray's order of 9 December 1986. Following suggestions offered by the special master and endorsed by sheriff and legal counsel on both sides, Judge Gray lowered the population cap to 1,296 inmates, but ruled that the cap would include only inmates in general housing areas on the third and fourth floors, and exclude the short-term traffic in the jail's booking area.

Orange County took various measures to reduce jail populations. The sheriff stopped housing state and federal prisoners (e.g., parole violators) awaiting hearings or transfers, as well as inmates returning to local courts to testify. Inmates were also released up to five days early to balance jail population counts, under section 4024.1 of the California Penal Code (Perlman 1986). Finally, under section 853.6, all misdemeanor suspects with warrants under $5,000 were cited and released after signing a promise to appear in court.

The special master recommended two alternatives to incarceration. The first was the development of a home-confinement program for those assigned to the county's work furlough program (Needham 1987a). A one-year pilot program of "supervised electronic confinement" (SEC) was implemented in October 1986, supervising 133 inmates (Schumacher 1987). The second suggestion was an increased use of county parole. Under this program, inmates may apply to a local parole board for early release (California Board of Corrections 1985). In the end, this alternative was used only sparingly (County Administrative Office 1986).

Numerous construction projects were planned to increase jail capacity, although a tangle of legal problems and community opposition kept them from being initiated. Environmental conditions introduced at the Trigger Stage continue to impinge upon the behavior of courts and county officials throughout a protracted lawsuit. Cities and community groups brought lawsuits over all of the proposed jail sites, and needed funding was never secured. One proposed jail site (Katella/Douglas in Anaheim) was put on hold after community opponents successfully challenged the validity of an Environmental Impact Report in Superior Court. The judge ruled that the report failed to sufficiently discuss the jail's possible economic and social effects on the surrounding community (Zoroya and Serrano 1988).

Organized community resistance to proposed jail sites used scare tactics, warning of the loss of family safety and drops in property values. Films and posters showed family-oriented persons being criminally victimized by people who had been released or who had escaped from the jail (Needham 1987b). Eventually, partisans began to suggest "better" places for the jail—either more remote locations or urban sites closer to the courts. Gypsum Canyon was the proposed site for a 6,200 bed maximum-security jail in Orange County. Its affluent residents complained that they would be able to see the jail from their homes, that it would attract an undesirable element in the form of visitors, and that dangerous offenders might escape into the community.

Even expansion of existing facilities met with community and local governmental resistance. Expansion of a medium-security jail in the city of Orange would have added 300 maximum-security jail beds and 700 medium/minimum-security beds. Because of local resistance, the board of supervisors decided that only medium-security beds would be built. The City of Orange, however, launched a lawsuit to prevent expansion of any sort (Zoroya 1988).

A combination of community resistance and poor planning prevented expansion of jail capacity at the James A. Musick Honor Farm in El Toro, originally designated as the county's long-term jail site. The board of supervisors was criticized for allowing private property development alongside this previously "remote" site. A county official explained:

> [T]hey went down and bought a sizable piece of property next to the Marine quarter in El Toro, and that got into some political activity that was questionable, and the next thing you know is, they say you can't use that 100 acres. This is the only planning we have ever done with the county, because now we have allowed single-family housing intrusion and industrial intrusion on the site, and we now have all kinds of problems in being able to utilize the only site that we did plan ahead.

As in many cases, new issues surfaced during the course of the litigation. One of these concerned allegations that sheriff's deputies indiscriminately detained disorderly inmates in the jail's "rubber rooms" without proper medical screening or attention for long periods of time. This practice, plaintiffs alleged, had resulted in one or more unnecessary deaths. In response, Judge Gray granted plaintiffs and their medical expert complete access to the jail's medical facilities and records (9 June 1987). Their difficulty acquiring records prompted further motions to Judge Gray and another order (22 October 1987), in which the judge explicitly granted plaintiffs' request for complete psychiatric, medical, and jail records of every prisoner held in a rubber room during the months of January, March, and September 1987, and the Module Security Log from 1 January 1987 through 12 October 1987.

Plaintiffs' counsel filed a motion to add conditions in the rubber rooms to the list of allegations to be litigated. They also proposed that court orders be extended to include all of the detention facilities operated by Orange County. Counsel argued that the sheriff had complied with population limits at the main jail by illegally shuffling inmates to the four branch jails, stuffing them far in excess of their capacities. Judge Gray refused the request (memorandum of 28 June 1988): "If the plaintiffs' counsel believe that the facts rise to such constitutional dignity that a United States District Court should become involved, they are entitled to file a carefully structured complaint in a new action that would focus upon those issues" (p. 2). Plaintiffs correctly perceived that the litigation was about to end, but they were not yet satisfied that conditions in the jail had been sufficiently improved. Judge Gray had been hinting for some time that the court would soon disengage itself from watching over jail conditions, and he now confirmed this.

> [T]his court has also expressed a disinclination to take over general supervision of the Central Jail, and for me to continue to entertain new claims in this action would tend to imply a willingness to maintain indefinite supervision. As is mentioned above, this case is thirteen years old and all of the original plaintiffs are long gone. I believe that the time has come to terminate this action, except to the extent that further modification of the Orders herein contained are sought or new contempt proceedings are brought for the alleged violation of such orders. (P. 2)

Judge Gray relinquished jurisdiction on 1 July 1988, satisfied that the county was now taking sufficient steps to reduce overcrowding. He did issue one more order to show cause regarding contempt at plaintiffs' request (12 September 1988): Plaintiffs alleged that the sheriff was in noncompliance with orders regarding eight hours of sleep for inmates, roof recreation, and disciplinary hearings. No contempt orders were issued; instead, Gray issued an order outlining further responsibilities of plaintiff and defendant counsel in the case (7 December 1988). Plaintiffs' ACLU attorneys were granted access to the central jail and the intake–release center at all reasonable times; they would advise county counsel in writing of prisoner complaints and other matters that needed correction. Only if counsel were unable to resolve matters informally were they to be brought to the court's attention.

Numerous times afterward, plaintiffs' counsel sought further redress and sanctions for noncompliance, with little result. Additional lawsuits have since been filed over conditions at all jail facilities, and the long-promised new jail has not materialized.

As in Santa Clara, the jail lawsuit was highly publicized. Federal judges, however, are less vulnerable than state court judges to criticisms by local politicians and the public, as one observed in an interview:

> I would think it would be more of an impact on the state judges than it is on us because they have to run for reelection. You know that if a state judge gets a bad reputation that the people don't like, he's likely not to get reelected. In federal court, we don't have that concern, but no judge likes to

make a decision that is considered to be obnoxious or absurd. . . . We're not here to please the public, we're here to apply the law.

In contrast to Santa Clara judges, however, Judge Gray rarely dictated *how* compliance was to be achieved. Over 13 years, Judge Gray was patient but persistent in seeking compliance with court orders, defining specific deadlines and sanctions for official performance (e.g., graduated jail population caps). Although the promised jail was never built and crowding continued to be a problem, Gray's persistence definitely improved the routine conditions and operations of Orange County jails (see Chapter 6).

### Highlights from Other California Cases

Resources and space limitations preclude a detailed examination of all 43 lawsuits, but a brief examination of other California cases highlights some of the trends we have already observed in the Postdecree Stage, including the influence of environmental factors, level of court, and judicial methods. Two important trends emerged from examination of court documents: state court judges were more likely to order and monitor revisions in local criminal justice policies and practices, and federal judges were more likely to leave policy discretion to criminal justice and government officials but set strict limits for compliance. The following discussion summarizes judicial methods in state and federal courts, illustrating the influence of other contextual factors at the Postdecree Stage.

*State Superior Court Cases.* A popular judicial technique in state court cases was to order regular status conferences between litigants to negotiate potential solutions. Because of differences in local political environments, this strategy is more successful in some cases than others. In Riverside (*In re Inmates of Riverside County Jail at Riverside v. Byrd* [Clark], 1987), a lengthy series of remedies emerged from such sessions. For example, an order following one such meeting specified construction of a 64-bed facility for women, with deadlines for beginning and completion (18 November 1987). Judge Howard M. Dabney later ordered the probation department to implement a pretrial house arrest program (23 February 1988, 13 July 1988). When this program proved inadequate to reduce jail populations, the judge ordered its cessation and directed instead that eligible inmates be considered for conditional release on their own recognizance (ROR). Probation further agreed to establish an intensive surveillance program for high-risk offenders.

In Santa Barbara (*Jahanshahi v. Carpenter; Inmates of Santa Barbara County Jail v. Carpenter et al., Consolidated Cases,* 1985), Superior Court Judge William L. Gordon ordered a jail taskforce consisting of agency heads to produce plans for ROR release, county parole, house arrest, and citation release, and directed them to formulate corresponding estimates of likely impacts associated with each program. The sheriff was directed to educate the police on the use of citations, so that misdemeanor suspects could be released with a promise to appear in court, without being booked into the county jail.

In Fresno (*In re Morgan, In re Ransbury, and Consolidated Cases,* 1983), Superior Court Judge Frank J. Creede suggested that the sheriff was responsible for recruiting needed cooperation from county agencies to reduce overcrowding: "The evidence does not persuade the court that the sheriff has done all that could reasonably be accomplished on an interagency basis as ordered by Judge Robert L. Martin on January 30, 1981 to accelerate available channels for release and issuance of citations" (12 January 1983, p. 29). Judge Creede suggested that more effective working relationships between the sheriff, courts, and the probation department could relieve overcrowding:

> Since the Sheriff has the responsibility by law of operating the jail, it is he who must perform the obligation of relieving overcrowding by requesting, and if other agencies fail in their assistance, *demanding* [original emphasis] that other agencies, i.e., police, probation, courts, health and other community agencies providing residential facilities for alcohol, mental health and low risk detainees, assist in providing alternatives to relieve the persistent overcrowding, additional means to relieve overcrowding or transfers to the branch jail, or accepting fewer state prisoners or reclassification of work furlough inmates. (12 January 1983, p. 31)

In response, the sheriff organized a meeting on 12 October 1983 which included presiding judges of the Superior and Municipal Courts, the chief probation officer, two representatives from the sheriff's department, the county administrative officer, and county counsel. County officials proposed creating a list of pretrial inmates eligible for ROR and a list of sentenced inmates for possible early release. Later, Judge Creede ordered that when overcrowding exists, the sheriff shall notify the Municipal Court, the Superior Court, and probation to see if ROR can be increased (27 March 1985, p. 3). In spite of resistance by local judges, Judge Creede eventually ordered the probation department to implement a full-scale ROR program (24 June 1986, p. 3) and screen all jail inmates for eligibility. The judge ordered the district attorney and public defender to attend a hearing three days later to voice their opinions about ROR screening and release.

In Humboldt County (*In re the Inmate Population of Humboldt County Jail and Connected Cases,* 1987), the county's failure to comply with its commitment to build a new facility elicited frustration from Judge John Buffington: "That new facility's site has yet to be found; that new facility's design has yet to be made; and the county has not yet learned how to properly operate the present facility" (16 May 1988, p. 6). Across county criminal justice agencies, the judge complained, "inertia, a result of local legal expectation and severe budget limitations leading to manpower shortages in all justice system departments, has prevented local justice officials from finding any successful consensus as to the jail" (23 January 1987, p. 12). He bluntly stated that "the local legal culture must change" (p. 11).

Judge Buffington ordered the district attorney and police to delay felony filings until investigations were complete, noting that too many weak cases wasted valuable court time. Further, the district attorney, public defender, legal counsel for plaintiffs and defendants, and law enforcement officials were ordered to prepare plans to expedite prosecution. The judge also ordered city and government officials to meet in efforts to plan for future county criminal justice needs. Later, he ordered local law enforcement agencies to cite and release all misdemeanor suspects under provisions of state law (Cal. PC 853.6).

*Federal Court Cases.* In San Francisco (*Stone et al. v. City and County of San Francisco,* 1982), parties signed an agreement on 30 June 1987 to build a new 300-bed minimum/medium-security facility, and Judge William H. Orrick set further hearings to review compliance. Frustrated with noncompliance, the judge eventually ordered: "The city shall ensure that funding for the capital improvements shall be available during the 1988–89 year" (13 May 1988, p. 3), and set deadlines for design, beginning of construction, and completion. Judge Orrick ordered that the construction contract include a "liquidated damages provision," requiring damages to be paid into a special fund for this litigation, if construction was not completed by the deadline. The judge later ordered fines levied if staffing orders were not followed ($100 per day per each position left vacant after the deadline), and fines in the amount of $1,000 per day if the new jail was not in full occupancy by 8 January 1989 (14 September 1988, p. 3). When overcrowding persisted two months later, Judge Orrick ordered the defendants fined $300 per day for each inmate who exceeded the rated capacity of individual housing units, with such funds to be targeted for the inmate welfare fund.

In Sacramento (*Mariscal v. Lowe,* 1981), a consent decree specified population limits at the main jail and set out plans for managing jail population. U.S. District Court Judge Lawrence K. Karlton noted that remedies contained in the consent decree were to be considered temporary remedial measures only, pending construction of a new jail facility (16 July 1981, p. 3). The judge also noted his willingness to reopen the case and issue further remedial orders if defendants were not able to construct a new facility within a reasonable period of time. Defendants agreed to develop and implement a new jail staffing and supervision plan within 90 days of the consent decree. The court retained jurisdiction in the case, and the county opened a new 1,250-bed, state-of-the-art main jail and court complex in 1989 at a cost of about $103 million (California Board of Corrections 1988).

In Sonoma County (*Cherco v. County of Sonoma,* 1982), population caps and plans for a new jail were specified in a 1982 consent decree. Judge Thelton Henderson set deadlines for completion of new facilities, issued numerous modifications regarding construction, planning, and renovations, and held numerous hearings to review time extensions. Judge Henderson appointed a special master who later served the same function in the Santa Clara case: Tom Lonergan. On 27 August 1985, the judge found defendants in contempt of court for failing to meet orders limiting the length of time that inmates could be detained in holding areas, and fined the county $5,000 dollars. He admonished county officials to work together more closely:

> [W]e remain persuaded that the most effective way of insuring further progress is for the parties to work informally and cooperatively. Specifically, the Court believes that in all instances the parties should attempt to resolve their disputes through the procedures developed pursuant to the Settlement Agreement (particularly by working through the Monitor), rather than assuming adversarial positions, and engendering this Court's involvement.

## Critical Factors in the Postdecree Stage

Critical factors influence outcomes at the Postdecree Stage, either facilitating or hindering jail lawsuit resolution. Each of these factors is dynamic and interactive. For example, we cannot separate with any degree of reliability a "tough-minded" judicial style from defendants' previous and current patterns of compliance/noncompliance. We cannot assume that the roles played by defendants, plaintiffs, and judges remain static over the life of the case. Each actor constantly changes and adapts behavior and strategies in relation to the others, and in relation to previous events and behavior. In this sense, analyzing litigation is somewhat akin to dissecting the moves in a chess game.

Consider "judicial methods." Only with difficulty can we encapsulate a judge's total performance with one all-encompassing label, even though there were observable differences in the styles used by each at different stages of litigation. As Figure 1 suggests, judicial methods at the Postdecree Stage are a function of conditions, actions, and events at previous and current stages of litigation: the legal and political environments, plaintiff and defendants' legal representation, legal jurisdiction and level of court, nature and number of violations alleged, bases for legal claims, incumbents serving as defendants, nature and number of remedies issued, judicial methods at the Remedy Stage, nature of negotiations between defendants and plaintiffs at the Remedy Stage, previous duration of the lawsuit, previous judicial methods and negotiations between defendants and plaintiffs, and previous mechanisms used to gain compliance. In spite of this complexity of interactions and the caveats noted above, some general trends can be summarized.

## Judicial Methods at the Postdecree Stage

Judge Leahy's early strategy in Santa Clara was to set population caps and allow defendants to sort out the mechanisms for achieving compliance. His role, as it appeared, was to set strict deadlines for compliance and monitor performance. As Judge Young would have said, defendants can "squirm . . . comply, or get out of the way for someone else to do so." In this sense, Leahy's initial style was similar to that of Judge Gray in Orange County—that of the Conscientious Monitor.

Judge Allen assumed a much more "interventionist" role in Santa Clara in the sense that he made orders that interfered with and occasionally assumed the decision-making power of the county executive, allocating county funds or determining county land use. Judge Allen perceived that compliance by defendants was impossible unless the court temporarily took over the management of the jail and related county functions. This role, only rarely enacted to this degree, can be called that of "Intervenor." A judge who employs this style, on a continuum from intrusive to autocratic, generally makes budgetary or operational decisions that limit or remove the discretion of county officials. The orders of the most active intervenors are likely to face serious appellate scrutiny.

Judge Premo adopted more of a managerial approach, orchestrating negotiations between litigants and county agencies. Premo warned of, but never enforced, contempt. His task-oriented and conference-holding style—a role we can label "Manager"—focused on making sure that people got together and communicated about the right issues in order to make progress toward a solution. Similarly, Judge Arneson in Contra Costa conducted informal discussions in his chambers, calling in plaintiffs and litigants, determining whether a problem existed, and calling for proposed solutions. Managerial roles, as in Contra Costa and some of the other California cases reviewed, are facilitated by an existing network of relations among county officials, and a smaller scale of local government. Judge Gray in Orange County also employed a managerial role at times, with the assistance of a special master skilled at mediating between different county officials and between plaintiff and defense counsel.

The fourth Santa Clara judge, Judge Avakian, wasted no time in identifying the primacy of the overcrowding issue and defendants' previous failure to comply with court orders. He warned of contempt and issued sanctions (jail sentences and fines) against county supervisors. His intention was clear, and he gave defendants ample opportunities to purge the contempt by demonstrating compliance. Judge Avakian, by deciding to sanction longstanding patterns of noncompliance, provides an example of another rare style, the "Enforcer."

The fifth judge in the Santa Clara case, Judge Ramsey, ruled upon several outstanding matters of compliance, but the major issue he inherited was the amelioration of overcrowding and other jail conditions. Judge Ramsey largely tied up legal loose ends while waiting for the county to complete construction of the long-awaited new jail. His goal was clearly to disengage upon sufficient demonstration of compliance with previous orders. At this point, a judge must carefully weigh plaintiffs' motions about remaining noncompliance. Only drastic noncompliance at this stage is likely to change the judge's mind to relinquish jurisdiction. A judge adopting this role can be called a "Conciliator."

I cannot say that events in Santa Clara would have been any different had the case been presided over by only one judge, or ten, rather than five. Perhaps the case required different styles at different points in time. Nor can I say that judges always adopt the appropriate style at the right time. For example, one could argue that Judge Allen acted as an "Intervenor" too early in the case, he overreacted to particular incidents of noncompliance, that his approach violated the separation of powers doctrine, or even that it poisoned the well by upsetting sensitive political relations between county officials. Alternatively, one might argue that his style was a justifiable and appropriate reaction to the county's blunt disregard of court orders. There is no doubt that the role adopted by Judge Allen's successor was strongly influenced by preceding judicial behavior and defendant responses. Judge Premo had learned from Allen's mistakes as well as his successes, recognizing the need for an improved jail information system, strict reporting, and the contribution of other justice agencies to planning. Sometimes events at a particular point in a case "pull" for a particular style.

In Orange County, we observed only one judge but several styles. Judge Gray, after 13 years of constantly monitoring jail population and conditions in Orange County, surrendered court jurisdiction upon submission of a reasonable jail plan and sufficient demonstration of good faith efforts to comply with court orders. Although he enforced contempt orders on one occasion, he more generally stated specific goals and deadlines for compliance and entertained suggestions from defendants, plaintiffs, and the special master. Frequently Judge Gray granted defendants' motions for exceptions and modifications to jail population caps. He used the special master extensively to gather information and facilitate negotiations between defendants and plaintiffs. It is difficult to characterize Judge Gray in terms of one role; rather, his role changed along with the circumstances of the case. Early in the case, he was mainly a Conscientious Monitor; later, after numerous delays and worsening noncompliance, he became an Enforcer. Even in the process of enforcing contempt fines, however, he was already moving toward the role of Manager by designating that fines be used to hire a special master to assist with information gathering, interpretation, and negotiation. In the end, although complete compliance was lacking, he assumed the role of Conciliator, refusing plaintiffs' continued attempts to reopen the case or apply new sanctions, but continuing to monitor jail conditions.

It is, in fact, unfair to characterize any judge as having a unique style, even though individuals may gravitate toward one. Judicial methods at any point largely depend upon the unique history and current events of the case. The behavior of a judge is a function of experience, expertise, and personality, no doubt, but it is also a function of the conditions he or she faces in the courtroom and the environment. Major influences on judicial behavior at the Postdecree Stage are summarized in Table 22.

## Negotiations at the Postdecree Stage

At various points in a jail lawsuit, but particularly in the Remedy and Postdecree Stages, defendants and plaintiffs come together to discuss problems and solutions. If they can agree that there is a problem,

**TABLE 22**
JUDICIAL METHODS AND MAJOR INFLUENCES AT THE POSTDECREE STAGE

| Judicial Methods | Likely Point in Case | Major Influences of Judicial Methods |
|---|---|---|
| Conscientious Monitor | Early | Judicial experience, expertise (high) |
| | | Level of court (federal) |
| | | Patterns of noncompliance (low) |
| Intervenor | Middle | Judicial experience, expertise (low) |
| | | Level of court (state) |
| | | Patterns of noncompliance (high) |
| | | Experience of plaintiffs' counsel (low) |
| Manager | Middle | Relations between officials (good) |
| | | Size of county (small)/number of actors (few) |
| | | Level of court (state) |
| Enforcer | Middle–late | Judicial experience, expertise (high) |
| | | Patterns of noncompliance (high) |
| Conciliator | Late | Patterns of noncompliance (low) |

and can come to an agreement on its nature and seriousness, they can attempt to negotiate solutions. Evaluating possible options requires consideration of at least seven criteria: feasibility (will it work?), potency (how much impact will it have on the problem), cost effectiveness (can we afford it?), consistency (are the conditions to be addressed stable or changing?), duration (how long will it take?), monitoring (how will we know whether it is being done?), and evaluation (how will we know whether it is working?). Given all these contingencies, the potential for derailment in negotiations is great. If jail conditions are bad, the problem is complex, solutions are multifaceted, and different actors are needed for agreement, more formal proceedings in chambers or in court are likely. Where negotiations fail, formal hearings and presentation of evidence are necessary. As we saw in Santa Clara, continual requests for appellate review are also likely under this "formal" litigation style.

In Santa Clara, the formality of negotiations rarely abated. County defendants were often unable to see eye to eye with each other, much less plaintiffs, outside of court. The single major exception to this style was, of course, the negotiation of a settlement agreement. That agreement came about only after several aborted attempts, however, and it was one thing to negotiate a settlement, quite another to enforce it. Although the judge and the special master were able to bring different parties to the negotiating table on several occasions, their effectiveness was gradually diminished by the mistrust between county officials, especially the sheriff and the board of supervisors. Judge Premo held numerous informal discussions between defendants and plaintiffs in his chambers, but this process suffered as conflict between defendants increased and tension between supervisors and the special master escalated. Eventually, the special master was shut out of county meetings, except where meetings were explicitly requested by Judge Premo.

Some argue that jail lawsuits are decided purely on matters of law, but the evidence suggests that the personal styles of opposing counsel and their interactions influenced the pattern of negotiations in each lawsuit. Bad blood between plaintiff and defendant counsel hampered negotiations early in the Orange County case. The plaintiffs' attorney had been involved in previous lawsuits over county jail conditions (both individual cases and class-action suits) and had already been stereotyped by defendants as a lawyer making a comfortable living off jail litigation. Particularly in the earlier parts of the case, defendants and plaintiffs were unable to reach agreement on any but the simplest issues (recall Judge Gray's list of 72 contested facts in his pretrial order). Later, relations between counsel for plaintiffs and defendants improved somewhat (largely due to a new lead attorney for the county), but effects of the initial polarization persisted. Special Master Grossman enjoyed some success as a mediator and go-between for county officials and legal counsel, but the real parties at interest—like the sheriff and county supervisors—met rarely. In contrast, all parties in Contra Costa (including the judge) knew one another, and informal discussions were frequent and productive.

The negotiation process in each of the three lawsuits examined was strongly influenced by the quality of relations among county actors and agencies. Officials in Contra Costa (sheriff, supervisors, police chiefs, district attorney, probation officials, public defender), as we witnessed, met regularly prior to the jail lawsuit, on both an informal and a formal basis. Plaintiffs' counsel was well integrated within this network of county officials. While we cannot ignore the influence of county size (fewer incumbents make for more highly integrated networks) or jail conditions (a recently constructed, modern, podular jail), relations among officials played a key role in facilitating negotiations. In contrast, relations among county officials in Orange and Santa Clara could be characterized as occasionally distant, acrimonious, or both. In Santa Clara, conflicts between county agencies and county supervisors preceded the litigation and were heightened by it. The sheriff and the probation department clashed over the sheriff's refusal to allow probation staff into the jail to assess inmates for ROR; the supervisors reprimanded the public defender's office when a staff member spoke to the special master. In Orange, relations between the sheriff and county supervisors were less strained prior to the litigation, and the sheriff enjoyed relative autonomy because of his own strong base of political power in the county. As a result, some of the key players in the jail lawsuit lacked a strong base of interaction that might otherwise have facilitated the negotiation of cooperative solutions to complex and interrelated problems.

Obstructive tactics by defendants in Orange and Santa Clara frequently hindered effective negotiations. Particularly in the early stages, defendants chose to contest almost every allegation raised by plaintiffs and every major order made by judges. In the most extreme form of this strategy, which I label "obfuscation," multiple motions and appeals may delay the case for lengthy periods. Some defendants disobeyed court orders outright, as when Santa Clara officials changed their plans for jail construction in contravention to the settlement agreement and without notifying the court of their intentions.

More frequently, however, a strategy of "broken promises" characterizes defendants' negotiation style. In both Orange and Santa Clara, judges repeatedly admonished defendants to submit both comprehensive jail plans and issue-specific plans to address deficits in jail conditions. Some defendants complied; in other cases, plans were delayed, were never implemented (witness Orange County's futile attempt to select a jail site), or were seriously flawed (Santa Clara, for example, failed to distinguish different types of housing for different security classifications). At those specific points in the case, if not indefinitely, "broken promises" raised hostilities and brought negotiations to a halt.

Any progress in negotiation requires, at a minimum, that both parties be willing to explore different solutions, and that each party have a certain level of competence and knowledge regarding the matters to be discussed. In Contra Costa, the sheriff and the judge brought the necessary sources of expertise and authority together. In both Orange and Santa Clara, the sheriffs' competence was at times questioned not only by plaintiffs' counsel, but by expert witnesses and county officials. In Santa Clara, for example, the information system was inadequate for managing inmate classification and movement. Although resources certainly influenced resolution of this problem, the sheriff seemed to the court incapable of designing or implementing the necessary information system. In Orange, the sheriff and his staff were accused of a

**TABLE 23**
NEGOTIATION STYLES AND MAJOR INFLUENCES AT THE POSTDECREE STAGE

| Negotiation Styles | Major Influences |
|---|---|
| Formal | History of jail conditions (poor) |
| | Complexity of problems and solutions (high) |
| | Multiple actors needed for consensus (high) |
| | Personal relations between legal counsel (poor) |
| | Relations between county officials (poor) |
| Obfuscation | Defendants' willingness to comply (low) |
| | Defendants' competence to comply (low) |
| Broken promises | Defendants' willingness to comply (high) |
| | Defendants' competence to comply (low) |
| | Relations between county officials (poor) |

"flagrant disregard for constitutional principles" and a reluctance to acknowledge the legitimacy of court orders regarding changes in jail policies, including those related to segregating pretrial suspects from sentenced prisoners.

Judges find it hard to distinguish whether such obstacles stem from defendants' unwillingness or inability to comply, unless a persistent pattern of unwillingness or incompetence can be documented, as in Judge Avakian's summary of deliberate noncompliance by defendants in the Santa Clara case. It is clear, however, that any progress in negotiations requires a certain amount of willingness and competence on the part of defendants and plaintiffs. Each must be able to identify and weigh feasible solutions, and each must possess the competence to design, implement, or monitor their proposed courses of action. Different negotiation styles and major influences are summarized in Table 23.

## Remedy Modification

Even after a decision is rendered, conditions must constantly be monitored, and compliance is usually gradual (see also Chapter 4). New issues come up, progress stalls, negotiations ensue, further hearings are held, and orders are usually modified or added to account for changes in the legal and political terrain. As indicated by the number of additional and modified orders in jail lawsuits (see Table 21), the Postdecree Stage is often the most difficult phase of the case for all parties. Remedy modification, like judicial methods, is influenced by all the conditions, actions, and events that have characterized the case through its Trigger,

Liability, Remedy, and Postdecree Stages. Yet variations and major influences can be at least partly summarized.

"Give and take" characterized Judge Gray's approach to remedy modification. While he was firm in his demands for compliance, he was also reasonable in hearing defense requests for time extensions and modifications to orders. Thus, when the county had difficulty complying with population caps at the main jail, Gray temporarily raised the cap, but set graduated deadlines for reducing the population. Gray also allowed the county to exceed the cap on weekends, when intake was more unpredictable. He later agreed (with the assent of plaintiffs and the special master) to exclude inmates in the holding area from the population cap. Nobody could accuse Judge Gray of being inflexible in his decrees, but neither would one deny that he possessed ample ability and will to enforce the court's orders.

In Santa Clara, the events we have examined would have frustrated any judge who heard the case. But noncompliance, interference, and political conflict only partly explain the need for 143 modifications in this perplexing case. The large number of modifications also reflects a lack of continuity resulting from four changes in judges, judicial inexperience in hearing complex civil lawsuits, lack of a guiding intervention philosophy, and the inexperience of both defendant and plaintiff counsel.

The lack of continuity is suggested by the differences in judicial methods noted above. For example, did Judge Allen's "intervening" in county decision-making alter tense relationships between the sheriff and county supervisors? Would Judge Premo's "managerial" job have been easier if a special master had been appointed earlier in the case? Would Judge Avakian's "enforcement" style have differed had violations of court orders been sanctioned more severely in the past? Each judge responded to unique conditions at particular points in time, but it is likely that dramatic shifts in judicial methods made the outcomes of defendants' and plaintiffs' actions somewhat unpredictable.

Judicial inexperience also influenced the remedy modification process. Few state court judges, in contrast to most of their federal counterparts, have been involved in complex civil lawsuits against public officials. Experienced judges would have adopted a more gradual, incremental approach to change, avoided infringement on county executive decisions, and been wary of procedural errors like Judge Leahy's failure to summon the district attorney to represent the People's interests. Judge Allen might have avoided treading on executive decisions by ordering the county to hold a special election to determine jail funding. Judge Avakian might not have requested the sheriff (a real party at interest) to determine jail cell conversion requirements. Judges more experienced in civil litigation involving public officials probably would have set stricter limits for compliance and enforced sanctions much earlier in the case. (Recall that the three judges before Avakian threatened contempt but never enforced it.) The large number of modifications in the Santa Clara case partly reflects monumental resistance by defendants and judges responding by "getting tougher," but it also reflects judicial decisions that were at times less patient, less informed, less predictable, less consistent, and less objective than they might have been. Judges appeared at times to be "muddling around," trying almost anything that might work, and rapidly changing methods if it did not.

Added to this mix was the relative inexperience of county counsel and plaintiff counsel, at least relative to "repeat players" such as the ACLU in other cases. Judges do not introduce evidence, witnesses, or motions in a case. They must rely upon a court record shaped by defendants and plaintiffs over time, and judicial decisions are in a very real sense limited by the information they have at their disposal. Had plaintiffs' counsel been better versed in correctional law, more experienced in dealing with public officials, and more aware of defense tactics such as obfuscation and broken promises, perhaps they would have requested more clearly defined remedies and more legal resources, the aborted settlement negotiated in appellate court might never have occurred, and stricter provisions and sanctions for noncompliance might have been written into the settlement agreement.

More experienced county counsel might have advocated or permitted a less litigious stance on the county's part, and earlier attempts to settle rather than "win" the case. For example, the coldly asserted "client–attorney privilege" in the settlement phase of the case further alienated all parties, especially the special master. When opposing counsel are experienced, debates may be more lengthy and intense, but each is more likely to draw realistic boundaries around remedies, thus decreasing the need for continual modifications to court decrees. The two opposing styles of remedy modification and major influences are summarized in Table 24.

### Compliance and Monitoring

*Special Masters.* Special masters played a major role in monitoring and enforcing compliance with court orders in Orange and Santa Clara counties. The roles that special masters assume depend upon a host of

**TABLE 24**
STYLES OF REMEDY MODIFICATION AND MAJOR INFLUENCES

| Judicial Styles | Major Influences |
|---|---|
| "Give and take" | Judicial continuity (high) |
| | Judicial experience (high) |
| | Guiding judicial philosophy (strong) |
| | Plaintiff counsel's experience (high) |
| | Defense counsel's experience (high) |
| "Muddling" | Judicial continuity (low) |
| | Judicial experience (low) |
| | Guiding judicial philosophy (weak) |
| | Plaintiff counsel's experience (low) |

factors in addition to their experience, expertise, and personal styles. First of all, their specific role and range of powers are largely defined by the judge. Their role is also strongly related to the conditions, events, and actions that preceded their entry into the case: previous judicial methods and responses by litigants, interactions and negotiations between plaintiff and defendant counsel, the litigation strategies of plaintiff and defendant counsel, relations between county agencies, the nature and number of remedies specified, the level of court, the type of plaintiffs' legal representation, and historical and current jail conditions. Again, however, certain trends can be described and some major influences singled out.

The most common role of a special master, and the one people most frequently associate with that title, is that of Fact-finder. A special master, usually experienced in correctional operations and administration, can collect the information the court needs to monitor jail conditions and make decisions relevant to the court's decree(s). In both Santa Clara and Orange, court decrees specified that special masters were to be granted unlimited access to jail facilities and records. In Santa Clara, Lonergan was also explicitly granted access to all meetings of county officials regarding the agreement. The special master typically spends a lot of time in the jail or jails affected by court orders, observing conditions, interviewing workers, officials, and inmates, and inspecting jail records—bookings, admissions, classification and placement decisions, housing conditions, food service records, medical slips, and disciplinary notices. The special master is also likely to identify or clarify problem areas, such as the roots of overcrowding in inadequate pretrial release programs and alternative sanctions for sentenced offenders.

Lonergan's reports in Santa Clara and Grossman's in Orange County strongly demonstrate the abundance and diversity of information needed by the court to monitor jail conditions and compliance with court orders.

The special master can also serve as an Expert whose opinion the judge values and seeks. In Santa Clara, Lonergan made frequent recommendations to Judge Premo and Judge Avakian based upon his inspections and findings. For example, upon finding that all inmates in one unit had been punished for a fire without benefit of a hearing or finding of guilt, Lonergan recommended that appropriate hearings be held, and he called a meeting to ensure posting of consent decrees and familiarity with their terms by jail staff. Numerous reports addressed specific issues of noncompliance and recommended actions by county officials. In Orange, Grossman also made numerous recommendations to Judge Gray to reduce overcrowding and ameliorate other violations. In particular, his recommendations facilitated the development of alternatives to incarceration, an area in which he found the county lagging.

Noting the lack of an adequate enforcement provision in the consent decree, Judge Premo granted Lonergan's request for more extensive powers regarding monitoring, enforcement, mediating and negotiating between litigants, and recommending solutions. Lonergan began issuing numerous "notices of noncompliance," and recommended sanctions for noncompliance as well as appropriate remedies. In one incident the sheriff claimed that Lonergan had authorized the opening of a reserve site to relieve overcrowding. (Although Lonergan had the power to do so, he denied that he had given such permission.) Lonergan asked the court to employ its powers of contempt to enforce compliance, to issue a restraining order against the county when it attempted to prevent employees from providing him with information, and, as noncompliance persisted, to apply sanctions such as fines. When the county complained to Judge Avakian of Lonergan's recommendations, the judge ordered them to consult with Lonergan before making any further motions to the court.

Lonergan had wide powers in this case. He was granted the authority to order implementation of early release provisions, the use of reserve jail sites, and other methods to reduce jail population whenever the cap was exceeded. These powers, to some, constituted "managing" the jail. While his "managerial" functions were limited, his exercise of power and discretion was reminiscent of Judge Allen's "take charge" approach, exemplifying the role of Intervenor.

Grossman's role, in contrast, was that of "correctional consultant."

He made no recommendations regarding the application of sanctions, and had no authority, as did Lonergan, to order population reductions when caps were violated. For better or worse, Grossman's boundaries were much more tightly circumscribed than Lonergan's. Many (including Santa Clara County officials) took exception to Lonergan's extensive powers; others (particularly judges and plaintiffs' counsel) felt that the situation called for such measures. The opposite reaction was voiced in Orange: Plaintiffs' counsel felt that Grossman could have done more; county officials respected his role as messenger and communicator. It is ironic that in spite of hesitancy to use the term "special master" in Santa Clara because of the term's unpleasant associations for public officials, Compliance Officer Lonergan wielded much greater powers and engendered greater hostility than Special Master Grossman.

Lonergan continually emphasized the importance of getting the police, district attorney, probation officers, and other criminal justice actors to share responsibility for devising solutions to overcrowding. He enjoyed considerable success, particularly early on, in getting different actors together and seeking their opinions individually. As time went by and his own conflict with county supervisors escalated, Lonergan had more difficulty in carrying out his role as Mediator and Negotiator. Orange County officials praised Grossman for supplying them with information about jail conditions, and for his nonpartisan efforts in general. While much less active as a convenor of meetings or negotiations, Grossman served effectively as liaison and communicator. The roles of a special master and the major influences of each are summarized in Table 25.

*The Contempt Process.* While judges exercise diverse methods to gain compliance, they have limited powers of enforcement. Contempt is the most powerful sanction they can employ, carrying penalties of fines or even incarceration. They use it rarely, and for good reason. It escalates conflict with politically powerful defendants, and if the threat of contempt fails to bring about compliance, the judge's perceived power and credibility suffer immeasurably. Contempt is the "big stick" that judges carry but hope they are never forced to use. There are at least seven stages in the contempt process. The process can be derailed at any stage and only rarely proceeds as far as the seventh.

1. Threaten the use of contempt for noncompliance with court orders.
2. Issue an order to show cause.
3. Hold a hearing to decide on contempt.
4. Issue a decision finding defendants in contempt.

**TABLE 25**
ROLES OF SPECIAL MASTERS IN JAIL LAWSUITS AND MAJOR INFLUENCES

| Roles | Major Influences |
| --- | --- |
| Fact-finder | Judicial definition of powers (narrow)<br>History of jail conditions (poor)<br>Patterns of noncompliance (low) |
| Expert | Judicial definition of powers (broad)<br>Personal experience and expertise of master (high)<br>Patterns of noncompliance (high)<br>Defendants' willingness to comply (high)<br>Defendants' competence to comply (low)<br>Complexity of problems and solutions (high) |
| Intervenor | Relations among county officials (poor)<br>Patterns of noncompliance (high)<br>Defendants' willingness to comply (low)<br>Defendants' competence to comply (low)<br>Judicial experience, expertise (low) |
| Mediator/Negotiator | Relations among county officials (good)<br>Defendants' willingness to comply (high)<br>Defendants' competence to comply (high)<br>Multiple actors needed for consensus (high)<br>Personal relations among legal counsel (good) |

5. Specify sanctions for contempt.
6. Give defendants time to purge the contempt by complying, or file appeals.
7. Enforce sanctions.

The first attempt to gain compliance usually involves the issuance of a warning to defendants that they are in violation of the court's orders, and that they must take immediate action to avoid contempt proceedings. In Santa Clara, we saw Special Master Lonergan recommend contempt numerous times, and Judge Premo issue several warnings. Contempt proceedings often entered a cycle of futility at this stage: further warnings by the judge, partial attempts to comply by defendants, further warnings, and eventual backing off by the judge. If defendants were sufficiently motivated to comply the first time they were warned, the use of contempt would be a simple matter. If defendants decide to test the court's resolve, however, as in Santa Clara, the judge finds the court's credibility and sanctioning power progressively weakened.

In spite of numerous warnings, no order to show cause was actually issued until 7 March 1983, nearly a year after the settlement was signed. Even then, Judge Premo granted a defense motion to "quash" the contempt hearing on the grounds that insufficient notice of the basis for the hearing had been supplied. Varying decrees of noncompliance continued for over a year before Premo resigned. Despite repeated warnings of sanctions and even termination of the settlement agreement in favor of a new trial, neither further orders to show cause nor sanctions were issued.

Judge Avakian seemed determined not to let defendants escape sanctions so easily, but he did not initiate contempt proceedings immediately. It took six months before warnings of contempt were issued; it took another six months to issue an order to show cause. Two months later, following hearings, county defendants were found in contempt of court, and both fines and jail sentences for county supervisors were ordered. Judge Avakian gave defendants ample time to purge the contempt, but the county chose to appeal. The Court of Appeals ruled that the separation of powers had been violated, and the contempt was annulled. Contempt proceedings in Santa Clara under Judge Premo and Judge Avakian are summarized below.

*23 August 1983:* Lonergan recommends that Judge Premo issue a warning of contempt.

*4 January 1984:* Premo warns the sheriff of possible sanctions for noncompliance.

*1 February 1984:* Premo notes inadequate enforcement provisions in the settlement agreement.

*27 February 1984:* Lonergan asks for contempt against sheriff and county supervisors.

*7 March 1984:* Premo issues an order to show cause.

*23 March 1984:* Premo grants motion by defendants to quash.

*2 April 1984:* Premo holds evidentiary hearing; warns of specific sanctions: $5,000 for each supervisor, $25,000 for the county.

*24 June 1985:* Lonergan recommends termination of settlement due to noncompliance and interference with court orders.

*1 January 1986:* Judge Premo resigns from the case.

*17 June 1986:* Judge Avakian warns of fines for noncompliance with the single-cell requirement ($1,000 per day times number of beds needed).

*8 January 1987:* Avakian issues an order to show cause and warns that fines will be retroactive to June 1986 if a finding of contempt is justified.

*16 March 1987:* Avakian issues a finding of contempt, ordering fines of $1,000 for each county supervisor (except one) and sentences of five days in jail. Avakian issues a stay until 16 April (later extended to 30

April) to give defendants time to purge contempt or file appeals. The county subsequently appeals.

*17 September 1987:* The contempt order is annulled by the Court of Appeal on two counts: improper judicial delegation of powers to sheriff, and vagueness of orders forming the basis for contempt. Judge Avakian subsequently resigns from the case.

In Orange, contempt proceedings were less frequent and more successful. Judge Gray was patient in awaiting defendants' assessment of jail needs and plans for a new jail. After six years of delays, increased overcrowding, and lack of a feasible plan, plaintiffs' counsel requested and received a finding of contempt. Gray refrained from the threat of contempt until he was ready to use it. When he did use it, Gray swiftly enacted all seven stages of contempt, demonstrating that he took the matter seriously and was not making idle threats. Judge Gray relied upon a strong court record and presentation of supporting facts by plaintiffs' counsel in this process.

Following the contempt findings, a special master was hired, using the fines levied against the county. In early 1986, a second order to show cause was issued over violation of population caps. While maintaining persistent monitoring of compliance during hearings, Gray was flexible in hearing both defense and plaintiffs' motions. No contempt finding was made, and Gray agreed to modify population caps. Although Gray issued one more order to show cause just before the court's disengagement from the case, the action represented a final warning to defendants to maintain jail conditions consistent with the court's orders. Major events in the Orange County contempt proceedings are outlined below.

*21 November 1984:* Plaintiffs file a motion for contempt and request appointment of a special master.

*20 March 1985:* Judge Gray issues a finding of contempt and orders fines of $50,000 (to be used to hire a special master) plus $10 per day for each inmate who slept on the floor more than one night.

*10 July 1985:* Gray reduces defendants' lump fine to $25,830.

*4 March 1986:* Gray issues an order to show cause regarding violation of population caps.

*6 May 1986:* No contempt finding; Gray permits modifications to population caps.

*9 December 1986:* Gray permits further modifications to population caps.

*12 September 1988:* Gray issues an order to show cause at plaintiffs' request.

## TABLE 26
### MAJOR INFLUENCES ON THE USE OF CONTEMPT IN JAIL LAWSUITS

| *Influences Favoring Judicial Use* |
| --- |
| Strength of court record (strong) |
| Nature and patterns of noncompliance (high) |
| Judicial methods (enforcer) |
| Judicial experience (high) |
| Perceived reaction by appellate court (favorable) |
| Nature of plaintiffs' legal representation (ideological) |

*7 December 1988:* Gray issues finding of no contempt and defines further responsibilities of plaintiff and defendant counsel.

Contempt is thus an empty threat unless it is enforced and unless a strong record supports findings of contempt. Idle threats, hesitation, judicial error, a litigious posture by the county, and a hostile appellate court all weakened judicial sanctioning power in Santa Clara. By contrast, Judge Gray used contempt sparingly but forcefully, and relied upon a strong court record shaped by plaintiffs. Gray's findings were bolstered by his previous success with appellate review in this case, and his sensitivity to the obstacles the county faced, including community opposition to jail construction.

Judge Gray's considerable experience, patience, and persistence served him well in this case. He was aided by a county board of supervisors who took his contempt findings seriously, in part because of advice received from county counsel, and in part because of the reputation and credibility of plaintiffs' ACLU counsel. The question of whether and to what degree contempt findings had the desired impact on compliance remains to be explored in detail in Chapter 6. Major influences on the use of contempt are summarized in Table 26.

## Summary

Jail lawsuits, like other remedial decree cases, involve polycentric problems and present considerable difficulties for defining and obtaining compliance. Although the nature and number of remedies influence litigant and judicial behavior in the Postdecree Stage, there is no simple relation between original remedies and postdecree outcomes. Actions, conditions, and events from previous stages of litigation continue to exert an influence on lawsuit duration, judicial methods, remedy modification, nature of negotiations, and mechanisms of monitoring and compliance.

Not surprisingly, jail lawsuits last a very long time. However, lawsuit duration is itself difficult to define. It is not always clear at which point defendants are in "substantial" compliance with remedial orders, nor at what point the court should disengage. Judges sometimes define very specific standards and time parameters for compliance. In other cases, the conditions required for disengagement of the court are nebulous. Environmental conditions such as jail overcrowding may change, creating new issues or new problems, not only during the case but long after defendants were thought to be essentially in compliance. For example, dynamic conditions in the local environment present a myriad of concerns that policymakers tend to downplay or ignore. Plans to construct new jail facilities frequently fail to account for volatile public opinion and opposition to increased taxes.

Type of court was the strongest predictor of lawsuit duration in this study, although the involvement of county supervisors and the nature and number of remedies specified were also influential. Federal judges possess greater experience in remedial decree cases and show greater persistence and independence from environmental constraints than state court judges.

Government defendants and plaintiffs' counsel have a variety of methods at their disposal for negotiating remedy modification and defining compliance. More formal negotiations in court, rather than informal discussions or meetings between litigants, are called for when jail conditions are and have been poor; problems and solutions are complex; many actors are needed for consensus; opposing counsel are antagonistic; and relations among county officials are strained. Defendants may use negotiations to resist or delay compliance by refusing to submit required plans, or by filing an inadequate plan (obfuscation). Defendants may also submit undifferentiated, multiple plans that allow them to claim compliance while judges and plaintiff counsel wade through and evaluate them (broken promises). In some cases, defendants submit "leverage" plans: plans that local governments lack the will or resources to implement, but can use to extract additional resources from state or federal governments. Ideological attorneys, in contrast to private or public counsel, show greater persistence in seeking compliance, and possess the skills and experience needed to recognize and counter stonewalling by defendants.

Judges adopt different methods in remedy modification, negotiating, and monitoring compliance, and they do so at different stages of a case. Early in the Postdecree Stage, judges often adopt a Conscientious Monitor or Manager role, attempting to facilitate negotiations between litigants and stimulate specific plans of action. Over time, many judges find it necessary to set limits as negotiations succeed in some areas and fail in others. They may shift toward a more active Intervenor role, whereby they still ratify some plans presented by litigants but begin adding remedies that narrow official discretion. Judicial options are more limited when resistance by defendants is pronounced, leading to potential conflict and a shift toward an Enforcer role. When defendants demonstrate substantial compliance or at least good faith attempts to comply, judges shift toward a Conciliator role, attempting to tie up legal loose ends and disengage from further court involvement.

Judicial methods are also influenced by court venue. State court judges, for example, were more likely to enact the roles of Manager and Intervenor. They tended more often to get involved in the *means* of compliance, by intervening in the affairs of local criminal justice agencies or engineering negotiations between key actors. Those who did so successfully benefited from their familiarity with local incumbents and the local justice system. Federal judges were more likely to enact the roles of Conscientious Monitor and Enforcer, specifying specific *outcomes* to be achieved and persistently monitoring and sanctioning noncompliance.

Remedies are often modified many times in jail lawsuits. A judge with a "give and take" style listens carefully to arguments from defense and plaintiffs' counsel and relies upon a strong court record shaped by each. He or she gives credibility to both defendants and plaintiffs, and is likely over time to give something to each. Experienced counsel tend to define legal issues and actions required for compliance more narrowly, as do more experienced judges. In contrast, a "muddling" style reflects uncertainty on the parts of judges and opposing counsel, overly vague definitions of problems and the actions required for compliance, low familiarity with correctional law, and a weak or absent guiding intervention philosophy.

Special masters assume diverse roles at this stage, including those of Fact-finder, Expert, Mediator/Negotiator, and Intervenor. Like judicial methods, such roles vary at different times in the case and depend upon factors such as judicial definition of powers, the expertise and experience of both the judge and the special master, historical jail conditions, and patterns of noncompliance. The considerable influence and flexibility of special masters observed in jail lawsuits challenge several commonly held assumptions: that judges must assume a "generalist" position; that legal reasoning is nonprobabilistic and absolute; and that judicial decision-making is "piecemeal" rather than comprehensive (Horowitz 1977).

Contempt can be a forceful method to gain compliance, although its use in jail lawsuits is rare. Its successful use requires judicial resolve, patience, and experience; acceptance of legitimacy by defendants; a strong court record shaped by plaintiffs' counsel; and expectation of favorable review by the appellate court. Continual derailment of contempt proceedings and unenforced threats of contempt weaken judicial credibility and sanctioning power.

The Postdecree Stage, focused on the implementation, monitoring, modification, and sanctioning of court orders, is often the most difficult and frustrating stage of any jail lawsuit. Conditions, events, and actions from the Trigger, Liability, Remedy, and Postdecree stages continue to be influential even as the diverse impacts that are the subject of the next chapter begin to emerge.

# CHAPTER 6

## The Impact Stage

[W]e were literally talking about closing the doors to senior citizens' centers, on libraries, on all that stuff. We're going to have to do that if we have a new jail.

—**An Orange County official**

Politically, it helps the sheriff to have a court order because then it's not just liberalism sneaking through into the sheriff's political agenda, it is the court telling the sheriff you must take care of this problem, and you must take care of it in a responsible way.

—**A Contra Costa County official**

Until there is commitment from each agency in the criminal justice system . . . the problem with population control and management by crisis will continue.

—**Compliance Officer Thomas Lonergan,
report on *Fischer v. Winter*, 26 December 1987**

HAVE COURT ORDERS brought about changes in jail conditions? The evidence is mixed. In some cases, orders have resulted in reductions in inmate populations, increased visitation and recreation, better medical care, improved disciplinary standards or procedures, enhanced staffing levels and personal safety, and improved sanitation and maintenance (UCLA Law Review 1973; Feeley and Hanson 1986, 1990; Harris and Spiller 1977). But where positive change has been achieved, conditions are often raised only to minimal constitutional standards. The worst abuses may have been removed, but significant reform has only rarely been achieved (Harris and Spiller 1977; Thomas 1980; Yackle 1989).

In general, correctional administrators strongly resist court-ordered change (Harris and Spiller 1977; Huff and Alpert 1982; Martin and

Ekland-Olson 1987). Compliance varies according to officials' willingness and ability to comply, the organizational and political climate,
local governmental structure, the choice of defendants, public opinion,
media exposure, judicial persistence and determination, and the participation of key actors in formulating the decree.

The *Ruiz* litigation in Texas provides a case in point (see Alpert,
Crouch, and Huff 1986; Crouch and Marquart 1989; Ekland-Olson and
Martin 1988). Opinions vary on whether *Ruiz* made things better or
worse. One school of thought holds that court orders actually increased
violence in Texas prisons. According to the "theory of rising expectations" (Alpert, Crouch, and Huff 1986), initial court-ordered change led
inmates to expect improvement in general and specific conditions of
confinement. Once it became clear there was no guarantee that court
orders would be implemented in a timely manner, or even upheld by
appellate courts, the inmates' disappointment contributed to short-
term increases in violence and rule-breaking following court orders.
Others attribute increased violence to the temporary power vacuum
that followed the court-ordered elimination of institutional control via
the oppressive inmate trustee ("building tender") system (Crouch and
Marquart 1989).

Certainly, the *Ruiz* litigation resulted in large-scale personnel
changes and in the reorganization of the Texas Department of Corrections, as well as significant refinements of correctional rules and procedures (Martin and Ekland-Olson 1987). The prison system moved from
a rigid "control-oriented" or "repressive" model of prison management
(pre-1982) to a "legalistic order" (1982–1985) characterized by decree
implementation and compliance pressure, and later into a more "bureaucratic" (post-1985) rule-oriented phase (Crouch and Marquart
1990). Observers disagree, however, about whether such change has
resulted in a "better-run" prison system (Crouch and Marquart 1990;
DiIulio 1990; Ekland-Olson and Martin 1990).

Paradoxically, benefits can also accrue to correctional officials as a
result of litigation. Court orders to reduce overcrowding and improve
conditions in the Texas prison system may actually have supported the
agenda of prison officials, producing desired increases in personnel,
wages, the physical size of the system, budget, and influence in the
form of a higher political profile (Alpert, Crouch, and Huff 1986). Litigation can thus provide leverage for correctional officials seeking budgetary or policy priority.

In the most thorough review of the literature on court-ordered correctional reform to date, Feeley and Hanson (1990) summarize the effects of court orders:

1. Litigation has affected the organizational structure of prisons, jails, and correctional systems in significant ways.
2. Courts have stimulated states and counties to develop more policies to deal with living conditions and overcrowding.
3. There is little evidence that court orders have led to improvements in the quality and type of services provided to prisoners.
4. The capacity of the courts to effect meaningful change in jails and prisons is not clear.

While court orders have had a "significant impact both within individual institutions and in entire correctional systems" (Feeley and Hanson 1990, 16), findings have been limited by the fact that "we know most about a small number of atypical cases, those that are large, dramatic, or especially controversial. There are few systematic studies of smaller cases" (p. 40).

At least three general recommendations follow from these observations. First, we need to direct more attention toward the multiple-order consequences of laws: "If we think of the adoption and attempted implementation of law as an intervention in a social or political system, we should expect change to reverberate throughout the system" (Brown and Crowley 1979, 272). Second, many standards of success and failure are possible, and legal impact studies must consider different standards in order to avoid erroneous inferences. Third, more emphasis needs to be directed toward explaining different types of impact across different cases.

Unintended effects of legal directives have received little attention (see, for example, Brown and Crowley 1979; Horowitz 1977; Kidder 1975). Legal actions are transformed by their encounter with the real world, producing "side effects" (Kidder 1975) or "latent effects" (Merton 1968). For example, desegregation of public schools contributed to "white flight" from the cities, unintentionally increasing housing segregation, weakening the financial base of cities, and contributing to urban decay (Brown and Crowley 1979). Of course, research has demonstrated neither the conclusive failure nor the success of law in achieving social policy goals. There are many situations in which the law can be, is, and should be used to achieve important social goals, such as civil rights reform.

As diverse impacts exist, so do different ways of assessing them. A major distinction concerns the methodology of case studies versus the comparative approach. Major sources of data for case studies include interviews, court documents, archival records (e.g., agency reports, newspaper stories), and observations of courtroom dynamics and jail operations. Comparative studies tend to use more quantifiable measures of causes and effects across different cases, although other methods, such as interviews, are often used to supplement statistical findings. Each method has implications for questions and answers about court-ordered reform.

Case studies of court-ordered reform in Texas and other jurisdictions have given us a richly detailed picture of litigation process and organizational reform in cases that involve complex parties and legal issues. On the other hand, case studies are limited by a lack of unifying theoretical constructs, few comparisons of findings across different jurisdictions, and insufficient attention to city- or county-run jails as opposed to state prisons. For this reason, overgeneralization of findings from prison studies and case studies must be acknowledged as problematic.

Comparative studies, which examine the impacts of court-ordered correctional reform across different cases using diverse methodologies, have confirmed some outcomes suggested by case studies, questioned others, and suggested additional impacts to be studied. Obviously, each type of methodology has its trade-offs: Case studies risk lack of generalizability; comparative studies risk some loss of depth in detail. For example, one study (UCLA Law Review 1973) examined diverse impacts across a number of prison sites, but used only one type of data (self-reports of correctional administrators); a second (Harris and Spiller 1977) reported diverse impacts derived from detailed qualitative research, but examined only four jurisdictions. A third type of study (Harriman and Straussman 1983; Taggart 1989) used more sites (10 in one study, 14 in another) but examined only one outcome (changes in correctional expenditures). Each study has improved our knowledge about the effects of court orders and identified important questions.

Correctional administrators have vocally decried the effects of court-ordered reform. An early survey of correctional administrators in California (UCLA Law Review 1973) examined the effects of court intervention on California state prisons. Although survey data were collected across different prison sites (enhancing generalizability), the self-report methodology limits the validity of the findings: Correctional administrators' perceptions cannot automatically be interpreted as unbiased. Many of these *perceived* impacts, however, are consistent with the more recent statistical and interview findings reported by observers of the *Ruiz* litigation in Texas. Such convergent findings, across different sites and time periods, highlight the importance of using diverse methodologies and cross-site comparisons and replications to support valid conclusions.

Administrators' perceptions of court review range from "inconvenience" to a suspected threat to their professional expertise and competence. Many administrators complained of problems in maintaining discipline and control within the institution as a result of outside interference from the courts. Some perceived a decline of respect in inmates toward personnel, and in some cases an increase in verbal and physical assault. Where such increases in violence are supported by empirical data, as in Texas, these effects cannot be attributed to court orders only. Increased violence is at least partially a result of the severe overcrowding and poor living conditions that precede or accompany the lawsuits leading to court orders.

Administrators suggest that prisoners are "emboldened" to violate rules more frequently after successful litigation. The courts, they argue, create a more adversarial relationship between staff and inmates, in contrast to a cooperative or therapeutic one. While "exchange relationships" certainly exist between guards and inmates (Sykes 1958), it can easily be argued that such relationships are predominantly coercive rather than therapeutic, and deteriorate as prison conditions worsen (Huff 1980; Irwin 1985; Thomas 1980).

Administrators report staff resentment that inmates can use the courts to challenge official authority. Staff experience lower morale and efficiency, as well as insecurity as a result of not knowing their legal rights and obligations. Uncertainty may translate into hesitation to act and less flexibility. On the other hand, administrators acknowledge (at least to some degree) their own responsibility to educate and train staff regarding changes in their duties and responsibilities under newly imposed court decrees.

Administrators perceive an increased need to lead staff to accept new policies stemming from court orders, and a need to be decisive. In some cases staff members have concluded that the brass were "selling the ship away" by entering into consent decrees. Administrators also express concern about security and transfers: Such issues, dependent upon specialized knowledge of correctional administration, should not be within judicial review, they suggest.

Other effects of court orders perceived by administrators include curtailment of recreation, education, and other programs due to resource reallocations necessitated by court orders, and increased personnel costs to meet court-ordered staffing and training standards. Personnel costs may be increased by orders stipulating freer inmate access to outside reading materials (more processing of mail), freer communication with courts (more access to books and libraries), increased visits by attorneys (more escorts needed), and taking inmates to court for hearings (more transfers). The majority of correctional administrators surveyed felt that costs were higher as a result of court intervention, and that such costs have significantly influenced the correctional decision-making process, causing the elimination of some programs or services, or budget reductions in other areas. Perceived increases in expenditures, however, have not been well supported by empirical studies so far.

Correctional administrators see five court-ordered changes as having the most negative influence on prison operations: increased visits by attorneys; freer access to outside reading material; privileged communication with attorney by mail; increased use of writs to challenge staff activities; and inmate initiation of damage suits against staff. These are the changes that involve the greatest "boundary" intrusions into administrative routines (Ekland-Olson and Martin 1988).

Judicial intervention has produced improvements in at least three areas: conditions of confinement, management of correctional systems, and public and official attitudes toward corrections, according to Harris and Spiller (1977), who examined the Baltimore City Jail, the Orleans Parish Prison, the Jefferson Parish Prison in New Orleans, and the Arkansas state prison system. Their research included site visits, interviews, analysis of court documents and newspaper clippings, and examination of agency budgets and annual reports.

The four case studies revealed improvements in medical care, disciplinary standards and procedures, personal safety, sanitation, recreation, race relations, staffing levels, and the physical condition of institutions. In each case, however, conditions were raised to minimal standards only. Overcrowding persisted; counseling, education, and other programs were still not available in any meaningful sense; and fear still prevailed in each institution.

Litigation also created pressure for new organizational structures, increased funding, new administrators, changes in personnel policies, new facilities, additional personnel, and improved management procedures. Arkansas, for example, also tried to hire more qualified people to work in its institutions, offering better training, better pay, and improved communication between upper-level staff and line officers. Similar findings were reported in the California and Texas studies discussed earlier.

Litigation, according to Harris and Spiller, created a more receptive climate for reform by raising the awareness of the public and government officials. Interviews with correctional administrators (no systematic public or policymaker surveys were conducted) indicated a belief that court orders had shifted public attitudes toward correctional reform in each of four case studies. In a sense, they suggested, the court could be used by correctional administrators as a scapegoat for changes that were long overdue. Public support for reform crystallized as a result of new information on conditions and practices that were at odds with public norms and expectations; repeated confirmation of brutal conditions and practices from credible sources; and broader social and political trends, including growing national sensitivity to civil rights. The news media, they suggested, played an influential role in this process of public sensitization; in Arkansas, legislators finally took action to avoid being perceived as "condoning barbarism" in the prisons.

Significantly, litigation encouraged correctional administrators to keep abreast of courts and standard-setting bodies, and to make appropriate changes *without* being ordered to do so. The concept of "negative reinforcement" (Schwartz 1978) explains that people may act not to receive a reward, but rather to *avoid* an aversive outcome. Policymakers may initiate proactive reforms to avoid potentially embarrassing, costly, and sweeping court-ordered changes. One of the major, unintended effects of prison and jail litigation, then, may have been to create an "official conscience." Whether that conscience has become internalized, however, is unclear; it may exist only so long as judges carry a big stick.

The need to reduce correctional populations has also supported a resurgence of alternatives to incarceration (more recently relabeled "intermediate sanctions" to gain public support), such as work furlough, community service, supervised electronic confinement, halfway houses, and improvements or expansion of pretrial release mechanisms (Byrne, Lurigio, and Petersilia 1992; Feeley and Hanson 1986).

Controversy over the "judicial power of the purse" (Frug 1978; Glazer 1978; Taggart 1989) focuses on the notion that courts are improperly directing the allocation of public funds by ordering governments to correct existing deficiencies. The question of increased costs due to court intervention has received much speculation but little empirical attention (Johnson and Canon 1984; Taggart 1989). Short-term correctional expenditures undoubtedly increase following court orders (Feeley and Hanson 1986; Harriman and Straussman 1983; Taggart 1989). Correctional reforms involving staffing levels or expansion of facilities require additional expenditures (Feeley and Hanson 1986; Harris and Spiller 1977; UCLA Law Review 1973). We still do not know whether these short-term increases persist over time, how government resources are redistributed, if at all, and how much judicial directives shift governmental policies and decision-making.

In the first detailed study of the budgetary impact of court decisions against prisons, Harriman and Straussman (1983) examined two types of expenditures: capital expenditures (e.g., prison construction and renovations), and prisons' operating expenditures (e.g., expenditures per prisoner). The 14 states under consideration all responded to court orders through capital expansion, and all experienced larger increases in planned beds. Researchers concluded that courts have affected state spending on corrections, increasing capital expenditures and corrections spending as a percentage of the state budget; that levels of prisoner spending in court-ordered states were, in general, lower than those in other states; and that the states with the most serious overcrowding problems have faced legal action.

More recently, Taggart (1989) examined the budgetary impact of court orders in 10 states. Court orders increased correctional expenditures in 5 of those states, but "most of the increases were on the capital side of the budget" (1989, 267). Prolonged increases in operating expenditures were not nearly as pronounced. Feeley (1989) points out that the 5 states that increased correctional spending were all in the South. He suggests that court intervention upset the traditional "plantation" model of self-sufficiency by rejecting "a model, an entire way of thinking about prisons that for some had been a moral vision of what prison and imprisonment were all about," along with "such features of the plantation model as forced labor, the use of convicts as guards, arbitrary discipline, the withholding of food, and the failure to supply medical treatment" (Feeley 1989, 279–280). Court intervention may have had the greatest impact in states that substantially deviated from emerging federal standards of correctional conditions and administration.

The budgetary impact of court orders has created one of the greatest controversies in the debate over court-ordered reform. The time has come for empirical investigation of how court orders against jails affect county finances, correctional expenditures, and policy choices.

A wide range of outcomes may result from court intervention, ranging from very *localized* impacts (within the jail) to *systemic* ones: changes in institutional conditions and service delivery; structural and organizational impacts; changes in correctional expenditures and policy priorities; and systemwide effects, altering relationships between agents and agencies in fundamental ways, sometimes with unintended consequences.

The rest of this chapter examines these four main categories of impacts. Using statistical data, court records, and observational and interview methods, I examined comparative data from 43 lawsuits in 58 California counties, focusing on three case studies in detail. We will also explore contextual factors in the legal and political landscape that dynamically shape and limit the effects of court-ordered reform.

## Changes in Institutional Conditions

As we saw in Chapter 4, court decrees have addressed overcrowding, medical care, visitation, access to courts, recreation, personal hygiene, food services, sanitation, staffing, and classification. These issues define the basic quality of life in jails, although issues of jail capacity and staffing were paramount. Although neither judges nor litigants in California were always completely satisfied with the outcome of cases, most parties agreed that significant improvements in conditions had been made.

In Santa Clara, jail conditions improved and the orders and agreement achieved their intended effects: "The end result which was sought in the agreement was a constitutionally clean jail system, adequate to handle the criminal business of this area. That's what they have," stated one of the trial judges. Yet it is apparent that conditions had to reach extremes before anything was done (see Chapters 4 and 5). I asked one judge how he went about deciding whether jail conditions reached the threshold of constitutional violations. Extreme conditions spoke for themselves, he observed.

> You have to consider the whole context. . . . [T]he quality of food at the Elmwood jail was an issue. How do you decide whether they should have a cheese sandwich or a bologna sandwich? You can get bogged down totally in details. On the other hand, if someone says, "We haven't had a hot meal in three days," then you're getting closer. . . . I remember one day, they pulled the sink away, and they had—literally this is true—40 pounds of maggots behind the service table where the food was. Okay. Now, does anybody have a doubt that that is not a safe and sanitary way to feed [2,000] people?

When asked about unintended effects of litigation, a Santa Clara judge replied, "I think that anything that was done had to be an improvement because things were so bad that we could only look up."

Reports by the compliance officer in the Santa Clara case showed several remaining problem areas even as the court was preparing to relinquish jurisdiction and the county was transferring control of the jail from the sheriff to the new County Department of Correction. In particular, stipulated staff positions had not been filled (2 November 1988) and staffing shortages persisted (6 March 1989); inmate supervision and mental health procedures were inadequate (17 January 1989); food services remained problematic (3 February 1989); and prescribed procedures for medical care were not being followed (6 February 1989). While some difficulty can be attributed to the transition to a new facility and a new administrative body, such implementation problems are pervasive in the Postdecree Stage of lawsuits. Conditions must be constantly monitored, and longstanding deficiencies are not easily or completely remedied.

In Orange County, a federal judge felt that significant improvements had been made in such basic needs as clothing, meals, and beds for all inmates. While not all orders achieve the desired change, "the judge's order has an effect many a times." In a report to the county on jail conditions (Correctional Consultants of California 1988), the special master noted that "the central men's jail is in compliance with *Stewart v. Gates* and most Minimum Jail Standards and American Correctional Association Standards," and "the Central Women's Jail and the branch jails are essentially in compliance with *Stewart v. Gates* and MJS and ACA standards. We use the phrase 'essentially in compliance' because there are a number of areas that have been identified where compliance is lacking" (p. 2). In particular, staff implementation of some procedures—notably the handling of inmate medical request slips, exercise, and disciplinary hearings—was less than desirable. In general, both funding and staffing levels were seen as inadequate.

Plaintiffs' counsel was dissatisfied, but inmates were ensured at least minimum standards of visitation, access to courts, hygiene, food service, and so on, even though they faced subtle retaliation in the form of transfers or less recreation. Orange County had in fact provided a "bad example" of what could happen to other counties, and created more awareness about the need for constitutional jail conditions. In general, however, court-mandated "minimum" standards became the *maximum* that inmates were afforded.

## Structural and Organizational Impacts

*Comparative Analyses*

To what degree are changes in jail population, capacity, and staffing attributable to court intervention? I explored this question using statistical data compiled for all 58 California counties.

County size is a major factor that mediates litigation onset and impact. Counties under court order are disproportionately likely to have large jails. Data from the 1988 jail census confirm a striking relationship between the risk of court orders and jail size. Of 3,316 jails in the 1988 census, 404 (12 percent) were under court-imposed population caps to reduce overcrowding (U.S. Department of Justice 1988). Jail size proved a most relevant discriminating variable (see Table 27). A majority of jails (62 percent) with capacities over 1,000 were under court order; only 7 percent of jails with capacities of fewer than 50 inmates were.

Does the national relationship between jail size and court orders hold for California counties? Table 28 presents patterns of expansion in jail population and jail capacity for counties under court order; Table 29 presents patterns of expansion for counties not under court order. A brief inspection of Tables 28 and 29 confirms that counties under order have much larger jails than counties not under court order. When a jail reaches a population of 500 in California, a court order is almost guaranteed.

The next major question is whether court orders cause jails in court-ordered counties to expand faster or slower than jails in counties not under order. Some argue that court orders give administrators the leverage they need to expand their facilities; others argue that court orders intentionally slow growth in jail populations. Comparisons of jail population and jail capacity for these two groups are shown in Tables 28 and 29. Rates of change in jail population were slightly lower in counties under order (131 percent) than in those not under order (136 percent). Counties under order showed a greater increase in jail capacity

**TABLE 27**
**JAIL SIZE AND COURT ORDERS TO LIMIT POPULATION**

| Jail Size (Rated Capacity) | Court Orders to Limit Population | |
|---|---|---|
| | No | Yes |
| 1–49 | 1,846 (93%) | 141 (7%) |
| 50–249 | 886 (85%) | 160 (15%) |
| 250–499 | 109 (72%) | 42 (28%) |
| 500–999 | 56 (61%) | 36 (39%) |
| 1,000 + | 15 (38%) | 25 (62%) |
| TOTAL | 2,912 (88%) | 404 (12%) |

Source: Census of local jails, 1988.
Note: Pearson chi-square (4 df) = 249.12, p < .001.

## TABLE 28
CALIFORNIA COUNTIES UNDER COURT ORDER: CHANGES IN AVERAGE DAILY JAIL
POPULATION AND BOARD-RATED CAPACITY, 1976 AND 1986

| County | Average Daily Jail Population | | Percent Change[a] | Board-Rated Capacity | | Percent Change[a] |
|---|---|---|---|---|---|---|
| | 1976 | 1986 | | 1976 | 1986 | |
| Alameda | 1,364 | 2,885 | +111 | 1,851 | 2,515 | +36 |
| Butte | 87 | 236 | +172 | 173 | 173 | 0 |
| Contra Costa | 316 | 867 | +174 | 315 | 689 | +119 |
| Fresno | 600 | 1,229 | +105 | 848 | 910 | +7 |
| Humboldt | 102 | 171 | +68 | 188 | 174 | −7 |
| Imperial | 228 | 416 | +82 | 348 | 388 | +11 |
| Kern | 642 | 1,754 | +173 | 658 | 1,776 | +170 |
| Lake | 31 | 74 | +139 | 55 | 72 | +31 |
| Los Angeles | 8,022 | 20,125 | +151 | 8,960 | 12,696 | +42 |
| Madera | 98 | 277 | +183 | 119 | 239 | +101 |
| Marin | 167 | 235 | +41 | 184 | 262 | +42 |
| Mendocino | 44 | 85 | +93 | 48 | 153 | +219 |
| Merced | 200 | 367 | +84 | 259 | 273 | +5 |
| Napa | 58 | 124 | +114 | 60 | 104 | +73 |
| Nevada | 44 | 114 | +159 | 64 | 102 | +59 |
| Orange | 1,173 | 2,862 | +144 | 1,395 | 2,567 | +84 |
| Placer | 61 | 139 | +128 | 37 | 146 | +295 |
| Riverside | 628 | 1,039 | +65 | 784 | 790 | +1 |
| Sacramento | 1,040 | 1,821 | +75 | 1,237 | 1,604 | +30 |
| San Bernardino | 773 | 1,668 | +116 | 1,565 | 1,337 | −15 |
| San Diego | 1,588 | 2,978 | +88 | 1,573 | 2,328 | +48 |
| San Francisco | 837 | 1,454 | +73 | 1,092 | 1,466 | +44 |
| San Joaquin | 437 | 834 | +91 | 770 | 756 | −2 |
| Santa Barbara | 186 | 547 | +194 | 383 | 544 | +42 |
| Santa Clara | 958 | 3,111 | +225 | 1,276 | 2,668 | +109 |
| Santa Cruz | 155 | 426 | +175 | 238 | 391 | +64 |
| Siskiyou | 31 | 53 | +71 | 54 | 42 | −22 |
| Solano | 152 | 516 | +239 | 224 | 388 | +73 |
| Sonoma | 226 | 435 | +92 | 344 | 407 | +18 |
| Tehama | 40 | 80 | +100 | 73 | 82 | +12 |
| Trinity | 9 | 15 | +66 | 14 | 14 | 0 |
| Tulare | 292 | 592 | +103 | 485 | 660 | +36 |
| Ventura | 477 | 1,171 | +145 | 533 | 921 | +73 |
| Yolo | 119 | 221 | +86 | 187 | 151 | −20 |
| Yuba | 72 | 140 | +94 | 145 | 138 | −5 |
| TOTAL | 21,257 | 49,061 | +131 | 26,539 | 37,926 | +43 |
| MEAN | 607 | 1,402 | +131 | 758 | 1,084 | +43 |

[a]Percent Change = [(1986 figure − 1976 figure)/1976 figure] × 100

**TABLE 29**
CALIFORNIA COUNTIES NOT UNDER COURT ORDER: CHANGES IN AVERAGE
DAILY JAIL POPULATION AND BOARD-RATED CAPACITY, 1976 AND 1986

| County | Average Daily Jail Population | | Percent Change[a] | Board-Rated Capacity | | Percent Change[a] |
|---|---|---|---|---|---|---|
| | 1976 | 1986 | | 1976 | 1986 | |
| Alpine (no jail) | — | — | — | — | — | — |
| Amador | 11 | 26 | +136 | 20 | 42 | +110 |
| Calaveras | 20 | 33 | +64 | 49 | 47 | −4 |
| Colusa | 26 | 46 | +76 | 96 | 94 | −2 |
| Del Norte | 25 | 56 | +124 | 78 | 64 | −18 |
| El Dorado | 57 | 142 | +149 | 98 | 110 | +12 |
| Glenn | 25 | 47 | +88 | 49 | 55 | +12 |
| Inyo | 15 | 35 | +133 | 32 | 47 | +47 |
| Kings | 90 | 374 | +315 | 152 | 193 | +27 |
| Lassen | 20 | 34 | +70 | 40 | 41 | +3 |
| Mariposa | 8 | 17 | +112 | 13 | 19 | +46 |
| Modoc | 7 | 17 | +161 | 25 | 14 | −44 |
| Mono | 7 | 9 | +29 | 27 | 22 | −19 |
| Monterey | 188 | 689 | +266 | 405 | 483 | +19 |
| Plumas | 6 | 24 | +287 | 12 | 13 | +8 |
| San Benito | 30 | 56 | +90 | 29 | 29 | +193 |
| San Luis Obispo | 88 | 243 | +176 | 138 | 199 | +44 |
| San Mateo | 435 | 800 | +84 | 431 | 622 | +44 |
| Shasta | 121 | 337 | +177 | 124 | 367 | +196 |
| Sierra (no jail) | — | — | — | — | — | — |
| Stanislaus | 394 | 714 | +81 | 504 | 653 | +29 |
| Sutter | 38 | 99 | +161 | 45 | 133 | +195 |
| Tuolumne | 21 | 58 | +176 | 46 | 41 | −10 |
| TOTAL | 1,632 | 3,856 | +136 | 2,413 | 3,288 | +36 |
| MEAN | 78 | 184 | +136 | 115 | 157 | +36 |

[a]Percent Change = [(1986 figure − 1976 figure)/1976 figure] × 100.

(43 versus 36 percent). The tendency for jails under court order to show slower increases in jail population and greater increases in jail capacity suggests that court intervention produces counterbalancing trends supportive of both jail population control and jail expansion. Such effects are less contradictory than they may sound: Most jail facilities were already so badly overcrowded and deteriorated that few courts could realistically order jail population controls without permitting or encouraging some new jail construction at the same time.

Court orders were also associated with moderate increases in sheriff personnel. From 1976 to 1986, counties under order increased sheriff personnel by 36 percent; counties not under order increased personnel by only 26 percent. Thus, on average, counties under order displayed slower rates of growth in jail population, and increased jail capacity and sheriff personnel at a slightly greater rate, than counties not under order.

The *magnitude* of expansion in specific counties is important. A county that increases its jail population by 12,103 inmates over a 10-year period (as Los Angeles did) is going to have considerably more difficulty coping with change than a county that increases its jail population by only 85 inmates (El Dorado), even though the rates of increase (151 and 149 percent respectively) are almost identical. These figures translate into very different costs. For example, if a conservative figure of $10,000 per inmate per year was used to cover jail operating costs alone (McDonald 1989), El Dorado would have to spend an additional $85,000, while Los Angeles would have to spend an additional $121,000,000. If new beds have to be constructed, costs (and cost differences) become astronomical: Capital costs for minimum-security beds run about $30,000 per bed, while maximum-security beds cost about $70,000 each. Further, such differences in magnitude are certain to have differential impacts upon the ability of county criminal justice systems—law enforcement, courts, corrections, and probation—to process inmates.

## Case Analyses

Judges perceive jail capacity, physical condition of facilities, and staffing as absolutely critical issues in jail reform. In California, the courts have had a profound impact on physical improvements and staffing levels. Court documents and archival data from 13 of the 43 lawsuits I examined allow us to review the major changes.

In many cases, judges agreed with plaintiffs that building new facilities and achieving realistic staffing levels were required to obtain constitutional conditions. Such intervention may simply bring "offending" counties up to standards already met in other jurisdictions (e.g., Harriman and Straussman 1983). Even though court-ordered reforms may implicitly require increased county expenditures on jails, explicit court orders to expand jail capacity or increase staffing levels were not uncommon. In 34 of 43 cases examined (79 percent), there were orders to reduce overcrowding (usually population caps). In 13 cases (30 percent), there were direct orders to improve staffing levels.

In 16 cases (37 percent), there were orders to build new jails or make substantial renovations to expand existing capacity. We can illustrate these three judicial emphases with brief descriptions of court orders from several cases.

In Alameda County (*Smith v. Dyer,* 1983), Judge Richard A. Bancroft ordered the county to "proceed expeditiously to secure funding, design, and construction of a replacement for Greystone." "The time for footdragging is over," Judge Bancroft proclaimed. "Replacement must occur regardless of the source of funds." Clarifying the court's position, he stated: "The Court's power in this regard is a negative one: it cannot order respondent board of supervisors to appropriate funds. But it can, and will, order the facility closed, if necessary, to eliminate unlawful conditions." A new North County jail facility with a rated capacity of 576 was built in 1984, and a new 1,968-bed Santa Rita jail opened in 1989 to replace the previous, outmoded facility (California Board of Corrections 1988).

In Riverside County (*In re Inmates of Riverside County Jail at Riverside v. Byrd* [Clark], 1987), Superior Court Judge Howard M. Dabney ordered the county to build a 64-bed facility for women, setting both beginning and completion deadlines. He also ordered status reports on a planned 325-bed facility and ordered expansion of the Indio facility by 14 beds. Later, the construction of an additional 128 beds at the Banning facility was ordered. The judge also ordered extensive hiring of new staff to deal with recreation, visitation, transfer and other problems (13 March 1986). He stated that adequate staffing was needed to meet constitutional standards of confinement.

In San Francisco (*Stone v. City and County of San Francisco,* 1982), U.S. District Court Judge William H. Orrick issued three orders to reduce overcrowding, two orders to improve staffing levels, and four orders to expand or renovate jail facilities. On 30 June 1987, parties signed an agreement to build a new 300-bed minimum/medium-security facility. Frustrated with noncompliance, the judge eventually ordered the city to secure funding for physical improvements and set deadlines for design, beginning of construction, and completion. A "liquidated damages provision" required damages to be paid into a special fund if construction was not completed on time. The judge later warned of fines for noncompliance with staffing orders ($100 per day per position left vacant after the deadline) and startup deadlines ($1,000 for each day the new jail was not in full occupancy). When overcrowding persisted, potential fines were set at a rate of $300 per inmate per day for each inmate who exceeded the rated capacity of individual housing units. The special master later commended defendants for efforts to reduce overcrowding, but also recommended that previously threatened fines be imposed for failure to provide adequate medical staffing (3 April 1989). The county soon began construction on a new 300-bed jail at San Bruno, and remodeled the 56-bed Work Furlough Center.

In Santa Barbara (*Miller v. Carpenter*, 1982), Superior Court Judge Charles S. Stevens stated: "[D]etention facilities of the main jail are entirely inadequate to house the number of inmates being detained. . . . [S]aid jail facilities were inadequate when the construction of the jail was completed [1970]." Several years later, the county had still not substantially increased its jail capacity. On 13 February 1989, Judge William L. Gordon (*Jahanshahi v. Carpenter*, 1985) ordered the county to begin plans for new facilities immediately. In addition, the judge ordered construction of a new reception center at the main jail.

In Placer County (*Offield v. Scott*, 1977), the county grand jury had been recommending jail improvements and expansion for years before the courts took action (annual grand jury reports were attached to the original complaint). In 1971, they recommended remodeling of jail facilities. In 1972, they stated that "the jail's present capacity is inadequate." In 1973: "The physical condition of the building and capabilities are totally inadequate." In 1976: "We, the Placer County Grand Jury for 1975–6, are convinced beyond a doubt—after thorough observance and investigation—that the conditions existing in the Placer County Jail, relative to security, is like sitting on a pile of dynamite that is fused and the fuse is lit. . . . Apparently, the only thing between the continued use of the present jail for holding prisoners, and its condemnation, is a laxity on the part of regulatory agencies to enforce the law governing the operation of the facility." Finally, in 1977, Superior Court Judge William A. Newsom agreed: "The county jail is an antiquated facility designed to meet the needs of a different era" (12 May 1977, p. 1). Unless defendants could meet the court's orders within 180 days (later extended six months to allow for construction of new facilities), the jail would be permanently closed. The county met that deadline seven years after the initial grand jury report. A minimum-security/work furlough center with a rated capacity of 48 was opened in 1978 and remodeled in 1984; a new county jail with a rated capacity of 92 was opened in 1985.

Similarly, in Santa Cruz (*Sandoval v. Noren*, 1983), the board of supervisors had been repeatedly warned by the county grand jury of the inadequacy of the county jail. The court had previously noted that the jail "demands replacement, not repair" (26 August 1983, p. 1), and that court orders were designed to provide interim relief pending construction of a new pretrial detention facility, although it did not issue specific orders to build. The court relinquished jurisdiction in 1986 following completion of a new 26-bed women's/work furlough facility and a 134-bed addition to the main jail.

In Fresno (*In re Morgan, In re Ransbury, and Consolidated Cases,* 1983), overcrowding had been a serious, longstanding issue. Superior Court Judge Frank J. Creede issued 10 orders over a two-year period specifying population caps at the main jail: "The remedies set forth in this order are intended to be interim, remedial measures pending the construction of a new detention facility by the County of Fresno" (27 March 1985, p. 23). "Full compliance with recognized constitutional standards and with the 1980 California Minimum Jail Standards can be achieved only with the construction of a new detention facility" (p. 12). The judge required written plans for a new jail and threatened to re-open the case if one was not built. The county opened a new work furlough facility in 1985 (rated capacity 50) and a new satellite jail in 1986 (rated capacity 84); it renovated the branch jail in 1985 to increase its rated capacity to 384.

In Los Angeles (*Rutherford v. Pitchess,* 1978), Judge Gray compared jail holding cells to a "pig pen" and called his inspection of jail facilities a "repelling experience." The judge acknowledged that his orders would require considerable increases in space and staffing. Numerous renovations and additions to this massive jail system resulted (see Table 28).

In San Diego (*Hudler v. Duffy,* 1980), Superior Court Judge James L. Facht diagnosed the major jail problems as overcrowding and inadequate staffing, calling the jail an "architectural nightmare" that worked against proper supervision and observation of inmates: "Not the least of the Sheriff's problems is the abysmal design of the jail. Architecturally, the jail is a gross case of malpractice in design. . . . Edgar Smith, the assistant executive officer of the State Board of Corrections and a principal witness in the case, says, 'I can't compare overcrowding and understaffing with the other aspects of the jail problem. It surpasses and transcends all others in its importance,' and I agree" (12 May 1980, p. 21). Extensive orders were made to improve staffing levels and reduce overcrowding. The county planned a 296-bed addition to its Vista jail facility, a new East Mesa jail with 968 pretrial beds and 256 minimum-security beds, and a second, 1,500-bed pretrial facility. Although legal and financial problems slowed progress in increasing capacity

(California Board of Corrections 1988), the judge noted the county's good faith efforts: "[T]he Sheriff's budget since 1976 has gone up 15 percent a year, all locally funded money. It [the county] has been responsive to the Sheriff's request for increased personnel" (12 May 1980, p. 18).

In Tulare County (*Mendoza v. County of Tulare*, 1985), the Superior Court ordered a new jail facility built by 30 November 1986. In June 1986, the parties stipulated to an agreement to make renovations to increase jail capacity. Despite increased pressure from the court, and a motion for contempt filed by plaintiffs, the county did not open any new jail facilities until 1987. Overcrowding has persisted in spite of the addition of 714 new jail beds (California Board of Corrections 1988).

Tehama County's plans to increase jail capacity caused the court to vacate a previous consent decree that specified jail population limits (*Smith v. County of Tehama*, 1986). The county agreed to renovate the main jail and purchased an additional building to hold minimum-security inmates.

In San Bernardino (*Fuller v. Tidwell*, 1987), the District Court specified jail population caps in 1987, and defendants agreed to construct new jail facilities. The population caps were temporarily raised in 1988 pending completion of a planned 960-bed pretrial jail facility. The court, however, retained jurisdiction for at least the next eight years to monitor jail populations and conditions.

In Humboldt County (*In re the Inmate Population of the Humboldt County Jail and Connected Cases*, 1987), Superior Court Judge John E. Buffington observed that "Humboldt County is a county on the verge of bankruptcy" (23 January 1987, p. 10), but "inadequate resources can never be an adequate justification for the state's depriving any person of his constitutional rights." Overcrowding and staffing were seen as crucial: "[T]he inmate population must be reduced to the rated capacity *and* [original emphasis] the appropriate number of staff must be hired to operate the facility at the rated capacity" (23 January 1987, p. 10). The sheriff was ordered to hire the personnel "needed to properly and safely man the present facility" (p. 15). Over a year later, however, the county had been unable to comply with its commitment to build a new facility, eliciting frustration from Judge Buffington: "That new facility's site has yet to be found; that new facility's design has yet to be made; and the county has not yet learned how to properly operate the present facility" (16 May 1988, p. 6).

Court orders have clearly facilitated expansion in jail capacity and sheriff personnel, although the magnitude of effects varies considerably across individual counties. Three complementary judicial emphases were illustrated: the need to limit current inmate populations, the need to provide adequate staffing, and the need to renovate or expand existing jail facilities. Orders to reduce overcrowding (without necessarily ordering construction) were specified in 34 of 43 cases. Some judges threatened to close old, outmoded facilities unless new facilities were constructed; others used the threat of contempt orders to motivate defendants to build new facilities. Many judges warned that remedial orders were temporary, interim measures only, pending construction of new facilities. Even if not ordered to build, defendants often perceived that court-decreed constitutional standards could be met only by closing old, poorly designed, deteriorating facilities and building new ones.

Of 35 counties under court order, 17 increased their capacity between 1976 to 1986 at rates of 40 percent or greater. In comparison, only 8 of 21 jails not under court order increased capacity at this rate. There are exceptions to this rule, however. Of counties under court order, five (12 percent) increased their capacity by 10 percent or less; six (14 percent) actually decreased their capacity slightly.

As we have seen, diverse factors across legal cases (e.g., the behavior of judges and litigants) and counties (e.g., willingness and ability to comply, local punishment policies) interact to produce heterogeneous outcomes. Variations in jail expansion can be explained in at least three ways. First, court orders have forced most counties to *keep pace* with jail needs to a greater degree than they otherwise would have done, counteracting the tendency toward inertia. Second, court intervention has in several cases required closing old facilities and replacing them with new, but not necessarily larger, ones. Third, judges vary a good deal in their persistence and use of sanctions.

The examples provided suggest that judicial persistence and the threat or administration of sanctions are necessary but not sufficient to produce intended changes in jail capacity and staffing. Judicial orders requiring expansion are most effective when orders are clear and forceful, they specify sanctions for noncompliance in advance (including heavy fines, contempt orders, or reopening of the case), they spell out incentives for compliance (e.g., the court's relinquishing of jurisdiction, the removal of population caps, restoring authority for jail planning to county officials), and defendants are both willing and competent to implement prescribed changes.

## Effects on Correctional Expenditures and Policy

Despite much speculation and argument among litigants, policymakers and scholars, questions about the effects of court orders on correctional spending and policies have rarely been addressed by empirical evidence. Where they have—as in the studies by Harriman and Straussman (1983) and Taggart (1989) discussed above in this chapter—the focus has been state prisons and state correctional expenditures, rather than jails and county government expenditures. If fiscal crisis is chronic at the state level, it is severe at the county level. California's Butte and Humboldt counties have teetered on the verge of bankruptcy for some time (Geissinger 1990). Yet courts consistently rule out inadequate resources as an excuse for depriving inmates of their constitutional rights (e.g., *Gates v. Collier*, 1974; *Miller v. Carson*, 1975). As a result, court orders may exert even more influence on county budgets and policy priorities than on their state-level counterparts.

In this section, I use time series data, court documents, and interviews with government, corrections, and justice officials in three counties to explore the impacts of court orders on county correctional expenditures and policy priorities. Cross-sectional data from two constructed samples of matched counties allow us to compare expenditures in California counties under and not under court order.

### Case Studies

Proposition 13, passed by California voters in June 1978, severely reduced disposable county funds. It limited property tax rates and assessments in Contra Costa, Santa Clara, and Orange counties, according to county officials, and these are the major source of discretionary county revenues in California (Koehler 1983). Since county revenues received from state and federal governments are targeted for highly specific functions, such as education, health, and welfare, reductions in discretionary revenues significantly constrain budgetary options. California counties received 38 percent of their revenues from state government in 1988, and 19 percent from federal sources (California Office of State Controller 1988). One official I interviewed called Proposition 13 "a catastrophe which effectively destroyed local government." In addition, the Gann Spending Limits of 1979 (Proposition 4) prohibited county and state governments from retaining surplus revenues that exceeded their budgets. The net result of these reforms, in conjunction with a sagging national economy and jail populations that soared in the 1980s (Kizziah 1984) was that counties faced growing fiscal difficulties and jail crowding problems at the same time that judicial scrutiny of jails was increasing.

*Contra Costa.* Although Judge Arneson at no time explicitly ordered jail expansion or additional county expenditures, his orders enhanced the jail's priority on the county policy agenda. County officials unanimously commended the sheriff's efforts in dealing with jail problems, but they were not sanguine about the pressures jail litigation had put on county finances: "We're forced to shift those millions of dollars across. . . . it puts you in a box, which is somewhat irrational, of diverting millions and millions of dollars that we know we would be doing better as an investment for the public—drug treatment programs, prevention programs . . . greater education efforts." Indeed, officials in other county agencies suggested that jail litigation had increased competition for county funds by other justice agencies (see data on budgetary allocations in Chapter 2).

Jail litigation significantly affected county government and criminal justice system policy decisions, although the policy impact of court orders was not solely financial. Respondents indicated that the sheriff managed to gain interagency support for numerous pretrial and postsentence programs that helped keep jail populations at manageable levels (described in the next section, "Systemwide Impacts").

I used interrupted time series analysis to examine changes in annual correctional expenditures (1963–1988) as a result of court intervention.[1] Because of the brevity of the series and the recent date of court intervention (meaning that there are relatively few postintervention points), we must be cautious in interpreting statistical results. While 50 or more time points are often recommended for ARIMA analyses, shorter series are often interpretable (Cook and Campbell 1979, 288). A careful process of identification, estimation, and diagnosis is the proper guide for any time series analysis (McCleary and Hay 1980).

A general upward trend in expenditures was apparent (Figure 3), although no strong change in the level of the time series was visually apparent at the onset of the court order. Time series analyses (Table 30) showed that the court order had a negative effect on correctional spending (B = −.171). However, because total county expenditures were used as a control against annual inflation, the negative coefficient merely indicates that raw expenditures increased while proportional expenditures decreased (Table 31) following court orders. Correctional expenditures decreased from 9.6 percent of total county expenditures in 1985 to 8.8 percent of total expenditures in 1988.

Prelitigation jail expansion in Contra Costa may have contributed to the patterns of correctional expenditures observed for 1963 to 1988, since a modern, podular/direct-supervision jail opened there in January 1981 (see Wener, Frazier, and Farbstein 1987). The moderate decrease observed in correctional expenditures (as a percentage of total

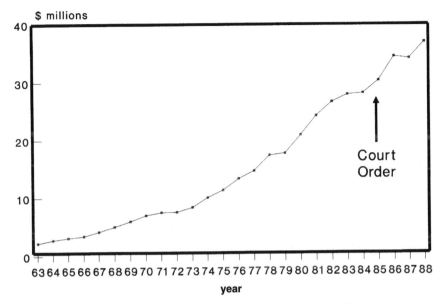

**FIGURE 3** *Contra Costa County, Annual Correctional Expenditures, 1963–1988*

expenditures) following the court order may therefore simply reflect the absorption of previous costs associated with the construction and startup of the new jail. One alternative time series model was constructed to examine spending patterns in connection with the new jail, with an additional impact parameter added to account for its construction in 1981. This parameter was nonsignificant, did little to improve the model, and was dropped.

The new jail may have provided significant symbolic benefits to the sheriff and the county, and probably helped the sheriff avert much more serious legal problems than those he faced four years later in *Yancy v. Rainey.* Many have argued that the podular/direct-supervision strategy ameliorates inmate complaints and legal problems by improving inmate and staff safety, meeting inmates' critical needs, and maintaining security (Zupan 1991). The Contra Costa jail in fact became a national showplace for the new-generation jail philosophy, and many corrections officials from around the country came to see it in operation. Though no county officials I interviewed explicitly said so, one can speculate that the presence of this innovative jail gave county officials symbolic clout by demonstrating *a priori* good faith and a sincere wish to meet or surpass constitutional requirements.

**TABLE 30**
PARAMETER ESTIMATES FOR TIME SERIES MODELS OF CORRECTIONAL
EXPENDITURES IN THREE CALIFORNIA COUNTIES UNDER COURT ORDER

| County | ARIMA (p, d, q) Model[a] | Constant | Court Order | Contempt Order | AR | MA | Logged Total Expenditures[b] |
|--------|---------|----------|-------|----------|-----|-----|--------------|
| Contra Costa | Lg(0,1,8) | .035* | −.171* | — | — | .745* | 1.000 |
| | | (.007) | (.063) | | | (.293) | |
| Orange | Lg(0,1,0) | −.013 | −.075 | .627* | — | — | 1.000 |
| | | (.018) | (.090) | (.090) | | | |
| Santa Clara | Lg(0,1,0) | .035 | .482* | — | — | — | 1.000 |
| | | (.041) | (.206) | | | | |

[a]p = order of autoregressive process (AR), d = order of differencing, q = order of moving average process (MA).
[b]The value of the total expenditures parameter in each model was constrained to 1.000 so that logged parameter estimates could be converted into their original scales and reexpressed as percentages.
*p < .05.

The time series results suggest two important conclusions. First, increased correctional expenditures in Contra Costa are not easily attributable to the effects of court orders. Second, the analysis challenges official perceptions of increased spending on the jail following court orders. Such perceptions may be partly explained by interagency competition for scarce county resources and the increased visibility of jail problems. Even if the jail was not getting more money, jail overcrowding and court orders were the topic of heavy media coverage and numerous meetings between county government and justice officials (Welsh and Pontell 1991). The observed decrease in proportional correctional expenditures following court orders suggests that the sheriff had temporarily used up his *budget* priority on the new jail but not his *policy* priority.

It is important to remember that court orders can have powerful symbolic effects in addition to their policy and budgetary impacts. The imposition and removal of the court order in this case may have averted future lawsuits against the jail by demonstrating that the sheriff was already in compliance with state and federal standards. If such action deterred litigious inmates or their advocates from filing new lawsuits, this legitimation alone would have been a substantial victory for the sheriff.

*Orange.* The short- and long-term costs of complying with court

## TABLE 31
### COUNTIES UNDER COURT ORDER: CHANGES IN GENERAL CORRECTIONAL
### EXPENDITURES (1963–1988) AS A PROPORTION OF TOTAL COUNTY BUDGETS

| County | Year of First Court Decision | Year of Decision | Percentage of Budget Allocated to Corrections | | | Percent Change | | |
|---|---|---|---|---|---|---|---|---|
| | | | 1963 | 1976 | 1988 | 1963–1976 | 1976–1988 | Court Decision–1988 |
| Alameda | 1983 | 9.35 | 7.05 | 9.07 | 8.94 | +28.6 | −1.4 | −4.4 |
| Butte | 1985 | 6.30 | 1.04 | 1.88 | 6.10 | +80.8 | +224.5 | −3.2 |
| Contra Costa | 1985 | 9.61 | 4.61 | 6.73 | 8.85 | +46.0 | +31.5 | −7.9 |
| Fresno | 1983 | 7.06 | 2.97 | 5.32 | 6.05 | +79.1 | +13.7 | −14.3 |
| Humboldt | 1987 | 4.98 | 2.35 | 4.16 | 5.73 | +77.0 | +37.7 | +15.0 |
| Imperial | 1973 | 5.18 | 1.78 | 6.19 | 10.49 | +247.8 | +69.5 | +102.5 |
| Lake | 1984 | 4.11 | 1.05 | 2.81 | 5.65 | +167.6 | +101.1 | +37.5 |
| Los Angeles | 1975 | 4.29 | 5.08 | 4.13 | 6.72 | −18.7 | +62.7 | +56.6 |
| Madera | 1984 | 9.26 | 2.37 | 4.65 | 6.98 | +96.2 | +50.1 | −24.6 |
| Marin | 1982 | 6.64 | 4.57 | 8.23 | 6.68 | +80.1 | −18.8 | +0.6 |
| Mendocino | 1983 | 3.66 | 2.14 | 2.76 | 5.12 | +29.0 | +85.5 | +39.9 |
| Merced | 1983[a] | 4.55 | 2.78 | 3.97 | 4.55 | +42.8 | +14.6 | 0.0 |
| Napa | 1988 | 5.84 | 1.62 | 5.59 | 5.84 | +245.1 | +4.5 | — |
| Nevada | 1983 | 5.62 | 1.51 | 4.37 | 7.50 | +189.5 | +71.6 | +33.4 |
| Orange | 1978 | 4.86 | 6.19 | 4.88 | 7.72 | −21.2 | +58.2 | +58.8 |
| Riverside | 1981 | 5.71 | 4.75 | 5.86 | 7.47 | +23.4 | +27.5 | +30.8 |
| Sacramento | 1981 | 7.27 | 4.00 | 6.88 | 6.64 | +72.0 | −3.5 | −8.7 |
| San Bernardino | 1987 | 5.80 | 4.33 | 6.87 | 5.87 | +58.7 | −14.6 | +1.2 |
| San Diego | 1980 | 6.44 | 4.80 | 5.64 | 6.93 | +17.5 | +22.9 | +7.6 |
| Santa Barbara | 1982 | 8.77 | 3.88 | 7.88 | 8.05 | +103.1 | +2.2 | −8.2 |
| Santa Clara | 1980 | 9.00 | 2.98 | 3.98 | 10.70 | +33.6 | +168.8 | +18.8 |
| Santa Cruz | 1983 | 10.11 | 2.05 | 5.53 | 8.30 | +169.8 | +50.1 | −17.9 |
| Siskiyou | 1986 | 5.26 | 1.81 | 4.04 | 5.09 | +123.2 | +26.0 | −3.2 |
| Solano | 1985 | 8.76 | 3.52 | 5.02 | 10.46 | +42.6 | +108.4 | +19.4 |
| Sonoma | 1982 | 6.78 | 2.66 | 5.10 | 10.94 | +91.7 | +114.5 | +61.4 |
| Tehama | 1986 | 6.14 | 1.54 | 4.48 | 7.60 | +190.9 | +69.6 | +23.8 |
| Trinity | 1986 | 4.36 | 0.14 | 0.43 | 5.16 | +207.1 | +1100.0 | +18.3 |
| Tulare | 1985 | 4.52 | 2.17 | 2.77 | 6.60 | +27.7 | +138.3 | +46.0 |
| Ventura | 1983 | 8.74 | 2.02 | 6.13 | 8.54 | +203.5 | +39.3 | −2.3 |
| Yolo | 1987 | 5.22 | 2.82 | 6.43 | 4.72 | +128.0 | −26.6 | −9.6 |
| Yuba | 1976 | 4.64 | 1.43 | 4.64 | 6.46 | +224.5 | +39.2 | +39.3 |
| MEANS | | 6.41 | 2.97 | 5.05 | 7.18 | +99.6 | +86.0 | +16.4 |

[a]Year of complaint. Decision did not follow complaint for another five years, but extensive negotiations occurred during that time.

orders had major impacts on budget decisions in Orange County, and court orders forced some difficult policy choices. County officials traced both judicial intervention and solutions to jail capacity.

> That has all come together when you don't have the facilities, you don't have the capacity to feed the people on time, to give them . . . the appropriate amount of recreation time. Hence the lawsuit in Federal Court that says, ". . . you had better expand your facilities. In the interim, you had better take measures to relieve the overcrowding."

Although Judge Gray never explicitly ordered expansion of jail facilities, he made it clear that constitutional conditions had to be achieved, whatever actions and expenditures were required.

The county increased its jail capacity from 2,159 in 1984 to 3,523 in 1987, an increase of 63.2 percent. Increased capacity, however, involved the expansion of current facilities and the erection of temporary facilities such as tents and portable trailers, rather than building the long-promised new jail that the court agreed was needed to replace the outmoded main jail. At the James A. Musick minimum-security jail, more than 320 inmates were being kept in tents. These temporary facilities are an extremely expensive way of coping with court orders, as one official noted: "We're throwing marvelous amounts of piles of money around and with very little return. We spent $8 million basically on Musick on temporary facilities. One of these days this facility is going to go bye-bye." A new intake–release facility with a rated capacity of 384 inmates opened in 1987, but the county's major construction plan envisioned a massive new $60 million, 6,200-bed jail for sentenced inmates, which a shortage of funds and numerous community challenges blocked (Welsh et al. 1990).

The funds required for a new jail carry serious repercussions for other county-provided services. One official warned that new jail construction, at a time of decreasing revenues from state and federal governments, would severely strain county finances and force cutbacks in other areas.

> Just because we have a new jail does not mean we're going to get one nickel more money. We're going to have to take 15 or 20 million dollars of public money we aren't getting any more; we're going to have to figure out sufficient cuts to be able to continue to still provide services. . . . It's going to be damned tough.

Eventually, following contempt orders against county officials, less capital-intensive pretrial and postsentencing options were considered.

A new jail could not possibly be on-line for several years, even if funding and site-selection problems could be resolved. Recommendations by the special master and county agencies led to the adoption of electronic surveillance, work release, and county parole programs to reduce overcrowding (see the section on "Systemwide Effects" below).

Although the contempt order of 1985 exerted a strong, positive effect on correctional expenditures, the original court order of 1978 did not (see Table 30). In Figure 4 we can see a break in the time series precisely at 1985, the time of the contempt order against county officials. As we saw earlier (Chapters 4 and 5), the original court order had resulted in little compliance prior to this time.

Court orders in this case appear to have halted and reversed a trend of decreased funding for county jails. Surprisingly, cross-sectional data (see Table 31) revealed a decrease in the allocation of county finances to county corrections from 1963 to 1976. Orange County was one of only two counties (with Los Angeles) to show such a decrease.

*Santa Clara.* Judge Allen issued the first of numerous orders challenging the authority of the county executive by explicitly requiring county expenditures (Chapter 4). He specified population caps at the main jail, warning that failure to comply would be punishable by contempt. He ordered the county controller to appear in court, take the

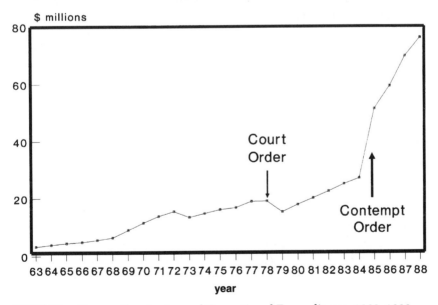

**FIGURE 4** *Orange County, Annual Correctional Expenditures, 1963–1988*

stand, and issue checks to pay for jail renovations; the county to plan construction of new facilities, and to refrain from cutting the sheriff's operating budget; the sheriff to hire an architect and bill the county, as well as to hire new deputies (Order 8a, 21 October 1982). Judge Allen also ordered defendants to expand current facilities and add temporary barracks to relieve overcrowding.

Frustrated by delays and resistance, Judge Allen boldly announced his intention to assume control over county jail expenditures: "The Court finds that the available prisoner housing in the county for medium and maximum security prisoners is full, and that the problems created by overcrowding in the main jail cannot be solved unless this court controls all expenditures for additional prisoner housing" (Order 16C, 7 February 1983). He ordered the county to prepare ordinances to raise taxes to cover jail costs. Such intrusive orders, unsurprisingly, were overturned by the state Court of Appeal.

Over the eight-year history of the case, court orders mandated various capital-intensive reforms. Five judges issued 14 orders to reduce jail populations, 10 orders to improve staffing levels, and 22 orders to increase jail capacity. In spite of resistance to court orders, judicial persistence contributed to increased capacity over the history of the case, from 1,292 in 1982 to 2,668 in 1986, an increase of 106.5 percent. An additional 1,000 beds were made available when the new central jail was opened in early 1989.

Time series analyses (see Table 30) supported a significant effect of court orders on county correctional expenditures. Overall, such spending rose from 3.0 percent of total expenditures in 1963 to 10.7 percent in 1988, an increase of 256.7 percent. An accelerated trend was apparent in the latter part of the time series from 1982 to 1988 (Figure 5), but no immediate increases were apparent at either 1979, the year of the initial court order about the women's jail, or 1981, that of the initial order about the men's jail.

Two events should be noted. First, the initial court order (1979) required immediate improvements in medical care, recreation, and capacity in the women's jail. The women's lawsuit was inactive from 1980 to 1982, at which time it was reopened by District Court Judge Peckham because of noncompliance. Second, the men's jail lawsuit resulted in an initial court order in 1981. After Judge Allen issued orders requiring direct jail expenditures early in 1982, the county filed appeals that tied up the case for most of the year. Near the end of the year, the Court of Appeal handed the reins back to Judge Allen, who ordered

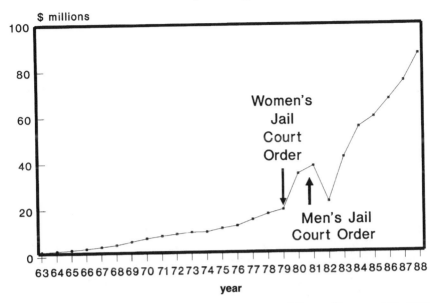

**FIGURE 5** *Santa Clara County, Annual Correctional Expenditures, 1963–1988*

further expenditures. Thus, a brief period of inactivity in both lawsuits between 1980 and 1982 partly explains the lag in effects of court orders. As we observed in Chapter 5, many more court orders followed.

The unusual and intrusive measures judges used in Santa Clara were justified, to some extent, by the resistance they faced. Various county agencies wanted to look tough on crime for political reasons, according to interview respondents, but were unwilling to provide commensurate resources. As in Orange, Santa Clara's problems were compounded by reluctance to use alternatives to incarceration. This bitterly contested lawsuit shows that judges can exert considerable influence, direct as well as indirect, upon county budgetary and policy decisions.

### Comparisons of Court-Ordered and Non-Ordered Counties

To facilitate cross-jurisdictional comparisons, I examined annual correctional expenditures for each county in California for 1963, 1976, and 1988, the beginning, mid-point, and end-point of the time span covered above. I considered the proportion of the budget allocated to corrections rather than raw expenditures so as to minimize differences due to the size and activity of different justice systems. The data included 31 counties under court order and 23 counties not under order in California for the period from 1963 to 1988.[2] Matched controls were constructed for counties of varying jail populations, including several small, medium, and large jails. Even matching on one variable (jail population), however, results in sample attrition, leaving 10 matched pairs for analysis. Matching resulted in two constructed samples with almost equivalent average daily jail populations of 632 and 688.

When we examine correctional expenditures for the 31 counties under court order (see Table 31), we see that the average proportion of budget allocated to corrections increased from 3 percent to 7 percent over a 26-year period, with considerable variation across counties. Indeed, from the year of the court decision to 1988, 18 of 31 counties showed positive change ranging from 0.6 to 103.0 percent; 2 counties showed no change; 11 showed negative change (−2.3 to −24.6 percent). Court orders have thus had strong impacts on county finances in some cases, but weak or negligible impacts in others.

Negative change suggests several possible mechanisms: (1) compliance with court orders may have been achieved through non-capital-intensive methods such as intermediate sanctions; (2) compliance may not have been achieved; (3) absent strong judicial intervention, some counties may have coped with budget crisis by reducing expenditures on a politically vulnerable victim (the jail); and (4) the postintervention period may be too brief in some cases to detect slowly emerging change. Patterns of change were further explored by comparing expenditures in matched control counties (Table 32).

Matched control counties (those with no court order) increased correctional expenditures at a similar rate for the time period 1963–1976 (a prelitigation period for all but one county). However, counties under order increased expenditures at a much greater rate (+174 percent) than counties not under order (+47 percent) for the period 1976–1988 (the most active period of jail litigation).[3] These are substantively significant differences, since even a small percentage change may translate into millions of dollars. Humboldt, for example, increased its correctional expenditures from $1,422,598 in 1976 to $4,481,227 in 1988, even though its rate of change for this period was only +37.7%. A matched-pairs t-test comparing rates of change (1976–1988) in counties under court order and not under order did not reach statistical significance (t = .92). Given the large variance and the small sample, we should interpret inferential statistics cautiously. It is clear, though, that court orders have had more impact on finances in some counties than others, and their effects are neither simple nor homogeneous.

## TABLE 32
### COUNTIES UNDER OR NOT UNDER COURT ORDER: CHANGES IN GENERAL CORRECTIONAL EXPENDITURES (1963–1988) AS A PROPORTION OF TOTAL COUNTY BUDGETS

| Counties Under Order | Year of First Court Decision | 1987 ADP[a] | Percentage of Budget Allocated to Corrections Decision Year | | | | Percent Change 1963– 1976 | 1976– 1988 | Court Decision– 1988 |
|---|---|---|---|---|---|---|---|---|---|
| | | | Decision Year | 1963 | 1976 | 1988 | | | |
| Humboldt | 1987 | 186 | 4.98 | 2.35 | 4.16 | 5.73 | +77.0 | +37.7 | +15.0 |
| Sacramento | 1981 | 2,124 | 7.27 | 4.00 | 6.88 | 6.64 | +72.0 | −3.5 | −8.7 |
| Butte | 1985 | 270 | 6.30 | 1.04 | 1.88 | 6.10 | +80.8 | +224.5 | −3.2 |
| Siskiyou | 1986 | 40 | 5.26 | 1.81 | 4.04 | 5.09 | +123.2 | +26.0 | −3.2 |
| Trinity | 1986 | 25 | 4.36 | 0.14 | 0.43 | 5.16 | +207.1 | 1,100.0 | +18.3 |
| Tulare | 1985 | 970 | 4.52 | 2.17 | 2.77 | 6.60 | +27.7 | +138.3 | +46.0 |
| Contra Costa | 1985 | 1,193 | 9.61 | 4.61 | 6.73 | 8.85 | +46.0 | +31.5 | −7.9 |
| Imperial | 1973 | 275 | 5.18 | 1.78 | 6.19 | 10.49 | +247.8 | +69.5 | +102.5 |
| Santa Barbara | 1982 | 659 | 8.77 | 3.88 | 7.88 | 8.05 | +103.1 | +2.2 | −8.2 |
| Sonoma | 1982 | 583 | 6.78 | 2.66 | 5.10 | 10.94 | +91.7 | +114.5 | +61.4 |
| MEAN | | 632 | 6.30 | 2.44 | 4.61 | 7.37 | +107.6 | +174.1 | +21.2 |

| Counties Not Under Order | Year of Decision in Matched County | 1987 ADP[a] | Percentage of Budget Allocated to Corrections Decision Year | | | | Percent Change 1963– 1976 | 1976– 1988 | Court Decision– 1988 |
|---|---|---|---|---|---|---|---|---|---|
| | | | Decision Year | 1963 | 1976 | 1988 | | | |
| El Dorado | 1987 | 185 | 6.78 | 2.31 | 4.51 | 6.92 | +95.2 | +53.4 | +2.1 |
| Kern | 1981 | 2,207 | 7.02 | 3.65 | 5.05 | 9.44 | +38.4 | +86.9 | +34.5 |
| Kings | 1985 | 326 | 7.36 | 2.31 | 4.70 | 8.31 | +103.5 | +76.8 | +12.9 |
| Lassen | 1986 | 46 | 3.75 | 1.05 | 2.18 | 4.37 | +107.6 | +100.5 | +16.5 |
| Mariposa | 1986 | 19 | 4.51 | 0.63 | 3.80 | 3.76 | +503.2 | −1.1 | −16.6 |
| Monterey | 1985 | 932 | 7.75 | 4.07 | 5.13 | 6.71 | +26.0 | +30.8 | −13.4 |
| San Joaquin | 1985 | 1,167 | 6.00 | 3.55 | 5.38 | 6.01 | +51.5 | +11.7 | 0.0 |
| San Luis Obispo | 1973 | 328 | 3.64 | 2.28 | 3.38 | 5.49 | +48.2 | +62.4 | +50.8 |
| San Mateo | 1982 | 895 | 12.49 | 4.87 | 9.81 | 11.90 | +101.4 | +21.3 | −4.7 |
| Stanislaus | 1982 | 775 | 6.89 | 3.44 | 4.59 | 5.83 | +33.4 | +27.0 | −15.4 |
| MEAN | | 688 | 6.62 | 2.82 | 4.85 | 6.87 | +110.9 | +47.0 | +6.7 |

Sources: California Board of Corrections (1988), *Report to the Legislature: Jail Standards and Operations Division—Jail Inspections and Costs of Compliance* (Sacramento: State of California); California Office of State Controller (1988), *Counties of California Financial Transactions Annual Report* (Sacramento: Office of the State Controller, Division of Local Government Fiscal Affairs).

[a]Average daily jail population.

In some cases, counties not under order actually showed greater increases in correctional expenditures than their court-ordered matches (see Table 32). Such results may reflect a greater attention to jail conditions in certain counties, and perhaps a desire to *avoid* court intervention. Similarly, the finding of lower rates of expenditures in several counties under order than in their matches suggests that the effects of the court are limited: Although cost-intensive improvements were made in several of the counties under court order, other counties may have been unwilling or unable to provide the same level of resources. A crucial variable in such cases is likely to be the persistence and resolve of the court. Counties may delay or stall before implementing court-ordered change, and even judicial persistence does not guarantee compliance (Welsh 1992a).

Patterns of change in counties under order were further explored by examining rates of change in correctional expenditures from the actual year of the court decision to 1988. The same baseline period of change was calculated for counties not under order to allow comparisons (see the last column in Table 32). Five of the 10 counties under order showed positive change ranging from 15 to 102 percent; the other 5 counties showed slight negative change ranging from $-3.2$ to $-8.7$ percent. One explanation for such results is the relative recentness of court orders. Changes in proportional correctional expenditures following the court decision were most pronounced in Imperial, which had been court-ordered much earlier (1973) than any of the other counties. The year of the decision provides a potential confound, since counties that have been under order longer experience a longer period in which expenditures drift upward. Again, matching provides a conservative strategy. Each county can be compared with its match to control for changes due to differential passage of time. We find that counties under order increased their expenditures by an average of 21 percent following court orders, while matched counties not under order increased by only 6.7 percent. A matched-pairs t-test comparing rates of change (year of decision to 1988) in counties under court order and not under order did not reach statistical significance ($t = 1.27$). Again, heterogeneous patterns of change in response to court orders are implicated.

Our analysis shows at least six mechanisms of response to court orders:

1. Non-capital-intensive responses (such as intermediate sanctions) may reduce the cost of compliance for some counties.
2. Although increased expenditures in several counties may signal cost-

intensive jail improvements, other counties may have been unwilling or unable to provide the same level of resources.

3. Judicial persistence may be a crucial mediating variable: without strong court intervention (using the Conscientious Monitor, Intervenor, or Enforcer style discussed in Chapter 5), some counties may have coped with budget crisis by reducing expenditures on a politically vulnerable victim: the jail.

4. The postintervention period may be too brief in some cases to detect slowly emerging change.

5. Counties not under court order but evidencing high rates of expenditures may be attempting to avoid court intervention.

6. Response depends partly upon the number and type of orders: Jails directly ordered to make capital-intensive improvements in staffing or to construct new buildings, for example, have less flexibility and a greater financial burden.

While judicial orders have not unanimously or unambiguously increased correctional expenditures, it is clear that judges have helped to make correctional issues a higher priority on local policy agendas, which may or may not translate into increased expenditures. Court orders likely exert the strongest impact on expenditures when: (1) counties resist using intermediate sanctions and cling to a "building" strategy; (2) a county's normative position with respect to spending (e.g., modern jail facilities) and policy innovation (e.g., intermediate sanctions) lags substantially behind other counties; (3) judges show great persistence in enforcing their orders, and specify clear sanctions and dates for compliance; and (4) those orders are of a capital-intensive nature (e.g., staffing, adding jail beds, adding medical facilities).

Resistance by defendants and persistence by judges in seeking compliance are key variables influencing financial impact. For example, the longer a county delays, the more likely it is that it will have to resort to temporary, expensive jail facilities and expansions, rather than short-term, capital-intensive solutions. Resistance also signals long-term neglect of jail conditions and greater hesitancy to commit resources to jails. If the court is persistent, resistance may only delay reform. It is not clear, however, that pronounced judicial persistence can in all cases overcome skilled and determined resistance by defendants, and the possibility remains that skilled resistance can avoid cost-intensive jail reform, translating into a low rate of change in correctional expenditures following court orders in some cases. Major factors influencing changes in correctional expenditures following court orders are summarized in Table 33.

**TABLE 33**
FACTORS INFLUENCING CHANGES IN COUNTY CORRECTIONAL
EXPENDITURES FOLLOWING COURT ORDERS

| Changes in Correctional Expenditures | Major Influences |
|---|---|
| High | Use of intermediate sanctions (low) |
| | Willingness to comply (low) |
| | Competence to comply (low) |
| | Judicial methods (Conscientious Monitor) |
| | Anticipatory prevention (high) |
| | Nature and number of remedies (capital-intensive) |
| | Normative lag (high) |
| Low | Use of intermediate sanctions (high) |
| | Willingness to comply (high) |
| | Competence to comply (high) |
| | Judicial methods (manager) |
| | Length of postintervention period (brief) |
| | Anticipatory prevention (low) |
| | Nature and number of remedies (non-capital-intensive) |
| | Normative lag (low) |

Resistance to judicial intervention, especially where the executive branch feels that its legitimate authority is being challenged, should not be unexpected.

> The likelihood of compliance is undermined, not enhanced, by detailed orders that fail to recognize the constraints on the political process. If the courts order the legislators and executives to do more than is possible, they invite understandable resistance rather than compliance; that resistance invites further orders, and the ensuing confrontation will lead not to better institutions but to political crisis. (Frug 1978, 791–792)

Such statements underestimate the potential flexibility of judicial orders and attempts to gain compliance, yet the court's options are indeed limited. Threats to fine (Orange, Santa Clara) or even imprison county officials for noncompliance (Santa Clara) may actually inspire county officials to resist and seek review of the orders by higher courts.

Some have suggested that courts should instead seek good faith compliance and set reasonable time limits for meeting goals (Brakel 1986; Frug 1978), even though "there is a human inclination, to which judges are as susceptible as the rest of us, to try to bypass the difficulties involved in the governmental process and demand immediate action"

(Frug 1978, 793–794). If court intervention fails, according to this view, the burden lies with the political branches of government and not the courts.

While the effects of judicial intervention on correctional policies and expenditures are limited by legal and pragmatic constraints, courts have stirred counties to action. Where unconstitutional conditions of confinement have been established, the judiciary has legitimately acted as a catalyst for change. It is only when judges seek to explicitly dictate, rather than initiate, legislative and executive action that the power of the purse takes on its negative connotations.

## Systemwide Impacts

Court orders against jails represent sudden changes in the local justice environment that put pressure on an entire criminal justice system to adapt by altering the routine processing of accused and convicted offenders. Jails interact extensively with law enforcement agencies, courts, probation departments, and local governments (Hall 1985, 1987). Local police departments decide whether to arrest and book accused offenders and thus control the major intake into jails. Local courts influence jail populations through pretrial release decisions and sanctions for convicted offenders. Changing decisions by district attorneys influence the efficiency with which pretrial suspects are processed. The probation department may administer both pretrial release programs, such as ROR, and alternative or "intermediate" programs for sentenced offenders, such as electronic surveillance and work furlough. County government is responsible for financial and personnel allocations to each of these agencies. Such agencies do not necessarily respond to change in a static or unified manner, however; nor are optimal decision-making strategies always followed (Cohen, March, and Olsen 1972).

Indeed, the criminal justice system is often viewed as a "nonsystem" because of its decentralized and fragmented nature (Eisenstein and Jacob 1977; Feeley 1983; Forst 1977; Gibbs 1986; President's Commission on Law Enforcement and Administration of Justice 1968; Reiss 1971; Rossum 1978). Dramatic changes in political environments, such as the imposition of court orders, create demands to tighten the "loose coupling" that normally characterizes American criminal justice organizations (Hagan 1989).

"Loose coupling" refers to organizational subsystems that are responsive to one another, yet maintain independent identities and a physical and logical separateness (Cohen, March, and Olsen 1972; Hagan 1989; Weick 1976). In such systems, "structural elements are only loosely linked to one another and to activities, rules are often violated, decisions often go unimplemented, or if implemented have uncertain consequences, and techniques are often subverted or rendered so vague as to provide little coordination" (Hagan 1989, 119). Demands for tighter coupling often lead to unexpected criminal justice impacts.

The distinction between proactive and reactive problem solving is crucial to understanding these effects. In proactive policing and proactive prosecution, for example, officials actively target certain problems for attention. Proactive problem solving, however, often requires a departure from the norm of loose coupling and a commitment to cooperation and planning from numerous agencies and actors. Reactive problem solving, on the other hand, usually means that officials within each agency respond independently to already-defined problems with the methods most familiar to their own organization.

Narcotics enforcement and white-collar crime prosecution require departures from loose coupling and normal routine. Narcotics work requires police to employ more controversial tactics to obtain evidence, including undercover work, entrapment, and the use of informants (Skolnick 1966). Police officers are more dependent upon prosecutors for feedback on the legal permissibility of evidence, and prosecutors are more dependent on police officers for extensive information and cooperation in the preparation of cases. Such information exchanges influence charging decisions and plea bargains. John Hagan argues that the proactive prosecution of white-collar criminals requires similar leverage to "turn witnesses." Judges must participate in these decisions as well, since their approval is necessary to implement charge reductions or negotiated sentences.

Contexts where the political environment has mandated departures from normal criminal justice operations offer great potential for understanding systems operations and outcomes. Interagency responses to court orders against county jail systems fall into this category. Although courts seek to stimulate more proactive responses by criminal justice subsystems to alleviate unconstitutional jail conditions, these agencies are more likely to respond, at least initially, in the more typical reactive style associated with loose coupling. A shift toward more proactive styles often occurs over time, but forced change is likely to breed resistance, especially if the targets of the intended change (county agencies) perceive the authority of the change agent (the courts) as illegitimate (Sieber 1981).

Reactive responses include denying or downplaying the problem, avoiding blame (Welsh et al. 1990), and struggling for resources and political power (Aldrich 1979). Proactive responses include formalizing exchange relations (e.g., jail task forces and interagency committees) and developing interagency innovations (e.g., new criminal justice policies and cooperative programs). I explore in this section how court-ordered change has altered interagency relations and social control policies in three counties.

## Case Studies

*Contra Costa.* Although interorganizational relations in Contra Costa reflected relatively tight coupling prior to court intervention, proactive responses increased following court orders. As noted in Chapter 3, a single judge heard all inmate complaints about jail conditions, and the sheriff and the judge often met with county officials when particular jail problems required attention. Many of those interviewed credited the sheriff with inculcating cooperative attitudes and developing effective interagency linkages surrounding jail issues. Tight coupling, however, may be inversely related to the size and scale of local government, as one official suggested.

> The bigger you get, the more problems you have. But in this county, I think we've been very lucky to have people who can communicate with each other. I think the current sheriff . . . and the prior sheriff before him had good working relationships with all the city police chiefs and with the courts. . . . So I think the individuals here—whether the system produces the individuals or otherwise, I don't know—but I think the sheriff and the judges and the police chiefs and the district attorney all try to work together.

Several new criminal justice committees emerged following the court order, and interagency contacts between sheriff, police chiefs, judges, district attorney, and probation officials increased. Such meetings, respondents suggested, helped air grievances, even if they did not always result in unanimous agreement: "I think those things help. At least people are communicating, so before somebody takes the public stand, you've had a lot of communication. . . . The edges get worn off. . . . I'm sure they don't always get what they want . . . but it helps for everybody to know what is really the cutting edge of grievances being espoused."

Committee discussions facilitated the cooperation required for proactive policy decisions to reduce overcrowding. Respondents from the sheriff's office and local police departments observed that discussions helped secure the cooperation of local police agencies to issue citations for misdemeanant suspects rather than booking them into the county jail.

> We have a number of committees that assist us in keeping that communication going. For one, as far as other law enforcement agencies, we have a Chiefs Association. . . . It's all the police chiefs in the county and [the sheriff] and the district attorney. And that is the body we use when we are talking about the citations. . . . We have a number of countywide protocols that are not mandated on anybody, but everybody has basically agreed to, and feel that that is a good way to operate.

Another useful committee, according to several respondents, was the Criminal Justice System Executive Counsel, composed solely of county officials: the sheriff, the district attorney, the presiding judge of the Superior Court, the chairman of the Judges' Association of the Municipal Court, the public defender, the chief probation officer, and a representative from the board of supervisors. This committee led to at least two innovations that helped to control jail populations by speeding offender processing: a video arraignment program that permitted inmates to enter a plea from the jail rather than awaiting transport to court, and the district attorney's early disposition program. In this program, developed in cooperation with the sheriff, the public defender, and the Municipal and Superior courts, pretrial inmates were screened soon after their admission to jail, resulting in speedier decisions to release, charge, or dismiss.

A county supervisor suggested that court orders gave the sheriff leverage to seek interagency cooperation for alternative programs: "Politically, it helps the sheriff to have a court order because then it's not just liberalism sneaking through into the sheriff's political agenda; it is the court telling the sheriff you must take care of this problem, and you must take care of it in a responsible way." Alternatives to incarceration and pretrial release programs were greatly expanded, including citation release by both sheriff's deputies and local police agencies, release on own recognizance, and work programs, including a work furlough center operated by the sheriff where inmates work during the day and return to minimum-security custody at night. Other sentenced offenders (between 700 and 800 per month, according to one respondent) work off their sentences rather than going to jail. The number of inmates on county parole quadrupled, according to interviewees, resulting in the release of about fifty convicted offenders in one six-month period. An electronic surveillance program, initiated with the cooperation of the probation department, allowed convicted offenders to serve a portion of their sentences confined to their own homes. The probation department worked closely with the sheriff on the electronic surveillance and county parole programs, and with the courts to screen potential inmates for pretrial release and alternative sentencing.

Emerging proactive adaptations, however, coexist in a state of tension with other responses more characteristic of loose coupling. For example, one police official felt that committees had led to more consistency in practices among county agencies, but he was skeptical about the motives of committee participants: "They're all working on their own political agenda." I observed other reactive responses.

When misdemeanor suspects at the jail were cited and released with a promise to appear in court (Cal. PC 853.6), one respondent saw a "revolving door" syndrome emerging: "Many judges in this county are not totally pleased with the citation process, especially when bench warrant cases are cited out. Failure-to-appear bench warrant cases come in, and they release them again. You can't get them back in court." While most officials felt that the sheriff's department did a good job of selecting the least serious offenders for citation release, some felt that dependence on citation release corrupted the integrity of the rest of the system.

Resource competition following court orders occasionally strained relations between county agencies. One probation official complained that jail spending diverted funds from other county programs.

> And where does the money come from to operate [the jail]? The very limited money they have under their discretionary control. . . . And one of the largest competitors for the discretionary monies of any county in the state of California is the sheriff's department and the probation department. We are almost entirely funded by the county; and so is the sheriff's department.
>
> **Q:** So, a little bit of competition . . .
> **A:** A little bit . . . to say the least!

Similarly, others suggested that the sheriff and probation got more resources as a result of court orders to reduce jail crowding, while the district attorney barely maintained previous levels of resources. Data only partly validated official perceptions (see Chapter 2). The sheriff received a greater proportion of the county criminal justice budget for jails in 1986 (19.2 percent) than in 1976 (8.7 percent), but the sheriff's allocation for law enforcement and other functions remained stable. In contrast, probation received far less in 1986 (19.9 percent) than in 1976

(30.1 percent). The district attorney's allocation remained constant from 1976 to 1986 (12 percent). These changes suggest that court orders tightened coupling without eliminating such reactive responses as resource competition and policy conflicts.

*Santa Clara.* Agency responses to court orders in Santa Clara were largely autonomous and reactive for about the first five years of the case (1981–1986). More proactive responses developed only after much urging and guidance by different judges and the court-appointed compliance officer, Tom Lonergan. Judges delegated to Lonergan significant powers to mediate between agencies and effect systemic solutions. In one of many detailed reports to the court, he diagnosed the loose coupling that characterized these subsystems: "There is a vast opportunity in the interaction of these governmental units for tasks to go unaccomplished, for responsibility to be ignored, for excuses to be offered instead of accomplished goals" (Report of Compliance Officer, *Branson v. Winter,* 1984, 5). More concerted efforts were needed if the courts were to end their longstanding involvement in the county's jail affairs. Lonergan suggested that interagency feuds had escalated the conflict and led to an unrealistic dependence upon the courts to resolve disputes.

> Until there is commitment from each agency in the criminal justice system
> . . . the problem with population control and management by crisis will
> continue. The local agencies must be made to realize that the solution lies
> within their own grasp and control and until they are willing to expend the
> effort necessary, will always elude them. Looking to the court to solve prob-
> lems created by local policy decisions is an abuse of process, and has led
> to the present stalemate. (Report of Compliance Officer, *Fischer v. Winter,*
> 1987, 10–11)

Some officials blamed court orders for a "siege mentality" whereby each agency attempted to protect its own interests. One official stated "that litigation created some of the most convoluted thinking I've ever seen." At one point, for example, the sheriff defied court orders by refusing probation officers entry into the jail to screen inmates for alternative programs.

The local legal, political, and organizational culture of Santa Clara contributed to the reactive stance demonstrated by county agencies. Santa Clara tripled its incarceration rate between 1976 and 1986, and experienced the greatest shortfall between jail population growth and jail capacity of the three counties studied (see Chapter 2). Several respondents suggested that individuals and agencies wanted to look tough on crime for political reasons, and found it convenient to blame "radical" judges for litigation problems.

Resource competition in the earlier stages of the case hindered proactive problem solving. In one view, litigation had had a positive effect on probation, "because it's got the probation department involved in the jail alternatives business . . . and we've been able to add staff." Indeed, probation increased its raw budget from 1976 to 1986, although its share of the total county criminal justice budget decreased by 8 percent. The sheriff's law enforcement and administrative budget experienced a more dramatic 21 percent decrease. Evidence suggested that this decrease was a direct result of conflict between the sheriff and the board of supervisors, and at least some of this conflict predated the jail litigation.

The board of supervisors, according to several respondents, accused the sheriff of deliberately overrunning his budget year after year, necessitating diversion of general funds from other county departments. The sheriff, perceiving that his interests were in conflict with those of the county, eventually hired his own legal counsel. One respondent noted: "There have been times when to interview the sheriff, for example, and a county executive, I'd have to have their lawyers present."

Attempts at proactive interagency solutions emerged, but only after persistent judicial prodding. Before the litigation, one official noted: "Everybody was doing their own thing. Everybody was behaving according to their statutory mandate, but in looking at a common issue, which is jail overcrowding, *nobody* is going to own that issue."

Numerous committees were eventually formed to deal with interagency issues related to jail litigation. Some committees lacked direction, frequently operating, according to one respondent, "in sort of an existential despair." The Justice System Steering Council, a loose, voluntary coalition of department heads, was compared to a dinner club; other committees, it was suggested, were dominated by "special interest groups" that pursued their own agendas. Certain agencies, according to one respondent, had not yet reached the point where officials could sit down as equals and negotiate: "There is an undertone of contest all the time between executive, judicial, and legislative branches in the county government." The Law Enforcement Executive Council (LEEC), which included police chiefs, sheriff's and probation representatives, the district attorney, and the county Department of Correction, received more positive reviews, "because we get down to the real nuts and bolts issues."

Numerous interagency reforms, including the use of alternatives to incarceration, were stimulated by court orders. After Judge Avakian took over the case in 1986, he ordered the sheriff to release all misdemeanor suspects with bails of $5,000 or less (*Branson v. Winter*, 7 May 1986). In 1988, 34,853 accused misdemeanants were cited and released at the jail. Further, on the theory that high-profile policing led to many unnecessary bookings into the county jail, a review of police charging practices was ordered (*Branson v. Winter*, 17 June 1986). Judge Avakian also ordered a review of prosecutorial screening procedures, suggesting that the district attorney took too long to file charges. Finding that county agencies were unwilling or unable to effect solutions on their own, the judge directed Lonergan to facilitate interagency cooperation in developing alternatives: "The compliance officer is authorized and directed to recommend and encourage the use by the various agencies involved in the arrest and detention of prisoners of all possible alternatives to confinement" (*Branson v. Winter*, 17 June 1986, 7).

The public service program (PSP), operated by the sheriff, expanded greatly as a result of court orders. Sentenced offenders performed community work, such as park and roadway maintenance, to reduce their sentences. An average of 400 inmates per month were on this program in fiscal year 1987–88 prior to the expiration of judicial supervision. The probation department, in cooperation with local courts, initiated a "Community Alternatives" program, which diverted sentenced offenders from jail and provided community service work, restitution programs, counseling, and other alternatives to incarceration. One respondent estimated that about 450 offenders were given this option over a three-year period. An electronic surveillance program, implemented in September 1987, processed 255 offenders in its first 10 months (Lang 1988). It was expanded to process about 200 people per month in early 1989. The probation department also increased screening of eligible offenders for county parole and work furlough as a direct result of court orders. About 200 people were on county parole in February 1989, and about 260 male inmates were on work furlough.

In Santa Clara, many interagency solutions emerged only after persistent pressure from the courts. The local legal and political culture resisted proactive problem solving, as five judges learned. Although court intervention increased interagency conflict, it also stimulated the proactive reforms needed to meet acceptable standards of jail confinement.

*Orange.* Court orders in Orange County were met at first by interagency conflict and competition. Until the county and the sheriff were found in contempt of court for noncompliance in 1985, the board of supervisors had left all jail matters to the sheriff. One official noted how relations changed following the contempt order.

> Before the contempt order . . . we really weren't getting this kind of information. . . . So the board really didn't begin to crystallize the issue. After that, there was a threat of contempt and that they would go to jail. Then they began to say, "Hey, wait a minute, we don't want to go to jail, and something's wrong here. For the last several years we have left it up to the CAO [county administrative officer] and the sheriff . . . to get recommendations for the board." And they weren't getting good recommendations. So then the board began to get actively involved directly into managing the jail.

After the contempt order, the board increasingly called upon the special master to supply information about jail conditions, demonstrating the loose coupling, and the information gap, that had characterized the system: "What happened was that the board used [the special master] as a go-between them and the sheriff [*sic*]. He really pointed out some things that we didn't know."

The sheriff's political power rivaled that of any board member. The board proceeded cautiously following court orders, while lamenting its lack of control over jail affairs.

> The board has some reluctance to get too deeply into some of this stuff in the sense that if the board starts imposing on the sheriff certain release dictates, then we're treading on the turf of a person who is powerful in his own right because he's an elected sheriff, . . . but also it exposes the board to some potential liabilities in terms of the jail overcrowding litigation that we really don't have muscle in that area.

As further evidence of loose coupling, some local judges complained that the sheriff had attempted to divert blame for jail problems to their own sentencing practices.

> When jail overcrowding first became a real hot issue, it looked to us as if the sheriff was attempting to put the judges in the middle, and to switch the blame from them to us: "Judges, look at all the people you're putting in jail; if you would do other things, we wouldn't have jail overcrowding." The problem is our job is to punish people. . . . So it was tempting to put us in a position of having to release people. And we weren't going to be put in that position. My position is: I'm going to put people in jail. If the sheriff wants to release them, that's the sheriff's business—not my business. I'm doing my job.

In contrast, some court officials were willing to broaden the responsibility of the judiciary to consider jail overcrowding: "We have to look for alternatives. We can be unrealistic about this and just say, 'Do crime, do time,' and turn to the Sheriff and say, 'That's your problem, buster.' We try to do that traditionally."

Alternatives to incarceration require proactive planning and coordination among multiple agencies. Until Judge Gray's 1985 contempt order, county officials had not seriously considered such alternatives: "[W]hen this whole jail overcrowding issue came to the forefront, then the board members began to take it more seriously [because] . . . the court was beginning to say, 'Well, look, you aren't providing the sheriff what he needs.' I think they then began to look at alternatives for incarceration."

In 1983, five years after Judge Gray's initial decision and order, Orange ranked fourteenth of 19 large California counties in the use of alternatives such as county parole, early release, and pretrial release (California Board of Corrections 1985). As one official noted, this aspect of the local political environment had already led to denials of the county's applications for state funding.

> We were turned away twice on the basis that the Board of Corrections was not convinced that Orange County had looked at alternatives to incarceration. At that point in time and history, I would have agreed with the Board of Corrections. I mean, Orange County was in a situation where if you asked them, "What have you done? What alternatives?" [they would say,] "Well, nothing. We still lock them up the old-fashioned way." Then they [the board] said, "Too bad. Go back and do your homework."

Other evidence (including agency reports) supports a causal relationship between court intervention and the county's serious consideration of alternatives. In a 1988 report to the board of supervisors (Correctional Consultants of California 1988, p. II-2), the special master, having then been appointed as a consultant to the county, stated: "Subsequent to the contempt of court finding, the county and sheriff initiated a series of actions designed to reduce overcrowding and meet the requirements of *Stewart v. Gates.*" Following the contempt order, the board requested that the County Administrative Office (CAO) conduct "a review of non–capital intensive alternative solutions to the jail overcrowding crisis" (County Administrative Office 1986, 1). The first serious attempts at coordinated problem solving now emerged: "To assist with the development of this document, the CAO has elicited input from the General Services Agency, the Environmental Management

Agency, the Courts, the Sheriff-Coroner, the Probation Department, the County Counsel in Orange County as well as other counties, and various state agencies" (p. 1).

Following the contempt order, Orange County created a supervised electronic confinement program in response to recommendations by the probation department and the special master. During a 12-month pilot program (Schumacher 1987), 133 inmates were placed on SEC. The sheriff also expanded his work release program, in which inmates work off their sentences at a rate of ten hours for one day off, and the courts have increased the use of community service, such as freeway clean-up, as a sentencing alternative (over 2,500 offenders in 1986). Under a county parole program implemented in response to court orders, 30 to 40 inmates were released in 1987, with plans for expansion. The CAO reported to the board of supervisors:

> With the impetus of meeting the steadily decreasing population limits set by the Federal Court and the estimation by the Sheriff of the need for additional bedspace to stay within those guidelines, the CAO requested County Counsel to review the applicable statutes and case law that set forth the provision for County Parole programs and the regulations pertaining thereto. (County Administrative Office 1986, 41)

As in Santa Clara, autonomous and reactive problem solving remained the norm in Orange County for a considerable time. Although Judge Gray attempted to stimulate coordinated planning by county agencies, loose coupling hindered proactive reforms and contributed, at least for a time, to competition and conflict among subsystems.

## Case Studies Summary

Responses to court orders varied according to the unique legal and political environments in each jurisdiction. Contra Costa revealed less resistance and more proactive interagency activity, thanks to the higher degree of interagency coordination that existed before the court orders. Contra Costa has a somewhat smaller population than the other two counties, and the tighter coupling observed is due in part to this difference in scale, as well as to punishment practices, budgetary allocations, and the behavior of key actors.

The leadership styles and attitudes of key actors (e.g., Stogdill 1974) were influential. Criminal justice subsystems certainly do not constitute rational forms of bureaucracy in the Weberian sense (Feeley 1973), but creative leadership from one or more officials may enhance tight coupling and expedite proactive solutions. Sheriff Rainey's efforts to build interagency support for jail and criminal justice reforms in Contra Costa helped avoid drawn-out litigation. The reverse is also true (e.g., McShane and Williams 1989); witness the acrimony between the sheriff and the board of supervisors in Santa Clara.

Judicial methods and mechanisms for monitoring and sanctioning compliance were also important influences on interagency relations. As judges sought to increase proactive and interagency responses by county officials, they did so with either a firm, guiding hand (the Conscientious Monitor) or with a task-oriented, conference-holding style (the Manager). Judges who intervened actively in the decisions of county government and justice officials were more likely to find widening rifts between those agencies and between the agencies and the courts. In Orange County, a contempt order was necessary to restart the planning process and motivate defendants. The role of Enforcer can thus be a useful one if used sparingly and consistently, and in the right circumstances (e.g., after more than ample time has been granted to submit jail plans). Major factors influencing interagency relations are summarized in Table 34 (for more detailed discussion of each, see Chapter 5).

Court-appointed special masters and group-level structures such as task forces and committees provide potentially powerful vehicles for developing a more proactive approach to criminal justice management and planning. The special master in Santa Clara was able to initiate and mediate productive discussions between highly polarized county

**TABLE 34**
**INTERAGENCY RELATIONS AND MAJOR INFLUENCES**

| Interagency Relations | Major Influences |
|---|---|
| Tight coupling | Preexisting relations among officials (good) |
| | Leadership by key actors (strong) |
| | County size (small) |
| | Roles of special Master (Negotiator) |
| | Threat or use of contempt (yes) |
| | Judicial methods (Conscientious Monitor/Manager) |
| Loose coupling | Resource competition (high) |
| | Historical jail conditions (poor) |
| | Preexisting relations among officials (poor) |
| | Leadership by key actors (weak) |
| | County size (large) |
| | Threat or use of contempt (no) |
| | Judicial methods (Intervenor) |

officials and subsystems, while some interagency groups and committees were particularly productive for developing cooperative solutions in Contra Costa. Neither special masters nor interagency committees provide panaceas, of course; each interacts with key actors and forces in the local environment. While frustrations are well known to special masters and members of interagency task forces, as witnessed by Orange and Santa Clara, key successes in each jurisdiction were also observed, particularly cooperation on the design of various alternatives to incarceration. Factors affecting the degree of success associated with each process are summarized in Table 35.

In both Orange and Santa Clara, the successes enjoyed by special masters were integrally dependent upon their technical as well as interpersonal skills, which allowed them to navigate the intricate political and organizational relationships encountered. Both had illustrious careers in corrections, and their technical expertise was beyond question. Firm support by the trial judge is essential: In spite of continual challenges to the special master in Santa Clara, successive judges upheld his authority and jurisdiction in almost every instance.

Key actors from different agencies must be (or become) willing and able to negotiate reforms. The passage of time and the persistence of judges, special masters, litigants, and other participants may bring some actors to a threshold of willingness to participate in cooperative reform efforts. In other cases, individual participants have, voluntarily or involuntarily, been removed from the search for solutions to jail problems. When the "body count" in Santa Clara got high enough, one official observed, negotiation began to seem wiser and more energy-

### TABLE 35
#### FACTORS INFLUENCING SUCCESS IN ACHIEVING PROACTIVE REFORMS

| Factors Influencing Success for Special Masters | Factors Influencing Success for Interagency Committees |
| --- | --- |
| • Judicial support for special master's recommendations <br> • Special master's technical knowledge <br> • Special masters' interpersonal skills <br> • Key officials' willingness and ability to comply <br> • Persistence by special master, judge, and participants | • Participation and leadership by key actors <br> • Key officials' willingness and ability to negotiate <br> • Clear group goals and purpose <br> • Formation of formal interagency agreements <br> • Persistence by special master, judge, and participants <br> • Size and scale of local justice system |

and cost-effective than obstruction of court-ordered reforms. Even in instances where neither firings nor unwanted transfers were imminent, key actors were highly motivated to end court monitoring and interference with their daily activities.

As noted above, court orders sharpened the perceived need for interagency solutions, as well as the need for the participation and creative leadership of key actors. Groups that made the most progress toward solutions were those that involved the appropriate decision-makers (as in Contra Costa), effective leadership (as in Contra Costa), clear goals (as with the LEEC in Santa Clara), and formal interagency agreements (as in Contra Costa's citation release program, Santa Clara's work release program, and Orange's work release and county parole programs).

Court orders sparked proactive reforms in the long run, but they also fueled conflict in the short run by requiring involuntary, increased coordination among agencies that typically handle problems in an autonomous, reactive manner. Of course, conflict may be necessary before organizational reform is possible (e.g., Brager and Holloway 1978; Coleman 1957). If loose coupling functions to protect organizational legitimacy by reducing accountability and hiding disjunctures between political claims and actions (Duffee 1989), forced interagency activity may be highly resisted. Judges who accurately diagnose jail problems as systemic in nature create demands to tighten the loose coupling that normally characterizes criminal justice agencies. The degree to which initial conflict leads to proactive and productive interagency responses depends upon the delicate mix of key actors (litigants, judges, special masters, politicians, justice system officials) and unique characteristics of the local legal and political environment.

## Summary

Court orders had an impact in four main areas: institutional conditions, structure and organization (e.g., population growth, jail capacity and staffing), correctional expenditures and local justice policies, and interagency coordination.

The degree and type of change involved depend upon the dynamic and interactive influence of various factors identified and discussed at each of the five stages of litigation (see Figure 1). Major "contingency" factors—those influencing observed variations in outcome—can be summarized under five main categories: environmental, judicial, plaintiff, defendant, and interagency (see Table 36).

## TABLE 36
### Factors Influencing Observed Variations in Outcomes

*Environment (before and after intervention)*

- Size and scale of the local justice system
- History of jail and punishment conditions
- Resource distribution and competition among county agencies
- Normative position relative to other counties in spending or policy innovation

*Judges*

- Nature and number of remedies specified
- Wording of court decrees and specificity of deadlines and assigned responsibilities
- Specification of clear sanctions and incentives for compliance
- Judicial methods and styles, persistence in monitoring and enforcing court-ordered reforms
- Limited mechanisms available to enforce compliance with orders
- Use of contempt proceedings
- Appointment of special master
- Judicial support for special master's recommendations

*Special Masters*

- Roles (fact-finder, expert, negotiator), technical knowledge, interpersonal skills, persistence, and innovation
- Lawsuit duration (court decision to measurement of outcomes)

*Plaintiffs*

- Breadth of alleged violations and bases for legal claims
- Type of legal representation, experience, and persistence in monitoring and enforcing court ordered reforms

*Defendants*

- Willingness and ability of key officials to comply
- Negotiation style (obfuscation, broken promises), skill, and determination to resist or delay compliance with court orders
- Willingness to use intermediate sanctions
- Anticipatory prevention

*Interagency Relations*

- Participation and leadership by key criminal justice actors in interagency planning
- Willingness and competence of key officials to negotiate interagency reform plans
- Clear group goals and purpose
- Formation of formal interagency agreements

Observed "impacts," as defined in any dynamic model, are only a part of the story of a jail lawsuit, not the end of it. We can distinguish between short-term and long-term impacts, depending upon the amount of time elapsed between the court decision and the measurement of outcomes, but we must make a choice to measure impact at a specific point in time, across some reasonable period before and after litigation. However, impacts measured at one time feed back into an ongoing, dynamic system (see Figure 1), and conditions defining this "new" system in any jurisdiction differ from prelitigation patterns in ways that can be empirically described—quantitatively, qualitatively, or both.

Historical conditions evolve and local environments change, setting the stage for an uncertain future. Will changes due to court orders persist over time? Will the courts prompt fundamental changes in local jails and justice systems? The next chapter summarizes findings from the five-stage model of litigation and discusses their implications for jail reform.

# CHAPTER 7

## Conclusions and Implications

What I was watching was what should have happened 10 years ago, and should happen every six months. You get a bunch of people in a room and they scream at each other until they get their system under control.

**—An attorney for plaintiffs in the Santa Clara lawsuit**

**M**Y GOAL in this book has been to explore jail reform litigation in a way that accounts for the dynamic interaction of actors, agencies, courts, and environments over time and across jurisdictions. With this exploratory journey behind us, it is germane now to return to broader questions. How and why is the law used to reform conditions of confinement in American jails, and with what results? How can counties avoid or end expensive litigation? This chapter summarizes the major findings and discusses implications for law, policy, and social change.

## Major Findings and Implications

First let us recall the five stages of jail litigation discussed above. In Stage 1, the Trigger Stage, conditions of the surrounding legal and political environment shape the onset of litigation. In Stage 2, the Liability Stage, a formal dispute is shaped by the interactions of plaintiffs' and defendants' counsel. In Stage 3, the Remedy Stage, remedies are shaped by preceding actions and events, and by further interactions between litigants, judges, and county officials. In Stage 4, the Postdecree Stage, remedies are modified and specific solutions are implemented, as litigants negotiate over acceptable conditions of compliance and disengagement by the court. In Stage 5, institutional, organizational, and systemic impacts emerge, leading to conditions that may or may not stabilize over time. These changes alter the environment and dynamically shape future policies and disputes. Major findings from each of the five stages are discussed below.

## The Trigger Stage

On a broad, national level, five interactive factors in the political environment have contributed to jail overcrowding and court intervention: public attitudes; demographic, social, and economic conditions; the organizational climate of jails; law enforcement and punishment policies; and resource shortages or imbalances. Increasingly harsh punishment policies since 1980 provide the strongest general explanation of pervasive jail overcrowding and litigation.

At the local level, historical jail conditions and punishment patterns affect a county's "risk" of court intervention. In general, counties characterized by more punitive punishment environments are more likely to face court intervention—those with high incarceration rates, highly overcrowded jails, low prisoner expenditures, and old or badly designed jail facilities. Indeed, such results are expected if there is any rationality to jail lawsuits at all. To justify court intervention, there must be at least some crude correspondence between *complaints* about jail conditions and *actual* jail conditions. Public officials' complaints that jail lawsuits are merely the product of "crazy lawyers" and "radical judges" are unsupported, as are relationships between crime rates and jail overcrowding, suggesting that such perceptions largely reflect self-serving organizational "myths" (De Neufville and Barton 1987) rather than reality.

Punishment patterns, while powerful predictors, are not the only factors that affect the likelihood of court intervention. Many small counties get sued, and many large ones do not, but the risk of court intervention increases and covaries with county population. The disproportionate risk of large urban counties for court intervention reflects at least partially the negative influence of criminal justice volume, large-scale bureaucracy, or both.

The volume of criminal justice business in large jurisdictions greatly increases the need for the efficient processing and detention of accused and convicted offenders. There are many more people to book, more people to arraign, more people to hold pending trial, more people to transport to court, more people to supervise, clothe, and feed, and more people to find beds for. If resources and official competence in large jurisdictions were commensurate with the huge criminal justice volume, perhaps all would be well. Unfortunately, large volume seems to tax both to the breaking point.

Resource shortage, imbalance, and competition all contribute to jail overcrowding and litigation. Resource shortages do not excuse constitutional violations, but the burden upon local government for justice expenditures has increased in recent years, and longstanding apathy toward jail conditions, combined with more recent budget shortages, strengthens predispositions toward lawsuits and court intervention. Shortages, in turn, have exacerbated resource competition among county justice agencies. An imbalance favoring courts and prosecution, and shortchanging probation suggests a "punitive climate" in many counties under court order. Ironically, those counties with the greatest difficulties in controlling their jail populations seem least cognizant of the burdens that such imbalance places on the jail: greater intake, fewer alternative dispositions, and less efficient outflow when, for example, probation terms tend to be tacked on to the end of jail sentences.

In large jurisdictions, the competence of officials to manage large jail populations effectively has long been questioned. There are certainly jurisdictions to be found where jail managers are competent administrators and leaders, and jail workers are well trained and well supervised. However, as discussed in Chapter 2, those who manage jails have traditionally had little specialized interest or training in corrections. Correctional training provided by cities or counties has often ranged from nonexistent to cursory, and poorly trained, poorly paid, and poorly supervised personnel have traditionally staffed American jails. Indeed, one could argue that improved standards for jail management and staff selection, training, and supervision over the past 15 years are among the major achievements of court intervention.

Legal environments in different states provide varying opportunities for jail litigation. California's liberal habeas corpus laws provided a climate favorable to prisoner litigation, so that the majority of jail reform lawsuits there were initiated in state rather than federal courts. Legal mobilization was also influenced by choice of plaintiffs' counsel. "Ideological attorneys" (repeat players such as the ACLU) targeted jails with the most grievous violations, usually in large urban areas, and filed a small number of cases, usually in federal court. Ideological attorneys, more familiar with federal law and more comfortable with federal judges, carefully chose important test cases in which to establish legal precedents. Private counsel, the most numerous plaintiff attorneys in jail lawsuits, also initiated jail litigation mostly in urban areas, but more frequently in state than in federal courts. Private counsel in this study were usually located near San Francisco or Los Angeles, which have a high density of skilled, "entrepreneurial" lawyers. Public counsel represented inmates exclusively in state court, generally in more rural areas where specialized attorneys were either unavailable or uninterested in the case.

## The Liability Stage

At the Liability Stage, both plaintiffs and defendants attempt to shape a strong court record to influence judicial decisions. The legal complaint filed by plaintiffs names certain officials as defendants, identifies specific violations of prisoners' rights, and offers legal bases for claims. Defendants, in turn, respond to the complaint, typically in a terse manner, contesting many or all claims by plaintiffs on procedural and substantive grounds.

Differences in legal "claiming" provide one of the most critical earmarks distinguishing jail reform lawsuits from their state or federal prison counterparts. Provisions of state law frequently provided the basis for legal claims by plaintiffs in jail lawsuits, in both federal and state courts. In California, the state constitution's ban against cruel and unusual punishment, the state Jail Standards, Penal Code, Health and Safety Code, Fire Code, and other provisions of state law were used in 86 percent of complaints resulting in liability decisions. State laws vary greatly, but they receive careful attention in jail lawsuits in any state, and findings of violations of state law are not easily subject to reversal by the Supreme Court.

After reading numerous complaints, I was struck by the similarity of wording. Violations alleged and legal bases for claims across jurisdictions seemed to repeat themselves. Particularly striking was the similarity to previously successful complaints filed in federal courts. Clearly, experienced litigators have learned a formula for successful "claiming" in jail lawsuits. Such similarities stem from the search for relevant legal precedents, with special attention to successful cases in one's own state. Similarities in complaints filed by plaintiffs' attorneys in different cases are also related to the open communication I witnessed between several of them, especially the "repeat players."

Certain core issues substantiated by state and federal law formed the major basis for complaints in California jail lawsuits. Federal law is, of course, consistent across the states, but the unique legal environment of any one state in conjunction with federal law offers unique opportunities for prisoner litigation. This legal environment helps to mold the core violations filed against county jails in a particular state. The claiming process is guided by three questions asked by plaintiffs' attorneys: (1) what seems to work in other jail lawsuits in this state?

(2) what is supportable by law? and (3) what is supportable by evidence? The violations most frequently cited by plaintiffs affected basic living conditions and were well grounded in state law and supported by federal case law. They included, in descending frequency, overcrowding, recreation, hygiene, access to courts, medical care, sanitation, food, heating and ventilation, visitation, lighting, inmate safety, and classification procedures. Empirical evidence enumerated inmates sleeping on floors or in gymnasiums, hours that inmates are allowed outside their cells, showers or changes of clothes allowed per week, requests for legal materials and staff responses, requests for medical care and staff responses, cell toilets in disrepair, meals served (quantity and nutritional value), average daily temperatures in living units, visits allowed per week, broken and unreplaced light bulbs in living units, reported assaults on inmates and on guards, and inmates assigned to different housing types and security classifications, such as general population or administrative segregation.

The number and type of violations alleged in a specific lawsuit set the initial boundaries for legal discourse among plaintiffs, defendants, and the judge. As this discourse over jail conditions, law, and evidence evolves, it shapes subsequent events in a lawsuit—the liability decision and specific remedies.

Ideological attorneys filed the most alleged violations in jail lawsuits, partly because of more serious jail conditions (high overcrowding and low prisoner expenditures), and partly because of a broader litigation strategy aimed at establishing important test cases. Ideological attorneys, as noted above, filed lawsuits more frequently in federal courts, partly due to their greater familiarity with precedents related to federal case law and constitutional law, and partly due to greater perceived expertise, autonomy, and powers of the federal judiciary.

The defendants named in jail lawsuits are the specific actors whom plaintiffs seek to hold accountable for illegal jail conditions. Those defendants play an important role in negotiating remedies, defining compliance with court decrees, and shaping eventual impacts of court decrees. County supervisors were named as defendants in fewer than two-thirds of jail lawsuits. The critical variable that determines whether plaintiffs name supervisors as defendants is the nature of plaintiffs' legal representation. Supervisors were almost certain to be named as defendants by ideologically committed attorneys; in contrast, they were named as defendants by private attorneys in about two of every three cases, and by public counsel in about one of every three cases. Legal complaints naming county supervisors as defendants also

evidenced more punitive but underfunded jail environments. More experienced "repeat players" targeted jurisdictions with more serious
conditions and attempted to assign responsibility to key government
officials as a means of achieving jail reform. Public and private counsel,
less experienced in jail litigation and more likely to possess direct or
indirect ties to the local political environment, showed greater restraint. As some have suggested (e.g., Kessler 1990), state courts exert a
"chilling" influence on social reform litigation, but the effect observed
here is only on the naming of certain defendants, and not on the decision to file a lawsuit in state court per se.

*The Remedy Stage*

Remedy formulation in jail lawsuits is shaped by the specific legal
claims and violations alleged, requests for specific relief, the litigation
strategies of plaintiffs and defendants, judicial methods for decree formulation, negotiations between litigants and judges, and the continuing influence of forces in the local legal and political environments.

In original court decisions, a higher number of specified remedies
was related to the number of violations alleged in the original complaint, the level of court (federal), the defendants named in jail lawsuits
(county supervisors), and strong legal bases and supporting evidence
for claims. A high number of violations alleged is related to more grievous jail conditions, but it also reflects the efforts of plaintiff attorneys.
Ideologically motivated attorneys target jurisdictions with more serious
violations, file more violations, and gain more relief. Similarly, lawsuits where county supervisors were named as defendants showed
greater patterns of jail violations. Ideological attorneys, because of their
greater experience and autonomy from local political environments,
were more likely to name supervisors in such suits. Federal courts
granted twice as many remedies to plaintiffs as state courts, suggesting
federal judges' greater persistence and independence from local political environments.

Over the history of a case, the influence of federal judges on the
total number of remedies specified diminishes (see Table 15). Federal
judges were more likely to grant relief only in specific areas where constitutional rights were clearly established, such as visitation and medical care. Total remedies were more strongly influenced, in the long run,
by the involvement of ideological counsel and supervisor defendants,
reflecting the more serious nature of jail conditions in those cases, as
well as the greater resources and persistence of ideological counsel in
holding county supervisors ultimately accountable for jail conditions.

Do plaintiffs get the relief they want? To answer this question, I compared the remedies granted in original court decisions with the relief requested in complaints. In original court decisions, the most common outcome per violation alleged is that no relief whatsoever is granted. The court's disallowing of claims was related to the weakness of evidence for some claims, but also to the influence of state courts, whose judges were more conservative in granting relief overall. Even when county supervisors are not named in lawsuits, state court judges are constrained by their ties to local legal and political environments, suggesting further "chilling effects" once a lawsuit in state court gets to the remedy stage.

Judicial orders to produce written plans addressing jail conditions were relatively common in original court decisions. In such cases, jail conditions were relatively stable, if not ideal. Providing that defendants also acknowledged certain deficiencies in jail conditions and expressed a willingness to ameliorate them, judges preferred to allow defendants time to develop and submit their own plans.

It is also relatively common for plaintiffs to get approximately what they sought in the complaint—increases in visitation and recreation time, improvements in food and medical care, and the like. This happened when prisoner needs were well demonstrated, legal bases for claims were well established, and claims were well substantiated by evidence. Plaintiffs rarely got more than they asked for. In one case inmates seeking a review of procedures for responding to requests for medical care did achieve an order of "greater" relief: After an intense review of evidence and state law, the county was required to construct and staff a small medical unit within the jail.

Because jail conditions often worsen between the filing of a complaint and the issuing of a decision, sometimes a remedy responds not to plaintiffs' original request for relief, but to present jail conditions. In the interim, new evidence is introduced, and new solutions are suggested and negotiated by litigants. For example, defendants may acknowledge that overcrowding is a serious problem, and the court may prescribe better pretrial release mechanisms to reduce jail intake, more postconviction release options to reduce jail time served, or the construction of new jail cells.

Finally, different types of remedies may be specified over the history of a jail lawsuit. The most common reforms ordered involved reduced crowding, improved medical care, hygiene, early release of convicted inmates, recreation, expedited release of pretrial inmates, sanitation, access to courts, food services, visitation, and classification procedures. Some of these remedies are directly related to overcrowding; others deal with conditions exacerbated by severe overcrowding.

All remedies are related to the strength of legal bases for claims and the strength of evidence presented, but we have seen that two constellations of remedies were additionally influenced by the level of court and the type of defendants named. Federal judges were most likely to order relief in the areas of medical care, recreation, visitation, and classification, where federal case law is well established. In a second group of remedies, judges held county supervisors uniquely responsible for several unpopular and expensive reforms: jail population caps and the early release of nonviolent offenders to reduce overcrowding; and increased staffing and improvements to the jail's physical plant (including new jail construction), which require budget allocations authorized by county supervisors. Such changes are directly and justifiably the responsibilities of county supervisors.

Defendants' participation in remedy formulation was related to six factors: leadership by key actors, seriousness of jail conditions, previous success at negotiations, the quality of relations among county officials, the complexity of problems and solutions, and the degree to which many actors are needed to reach a consensus decision.

Effective leadership by key actors—judges, sheriffs, county officials, counsel for defendants and plaintiffs—is necessary to get different parties who speak different "languages" together to negotiate. In Contra Costa, officials praised the leadership of the state court judge and the sheriff in bringing key county officials together to discuss solutions to jail problems. The judge had an office right across the street from the jail, and was familiar with jail conditions and jail personnel. While the judge's order left discretion to the sheriff, the sheriff immediately implemented a coordinated plan, delegating responsibility to specific personnel to address all issues defined by the order.

Serious jail conditions, especially if they get worse during the negotiation phase, increase both time and political pressures on discussants. Crises may derail negotiations. Although overcrowding in Contra Costa was still a concern at the negotiation stage, jail conditions were less urgent than in the other two counties studied because a new jail had opened four years before the court order. In contrast, Judge Leahy in Santa Clara emphasized early in the case the importance of addressing overcrowding that was reaching "crisis proportions." When defendants failed to carry out the plans they had offered, Leahy began ordering more unpopular population reduction methods, such as early releases of some sentenced prisoners. Similarly, by the time Judge Gray issued his decision in the Orange County case on 3 May 1978, over-crowding had worsened considerably, complicating potential negotiations and necessitating immediate action in the form of population caps.

Some previous success at negotiations, between the filing of the complaint and the issuance of the court's decision, can establish a critical foundation for later discussions between plaintiffs and defendants. Prior to issuing his only orders in Contra Costa, the judge brought county officials together several times to discuss jail problems and possible solutions. Officials had previously negotiated on numerous issues in addition to the county jail case. Negotiations in Santa Clara were tense in the early stages of remedy formulation (under Judge Leahy), and nearly absent in the middle stages (under Judge Allen). In Orange, three years of discovery, testimony, review, and stalled negotiations elapsed between the filing of the original complaint in 1975 and the court decision in 1978. Although defendants and plaintiffs in Orange were able to negotiate one stipulated agreement in 1977 over provision of medical and dental care, most issues remained contested until Judge Gray ruled on these in his Memorandum to Counsel of 26 January 1978.

Relations among county officials can facilitate or impede negotiations at the remedy stage. A participatory style of negotiation in Contra Costa was greatly aided by the fact that county officials already knew each other and the judge quite well, and communicated regularly on both a formal and an informal basis. Poor relations among Santa Clara County officials (particularly between the sheriff and the county supervisors) contributed to the county's early inability and unwillingness to negotiate. In both Orange and Santa Clara, strained relations between county officials made negotiations difficult.

The greater the complexity of jail problems in any jail case, the greater the demands upon discussants' patience, competence, and willingness to find solutions. Contra Costa's problems were relatively straightforward: 7 alleged violations and 8 remedies. In contrast, complaints in Orange and Santa Clara each contained 19 alleged violations. Twenty-nine orders were issued over the history of the Orange County case; 147 orders were issued in the Santa Clara case. By the time Judge Gray issued his 1976 pretrial conference order summarizing facts contested (72) and facts uncontested (7), it was clear that complexity would hamper negotiations in Orange.

Finally, negotiations are more complex and time-consuming when many actors are needed to reach a consensus decision. In Contra Costa, relatively few key officials were required to reach consensus on major decisions; in the larger, more urban counties, many actors in many county departments and agencies had input into decisions about funding, planning, land use, law enforcement, and courts.

How judges collected information, conducted negotiations, and formulated remedies depended on at least five factors: whether we examined the process early or later in the Remedy Stage; judicial experience and expertise; defendants' acceptance of judicial authority; needs for more evidence; and changes in jail conditions preceding remedy formulation. We observed two main styles of judicial method at this stage. We called the first the Conscientious Monitor. In the early stages of remedy formulation, judges often attempted to facilitate discussions between plaintiffs and defendants, dispose of contested issues, and encourage defendants to develop written plans to address jail problems. This strategy worked best when defendants accepted judicial authority, as in Contra Costa. Judge Arneson, having heard every petition filed by prisoners in Contra Costa for some years, had considerable experience and credibility in jail issues. In Orange, Judge Gray patiently reviewed evidence for 30 months prior to his original court decision. Experienced in complex civil lawsuits, with a reputation for being tough but fair, Gray had made it clear that he would limit the court's authority to clear constitutional violations, but would fully enforce whatever orders he felt necessary.

Later in the remedy formulation process, judges may become impatient with defendants' efforts and take on the role of Intervenor. In Santa Clara, challenges to judicial authority facilitated a shift toward greater intervention in the affairs of county justice and government. Despite encouragement, defendants failed to develop plans to address jail problems, and both Leahy and Allen showed impatience. As jail conditions got worse, judicial methods became more interventionist.

Leahy first issued population caps to leverage the county to develop its own plans. When the county's efforts failed, he began instituting more unpopular mechanisms, such as early release of sentenced offenders. After Leahy's disqualification, the entire Superior Court bench disqualified itself from hearing the case. Judge Allen, appointed by the state Judicial Council, became increasingly frustrated with the county's inability to develop cost-effective, useful, and adequate jail plans, while the county became increasingly deaf to the suggestions of the court. The judge began to issue "interventionist" orders, demanding (among other things) that the county refrain from selling land that could be used for jail expansion, and that it call a special vote to decide on tax increases for jail funding. The defendants appealed such orders.

Although both Leahy and Allen had extensive experience on the bench, neither had ever presided over a complex civil lawsuit against public officials. Greater experience might have fostered the patient but firm style of the Conscientious Monitor, along with a more incremental approach to change.

Small, gradual efforts to shape negotiations and remedies are appropriate where several public officials have conflicting or poorly conceived definitions of the problem, possible solutions, and the goals of change. The incremental approach relieves judges as well as public officials from the daunting responsibility of considering all possible policy options and their consequences at once. It allows for gradual experimentation and expects unanticipated consequences. It invites rather than avoids the accommodation of diverse interests affected by the courses of action considered. Modest rather than sweeping goals are set at any one time, followed by a period of gradual implementation, monitoring, evaluation, and review. As one advocate of the incremental approach suggests, those who adopt more autocratic or activist approaches to change are likely to be disappointed.

> "Fiery" politicians, neophyte social reformers, and "maverick" administrators tend to equate incrementalism with defeatism, "doing nothing," or "selling out." But those politicians, activists, and administrators who ply their trade long enough learn that incrementalism is often the best, or the only, approach to effecting and sustaining needed changes. (DiIulio 1990, 297)

## The Postdecree Stage

Jail lawsuits involving polycentric problems make it hard to define and obtain compliance. Actions, conditions, and events from previous stages of litigation continue to influence postdecree outcomes such as lawsuit duration, judicial methods, remedy modification, nature of negotiations, and mechanisms of monitoring and compliance.

As we have seen, it is difficult to say exactly how long a lawsuit should go on, or when defendants are in "substantial" compliance with remedial orders, or at what point the court should disengage. Changes in environmental conditions such as jail overcrowding may themselves create new problems, as when plans to construct new jail facilities are blocked by partisan neighborhood politics and inadequate county resources.

Many factors influenced whether lawsuits dragged on: the nature and number of remedies specified, the level of court, and the type of defendants. When the original court decision specified more, or more substantial, remedies, defendants had to work harder to comply, the court and plaintiffs' counsel had more to monitor, and difficulties were more likely to surface. Certain types of remedies, including population caps, fuel controversial policy choices such as jail construction and the use of intermediate sanctions. The planning, time, competence, and finances required for such options make delays in compliance likely.

Federal judges participate in longer lawsuits largely because they possess greater experience in remedial decree cases and show greater persistence. Judicial persistence spells longer periods of monitoring and greater reluctance to relinquish jurisdiction in the face of incomplete compliance. As one inmate attorney noted, "There are two extremes. At one end, the judge won't even hear the case. At the other end, judges are exceedingly firm in making an order and achieving compliance." Naturally, judicial persistence is associated with defendant resistance.

County supervisors displayed frequent noncompliance and resistance throughout the Postdecree Stage. More likely to litigate than capitulate, at least initially, county supervisors may, in extreme cases, wage a "war of attrition" to delay unpopular and expensive policy choices. This is a war that the federal courts and ideological counsel are best equipped to wage.

Defendants' and plaintiffs' counsel can negotiate remedy modification and define compliance in a variety of ways. More formal negotiations are called for when historical jail conditions are poor, problems and solutions are highly complex, many actors are needed for consensus, opposing counsel are hostile, and relations between county officials are strained. Defendants may use negotiations to resist or delay compliance by refusing to submit required plans, by filing an inadequate plan (obfuscation), or by submitting a large set of undifferentiated plans that allow them to claim compliance but force judges and plaintiffs' counsel to wade through and critically evaluate a mass of materials (broken promises). In some cases, defendants submit "leverage" plans: plans that local governments lack the will or resources to implement, but can use to extract additional resources from state or federal governments. Ideological attorneys, in contrast to private or public counsel, show greater persistence in seeking compliance, and possess the skills and experience needed to recognize and counter "stonewalling" by defendants.

Judges adopt different methods in remedy modification, negotiating, and monitoring compliance, and they do so at different stages of a case. Early in the Postdecree Stage, judges often adopt a Conscientious

Monitor role, attempting to stimulate litigants to develop specific plans of action. Over time, though, many judges find it necessary to set limits as negotiations succeed in some areas and fail in others. Depending on their own styles and such local conditions as the quality of relations between county officials, the size of the county, and the number of decision-makers, some judges may adopt the role of Manager, orchestrating negotiations with defendants and plaintiffs in chambers, facilitating their discussions, and focusing their attention on developing strategies to meet constitutional standards. Where these methods fail, judges may shift toward a more active Intervenor role and begin adding remedies that increasingly limit official discretion. In the extreme form of this style, as exemplified by Judge Allen in Santa Clara, an Intervenor may temporarily take over all decisions regarding jail operations and expenditures, limited only by appellate review. When resistance by defendants is pronounced, judicial options are more limited, leading to a shift toward an Enforcer role, with threats or application of sanctions. In Santa Clara, judges with different personal views took very similar actions, according to one observer:

> [A]ll the judges were very clear in their political waverings or leanings. No matter which end of the political spectrum they were on, they had the same reactions to and from county government in this case. It was not going to happen, and they were going to be frustrated and kind of bitter at the end. Each one of them, I think, towards the end, was extremely frustrated and bitter.

Much later in a lawsuit, when defendants finally demonstrate substantial compliance, judges shift toward a Conciliator role and attempt to tie up legal loose ends and disengage from further court involvement.

Judicial methods are related to court venue. State court judges, for example, were more likely to be Managers and Intervenors. They tended more often to get involved in the *means* of compliance, by intervening in the affairs of local criminal justice agencies and/or engineering negotiations between key actors. Those who did so successfully (for several examples, see Chapter 5) benefited from their familiarity with local incumbents and justice agencies, a high degree of credibility, and personal political power. Such judges correctly diagnosed jail problems as systemic and resolved to get multiple agencies to take responsibility for developing solutions. State court judges who lack familiarity, credibility, and political power, however, would be well advised to avoid the Intervenor role. Federal judges were more likely to enact the roles of Conscientious Monitor and Enforcer, specifying specific *out-*

*comes* to be achieved (such as jail population reduction), and persistently monitoring and sanctioning noncompliance.

Remedies may be modified many times in jail lawsuits, as the complex legal and practical issues in each case interact with judicial experience and methods and the experience and behavior of opposing counsel. A judge with a "give and take" style listens carefully to arguments from opposing counsel and relies upon a strong court record shaped by each. He or she attributes credibility to both defendants and plaintiffs, and over time grants something to each. Experienced counsel tend to define legal issues and actions required for compliance more narrowly, as do more experienced judges. A "muddling" style, in contrast, reflects uncertainty on the parts of judges and opposing counsel, overly vague definitions of problems and the actions required for compliance, low familiarity with correctional law, and lack of a guiding philosophy of change, such as incrementalism.

Special masters also assume diverse roles in the Postdecree Stage, including those of Fact-finder, Expert, Mediator/Negotiator, and Intervenor. Like judicial methods, the roles enacted by special masters vary at different times in the case and depend upon several factors: judicial definition of powers, the personal expertise and experience of both the judge and the special master, historical jail conditions, and patterns of noncompliance.

Contempt can be a forceful method of gaining compliance, although its use in jail lawsuits is rare. Its successful use requires judicial resolve, patience, and experience, acceptance of legitimacy by defendants, a strong court record shaped by plaintiffs' counsel, and expectation of favorable review by the appellate court. Continual derailment of contempt proceedings and unenforced threats of contempt weaken judicial credibility and sanctioning power.

As others have shown in public policy litigation settings, county defendants' eventual acceptance of judicial authority and their willingness and competence to comply remain crucial factors in the reform process. While the alignment of all three factors is rare at the onset of jail litigation, litigation can be the crucible that creates or strengthens defendants' acceptance, willingness, and competence.

## The Impact Stage

Diverse impacts evolve dynamically over the life of a jail lawsuit and beyond. Designating a separate conceptual "stage" following the Postdecree Stage does not imply that impacts emerge only in a linear fashion, at a single point in time, or in a static environment. Indeed, the threat of a lawsuit alone (the Trigger Stage) sometimes provides sufficient motivation to change jail or criminal justice operations. Changes can also emerge through negotiations at the Liability, Remedy, and Postdecree Stages.

We identified four major types of impacts, ranging from very *localized* ones (within the jail) to *systemic* ones that alter relationships between agents and agencies in fundamental ways.

*Institutional Conditions.* Court decrees have addressed overcrowding, medical care, visitation, access to courts, recreation, personal hygiene, food services, sanitation, staffing, and classification (Chapter 4). Although neither judges, litigants, nor county officials were completely satisfied with the outcome of cases, most parties agreed that significant improvements in jail conditions occurred.

Reviews of court documents, examination of statistical data, visits to jails in three sites, and interviews with county officials, judges, and litigants confirmed that the most extreme violations preceding court intervention have been alleviated. For example, overcrowding has been reduced, jail populations are much more efficiently managed in terms of intake, housing, movement, and release, and basic needs such as beds, clothing, and food are being provided. New jail facilities were often needed to meet basic standards of confinement.

In most cases jail conditions were improved to meet minimum standards required by the federal constitution, the state constitution, and the state's Minimum Jail Standards, Penal Code, Health and Safety Code, and Fire Code. On the other hand, at least two of the three case studies showed incomplete compliance. The court must eventually disengage, and it does so upon "good faith" demonstration of compliance, not complete compliance. Thus, in Santa Clara, we saw remaining problems with staffing, supervision of inmates, food service, and medical care. In Orange, difficulties remained with inmate medical requests, disciplinary hearings, staffing, funding, and jail facilities. The courts have encouraged county officials to pay much greater attention to jail conditions than in the past, but it is not easy to extend the official will and funding required to maintain, monitor, and improve jail conditions past the point of court disengagement.

To monitor and evaluate jail conditions over time, jails and prisons need better performance measures and states must regulate them more strictly. Court intervention has helped refine criteria for reasonable jail standards and performance, and has encouraged agencies such as the American Jail Association, the American Correctional Association, and the National Institute of Corrections to clarify standards and motivate

jails to "self-audit" (Feeley and Hanson 1990). Many states are reviewing their regulatory laws to specify more precise standards and mechanisms of accountability for jails. Accountability, however, requires
fiscal and political resources that have not always been forthcoming.
California's Board of Corrections (BOC), responsible for inspecting
county jails and monitoring compliance with state standards, has long
been understaffed, and the agency lacks the formal sanctioning power
needed to correct violations. Compliance with state jail standards has
generally been voluntary, and no county has ever lost its state funding
as a result of negative reports or recommendations made by BOC.

Precise standards for jail conditions and stronger mechanisms of
accountability require more unambiguous measures of performance
(Logan 1993) in at least eight areas: security ("keep them in"); safety
("keep them safe"): order ("keep them in line"); care ("keep them
healthy"); activity ("keep them busy"); justice ("do it fairly"); conditions ("without undue suffering"); and management ("as efficiently as
possible"). Institutional records and surveys of inmates and staff are
our two main sources of data, but it would be expensive to conduct
detailed jail audits on a consistent basis. Without clearly specified
sanctions and mechanisms for achieving compliance with state jail
standards, little progress can be expected from individual counties
after court disengagement.

*Structural and Organizational Impacts.* Court orders have facilitated jail expansion (increases in jail capacity and staffing) and slowed
rates of growth in jail populations, although the magnitude of effects
varies considerably across individual counties. This book illustrates
three complementary judicial emphases: the need to limit current inmate populations, the need to provide adequate staffing, and the need
to renovate or expand existing jail facilities. In many cases, judges diagnosed constitutional violations as stemming from overcrowding and
understaffing, and they frequently issued explicit orders to build or expand facilities and increase staffing levels. Even if not ordered to build,
defendants often perceived that the only way to meet court-decreed
constitutional standards for inmate safety and supervision was to close
old, poorly designed, deteriorating facilities and build new ones. Court
orders have therefore forced counties to *keep pace* with jail needs,
counteracting the tendency toward inertia. Judges vary a good deal,
however, in their persistence and willingness to use sanctions.

Judicial orders requiring expansion are most effective when the
wording of orders is clear and forceful, sanctions for noncompliance
are specified in advance (including heavy fines, contempt orders, or

reopening of the case), incentives for compliance are clear to defendants, and defendants are both willing and competent to implement prescribed changes.

*Correctional Expenditures and Policies.* County officials, we saw, responded to court orders in different ways, sometimes resisting cost-intensive jail improvements, because of unwillingness or inability to pay for them, sometimes increasing their use of less capital-intensive methods such as intermediate sanctions, to comply with court orders at lower cost. In the absence of strong court intervention, as applied by a Conscientious Monitor, Intervenor, or Enforcer (see Chapter 5), some counties have coped with budget crises by reducing expenditures on their politically vulnerable jails. Some counties not under court order spent more money on jail construction or operations, perhaps hoping to *avoid* potential court intervention—a policy of "anticipatory prevention." Some changes emerged too slowly to be detected in a brief post-intervention period. Responses to court orders depend partly on the number and type of remedies specified. Direct orders to make capital-intensive improvements in staffing or building give counties less flexibility and a greater financial burden.

Clearly, judicial orders have not unanimously or unambiguously increased correctional expenditures. Judges have, however, raised the priority of correctional issues on local policy agendas. Whether that translates into increased expenditures or not depends upon various contingencies. Court orders exert the strongest impact on expenditures when: (1) counties resist using intermediate sanctions and doggedly cling to a "building" strategy; (2) a county lags substantially behind others in its normative position with respect to spending (on modern jail facilities, for example) and policy innovations like intermediate sanctions; (3) judges are persistent in enforcing their orders and specify clear deadlines and sanctions; and (4) those orders are capital-intensive, dealing with staffing, adding jail beds, new medical facilities, and the like.

It is not clear that judicial persistence can in all cases overcome skilled and determined resistance. The possibility remains that stubborn defendants can delay or avoid cost-intensive jail reform, so that in some cases a low rate of change in correctional expenditures will follow a court order.

*Systemwide Impacts.* Court orders against jails represent sudden changes in the local environment that put pressure on entire criminal justice systems to alter the routine processing of accused and convicted offenders. Courts seek to increase county responsibility for jail and criminal justice planning, and court intervention creates pressures toward more proactive, interagency planning rather than the "loose coupling" that so often characterizes county government and justice systems.

Systemwide responses to court orders in each county depended on each one's unique legal and political environment. We observed that differences in "coupling" before court intervention were partly due to differences in county size and scale, although historical punishment practices, resource competition, and the behavior of key actors also had an effect. Strong preexisting relationships among officials tighten coupling and improve interagency planning, and so do judicial methods that require clear outcomes (comprehensive jail plans), specific deadlines, and firm monitoring (Conscientious Monitor style) and task-oriented interagency negotiation (the Manager style). Judges who intervened too actively in the decisions of county government and justice were more likely to find a widening rift between themselves and defendants.

Court-appointed special masters and group-level structures such as task forces and committees can help develop a proactive approach to criminal justice management and planning. Groups made the most progress toward interagency solutions when they included appropriate decision-makers and had effective leadership, clear goals, and formal interagency agreements. Neither special masters nor interagency committees provide a panacea, of course: Each interacts with key actors and forces in the local environment. While frustrations are well known to special masters and members of interagency task forces, as witnessed by Orange and Santa Clara, key successes in each jurisdiction were also observed, notably cooperation on the design of alternatives to incarceration.

The successes enjoyed by special masters in both Orange and Santa Clara depended on their technical as well as interpersonal skills and the expertise and prestige derived from distinguished careers in corrections. Firm support by the trial judge is also essential: Several judges in Santa Clara upheld the special master's authority in the face of repeated challenges.

No progress toward proactive solutions can be made until key actors from different agencies are willing and able to negotiate reforms. Over time, judges, special masters, litigants, and other participants can prod officials to discuss their own participation in cooperative reform efforts, though some can never be brought to this point. In many cases, such as *Ruiz*, recalcitrant officials are eventually forced out of their positions (Martin and Ekland-Olson 1987). Whether initial conflict leads to proactive and productive interagency responses depends, as we have seen, on the mix of players—litigants, judges, special masters, politicians, justice system officials—and the unique characteristics of the local legal and political environment.

## Needs for Research on Court-Ordered Reform

The analysis of jail litigation I presented here attempts to account not only for litigation process but also for the interactive and dynamic influence of local legal, political, and organizational environments on systemic adaptations to court-ordered reform. This diversity is not easily captured by research, whether it takes the form of "single case" studies of particular legal cases, "single issue" studies of particular factors, such as normative views about proper judicial roles, "single actor" studies of particular players (often judges), or "single snapshot" studies that examine one time-frame from the long lifespan of these lawsuits. The involvement of key players and the influence of different environmental factors shifts over time. A longitudinal perspective lets us do a better job of analyzing the causes, processes, and impacts of court-ordered jail reform. Because the jail lawsuits studied here were settled fairly recently, however, we will need to reexamine conclusions over time and test them against findings from other jurisdictions.

I have measured a subset of potentially relevant variables at each of the five stages of litigation, but it is still possible and desirable to use or develop better measures of events and actions at each stage: judicial methods, negotiation styles, leadership of key actors. Analyses of complex legal and social phenomena in jail reform litigation would also benefit from further interdisciplinary inquiry. Researchers could, for example, measure jail conditions more precisely (Logan 1993), as well as jail and prison organizational climates (e.g., Camp 1994; Cullen et al. 1993) and interagency relations among government and justice officials (e.g., Heinz and Manikas 1992).

The best way to strengthen the validity of conclusions is to use a variety of convergent methods—statistical measures, surveys, interviews, observations, and archival analyses, for example—to ask the same questions. Validity and reliability do not necessarily require quantitative measures; strong qualitative data face similar burdens. While there is still a need for carefully conducted case studies, others have convincingly argued the need for more systematic, comparative analyses of social reform litigation. Each methodology has its tradeoffs.

With case studies we face the danger of subjectivity and loss of generalizability; with comparative studies, the risk is loss of depth. We would do better to use both.

More surveys of judges, litigants, and public officials involved in jail lawsuits would also be beneficial. I conducted interviews with judges, litigants, and public officials in only three counties, so my interpretations on choice of court are supported largely by archival (court documents) and statistical analyses. As I have argued, state law in California facilitates the filing of claims in state court, yet state court is usually less favorable to plaintiffs in terms of remedies, unless a particular judge benefits from good relations with county incumbents, familiarity with local justice conditions, and strong resolve and political power. To examine such issues in sufficient depth, I would propose a series of studies using large samples of judges and litigants across different states.

Although I tried to use diverse research methods to converge on questions about jail reform, truncated and incomplete records of jail conditions and county punishment patterns, short series of data on county finances, and other gaps limited analysis in some instances. Cross-sectional data, wherever possible, were supplemented by archival and qualitative analyses using, for example, court records and interviews.

Every social scientist knows the truism that "correlation does not equal causality." I do not claim to have demonstrated causality: No single study—quantitative, qualitative, case study, or otherwise— has ever established causality. "Causality" can only be approached, never achieved, in nonexperimental research (Blalock 1964). It is approached through repeated studies, large samples, reliable and valid measures, replications, different methodologies, and convergent patterns of similar findings over time. I propose that the model I have defined here may guide more systematic inquiries in this area.

In general, researchers need to explore linkages between actions and events at different stages of litigation. For example, how do events and actions at the postdecree stage—judicial methods, the nature of negotiations, roles of special masters, use of contempt proceedings— relate to impacts such as institutional conditions, organizational expansion, correctional expenditures and policies, and interagency relations? I have combined qualitative and quantitative data to address some of these questions (Chapter 6), but greater depth of each type of data is needed. Again, wherever possible, use of convergent sources of data will enhance the search for "common denominators" to link actions and events at different stages.

## Law as a Means of Social Reform

Many have expressed skepticism about the use of courts as a means of social reform. Jail litigation is expensive and highly contested, and often results in minimal substantive reform. In many cases, however, the courts have pressured county agencies to take a more proactive approach to jail problems.

Some suggest that courts occasionally affect social conditions, but only when other political and social forces are already moving in that direction (Rosenberg 1991). With jails and prisons, this is clearly not the case. There is no indication that officials would have improved jail conditions or standards had the courts not intervened or threatened to do so; nor is there any evidence that they were moving in the direction of reform prior to the advent of court intervention. In some cases—that of Orange County, for example—court intervention clearly halted and reversed trends of decreased jail funding and rapid deterioration of jail conditions. Before intervention, forces in support of change were hard to find, particularly among jail administrators. Even though litigation has in some cases increased their budgetary and policy priority, defendants have displayed a degree of hostility and noncompliance that calls into question Rosenberg's (1991) claim that significant change occurs only where officials are already poised to move in that direction.

Critics of court intervention in social policy cases also charge that judges go too far, intervening in executive decisions regarding expenditures and policy choices. Yet Intervenors are in fact rare in jail reform lawsuits. The Court of Appeal largely blocked Judge Allen's attempt to take control of all of Santa Clara's jail expenditures and issue orders to the sheriff and the county controller. Other judges have ordered counties to build new facilities, but such orders were usually based on county officials' previous broken promise to do so.

Few judges (if any) wish to assume management of county jail systems. The federal judge who heard the Orange County case stated: "I didn't want to run the jail." And yet changes were necessary: "One of the inherent needs for incarceration is to treat the incarcerated person like a human being; and that is to give him a decent place to stay, and that costs money. It costs money in space, in equipment, bedding, personnel to watch over him—maintain him, and it remains a constant problem." Conflict between the judicial and executive branches is inevitable, as another judge suggested:

> That's the big problem with all jail litigation. It's basically asking the judge to supervise local government officials in the performance of their duties.

That's really what it amounts to, by mandate. . . . We issue orders to public officials to do their job a certain way. In this case, because there were defects and all sorts of problems, it required constant, round the clock, 24-hour supervision, which a court obviously cannot do.

A litigant observed another drawback in the use of courts as vehicles of jail reform: "The big problem with this litigation is that it doesn't lend itself to a litigation method of resolution, which involves lawyers and having witnesses in court, and the judge deciding cases. . . . It's the wrong kind of forum."

Given all the difficulties documented, is court-ordered reform of jails necessary and useful? It is useful: Courts have become the "final repositories of social trust" (Lieberman 1981) for marginalized and powerless groups, like inmates, who have no other forum to have their claims heard. When county officials abrogate their responsibility, judges have to take unpopular stands. Conflict is often necessary before any kind of reform is possible (Brager and Holloway 1978; Coleman 1957). Some respondents perceived litigation as the only way to get county officials to take responsibility for jail conditions:

> What I was watching was what should have happened 10 years ago, and should happen every six months. You get a bunch of people in a room and they scream at each other until they get their system under control. But it is so painful, and they are all talking different languages, that I understood why *Branson* had to be filed, and why we were still in *Branson* eight years later. Because nobody was willing to bite the bullet.

Jail litigation has been a catalyst for change and offers an opportunity to examine how public officials and organizations adapt to court decrees that mandate a departure from business as usual. Court orders open "small but potentially critical ruptures in the naturalness of legal order and social hierarchy" (Simon 1992, 940). The evidence I present here strongly supports this view.

Is jail litigation *necessary?* The answer is no—because it is possible and desirable for public officials to take ownership of jail problems.

Public officials have traditionally deflected blame for unpopular political choices onto other officials or onto external forces beyond their control (Welsh et al. 1990) Officials have blamed jail problems on increased crime, a punitive public, inadequate funds, radical judges, and "bleeding heart" inmate lawyers for quite some time now. In the face of persistent economic problems and increased public frustration, the old excuses have worn thin, and public officials increasingly face charges of mismanagement or incompetence for failing to deal with social problems. Simplistic "blame avoidance" and "blame pinning" strategies fail to locate jail problems within their proper sphere of responsibility.

Many public officials and social scientists tend to define any social problem and its perceived negative consequences as a "crisis."[1] This draws attention to a problem, but it also unwittingly encourages a tendency to respond to social problems with poorly planned, "knee jerk" solutions based on the perceived immediacy of the situation rather than a systematic analysis of the problem (Feeley 1983; Sherman and Hawkins 1981). Court orders have not created a public policy "crisis." Court orders have pushed public officials to face their responsibility to manage their local criminal justice systems effectively and efficiently.

## Policy Recommendations

Jail overcrowding is the result of complex social and political forces. Competing problem definitions and causal explanations are accompanied by uncertainty and a sense of urgency. Under such conditions, a "garbage can" model of decision-making prevails: Policymakers seize upon readily available solutions rather than weighing options and formulating an optimal plan (Cohen, March, and Olsen 1972).

This style of decision making leads to poor theories and poor policies. It fails to diagnose or link problems, causes, and solutions. It leads public officials to ignore critical events that could help them understand and address jail problems. It leads people to look at unidimensional events—such as early release of prisoners—in isolation from the forces shaping those events (in this case severe overcrowding and serious constitutional violations unaddressed by public officials). It leads to bickering, blame avoidance, and poor policy formulation. As a result, ineffective, inefficient, or inconsistent policies may be adopted. To counteract such tendencies, we need to pay more attention to structuring and defining the problem of jail overcrowding.

Successful court intervention forces public officials to develop and analyze accurate information about jail problems and their causes and solutions; to develop comprehensive jail plans; and to work with officials from different county agencies and county government. Where intervention has failed, the blame lies with public officials and not the courts.

Officials who seriously wish to avoid or end court intervention must reexamine their approaches to jail policy analysis and design. Ultimately, it is this process that judges have sought to influence through court intervention. A policy design approach focuses attention on matching problem definitions to proposed solutions. Seven aspects of policy design (adapted from Ingraham 1987) are relevant to ending court intervention in jails.

1. *Degree of goal consensus versus level of conflict.* At present, jail policies are rarely tied to explicitly stated goals, purposes, or fiscal limitations. Officials must devote more attention to the unique purposes of local jails, bringing their goals into line with practical and fiscal constraints. If consensus is not possible, reasonable compromises must be realized.

2. *Placement on the policy agenda.* Time and resources must be devoted to arriving at a solution. Conflict-resolution and group-building techniques have proven effective in a wide variety of policy settings (e.g., Gulley and Leathers 1977; Susskind and Cruikshank 1987); Kaufman (1985) describes the team-building techniques the National Institute of Corrections used to help state policymakers formulate solutions to prison overcrowding; Harland (1991) describes similar strategies used with New York jail policymakers.

3. *Availability of alternative choices.* Policymakers must articulate a complete list of policy alternatives and consequences. For example, neither new construction nor intermediate sanctions will be effective in all settings. Comprehensive needs assessments and jail audits in each locality will help define the need for future jail space, the feasibility of intermediate sanctions, and the costs (both financial and social) of pursuing different policy alternatives (e.g., National Council on Crime and Delinquency 1985, 1988).

4. *Diversity of stakeholders.* The more heterogeneous participants in the policy process are, the more likely is conflict over policy options. Jail overcrowding is the policy arena for diverse actors: county supervisors, district attorneys, sheriffs, probation departments, judges, and state legislators. Absent interagency cooperation, many policies meet unexpected resistance and noncompliance. The diverse views of key actors must be identified and considered if effective responses are to develop.

5. *Level of expertise required.* Expertise includes technical and political competence, extent of contact with the problem, and understanding of the problem. Policymakers must carefully locate and integrate expertise in a variety of areas: jail population forecasting; jail policy advocacy; design and administration of programs in jails, courts, probation, and other agencies; and planning. No one should assume

that policymakers themselves possess the necessary range of required expertise.

6. *Resources demanded by the policy versus resources available.* Once agreement is reached on problem definition and policy goals, it is essential to match resources to policy (Mullen 1985). Either resources must rise to the level required by policy, or policy must be tailored to meet resource constraints. No community should contemplate "get tough" sentencing, for example, unless it can ensure the necessary jail and prison space. Minnesota's sentencing guidelines are explicitly tied to resource considerations (Blumstein 1987; Miethe and Moore 1989).

7. *Implementation responsibility and determination of performance criteria.* Once other policy requirements are met—resources, agreement on problem and goals, commitment to achieving a solution—any new policy must contain a plan for monitoring its progress and evaluating its effectiveness over a specified period of time. A dearth of valid evaluations of new policies has seriously hindered progress in solving the jail crowding problem.

Careful planning and research can open the door for coordinated policy innovation rather than a "piecemeal political patchwork of minor ameliorations" (Mattick 1974, 822). Effective policy design is neither easy nor painless, but neither is court intervention. The major obstacle to more rational planning is the tendency to seize upon unrelated, simplistic solutions at the expense of more coordinated but complex plans informed by policy-relevant research. The dangers of faulty problem analysis, "knee jerk" change, and poor evaluations of change should by now be clear.

## Conclusion

Although court orders have produced short-term improvements, long-term responsibility for monitoring and evaluating punishment standards must lie with states, counties, and their constituents, not just the courts. Those who have studied court-ordered prison reform in detail have reached similar conclusions. Martin and Ekland-Olson (1987) write:

> Prison life in the future will be shaped by the reforms fashioned over the past two decades. If we allow our penal institutions to once again vanish from the public view, they could again develop into a law unto themselves. Above all else, the struggle over the past two decades demonstrates that prisons are an integral part of the social fabric. (P. 247)

Crouch and Marquart (1989) define a stronger need for outside scrutiny of prisons themselves and the unprecedented and rapidly increasing use of incarceration across the country: "What these and other Texas prisons will be like . . . is an open question. The answer lies in time and in society's recognition that extensive use of incarceration, together with ignorance of what that incarceration entails, is a formula for disaster" (p. 238).

Slater (1976) criticizes the "toilet assumption"—the belief that all our social problems can be flushed away with little trouble to the public because they are the responsibility of public officials and nobody else. If we operate by this assumption, we should not be surprised when the sewer backs up. If we are ever to get past the habit of making costly and messy emergency repairs, we must develop more coherent mechanisms of accountability, maintenance, and planning for our social institutions of punishment (Mullen 1987). In the end, we can understand jail overcrowding, jail litigation, and correctional reform only by placing these phenomena within the larger context of the social response to crime. Courts make a difference, but the problems of jails neither begin nor end at the courtroom door.

# APPENDIX: METHODOLOGY

## ANALYSIS OF COURT DOCUMENTS

*Procedure.* I collected court orders and complaints resulting in court orders against county jails for all 58 counties in California. Although jails face multitudes of claims by individual inmates every year (Thomas, Keeler, and Harris 1986), this study examined only lawsuits that challenged general living conditions in jails. Case selection was based on two criteria: The lawsuits involved jail overcrowding or general conditions, with at least three remedies specified, and orders were issued after 1 January 1975 but prior to June 1989.

Some court documents were obtained from the California Board of Corrections, the state agency responsible for inspecting jails. I spent an additional year contacting plaintiffs' and defendants' legal counsel, county sheriffs, the court where the case was heard (either U.S. District Court or the local state Superior Court), or all of the above. Copies of the complaint, the original order or decree, and any additional orders were requested; respondents were offered a copy of the study results upon completion. I obtained 43 cases, although some counties had multiple lawsuits (Los Angeles had 3; Madera, 2; Placer, 2; Riverside, 3; Santa Barbara, 2; and Santa Clara, 2). Thirty-five of 58 counties (60 percent) faced court orders.

I analyzed court documents from each county—complaints, decisions, orders, status reports, and the like—to prepare a chronology of litigation events. The next step was to examine court documents for orders, plans, recommendations, and outcomes related to responses to county jail problems. Third, I coded major dimensions of litigation for each lawsuit, including number and type of alleged violations, and number and type of orders.

*Coding Instrument.* The coding covered type of plaintiff's legal representation (ideological/private/public), level of court (state/federal), type of defendant (county supervisors/jail commander/sheriff), lawsuit duration (in months), use of contempt (yes/no), and use of special masters (yes/no), as well as 37 potential violations (medical care, overcrowding, etc.). For the complaint, violations were coded on a yes/no basis (violation of law alleged or not). For the initial court decision, I followed two coding steps, first recording which (if any) of the 37 possible violations resulted in remedies (yes/no). Then, if a remedy was specified, I coded what relief the plaintiffs received (0 = no relief; 1 = written plans only; 2 = less relief than sought; 3 = relief approximately equal to that sought; 4 = relief greater than sought; 5 = relief for issue not alleged in complaint). Additional orders and modifications by the trial court and any reversals by the Court of Appeal were also coded (yes/no; total number of additional orders).

I tested interrater reliability by comparing independent raters' codings of each of 37 potential violations and remedies with my own for each case. I examined orders first on a yes/no basis (agreement about whether a specific order was made or not) and on overall agreement on the 0–5 scale. For complaints, 29 items (78 percent) resulted in perfect or substantial agreement, as evidenced by kappa coefficients exceeding .60 (Landis and Koch 1977). For orders (yes/no), 31 items (83 percent) showed substantial or perfect agreement; on the 0–5 scale, 27 items (73 percent) showed substantial or perfect agreement.

## CROSS-SECTIONAL DATA

Cross-sectional statistics (1976–1986) reflecting county punishment practices were coded from Annual County Profiles, provided by the California Bureau of Criminal Statistics (1986, 1987). County profiles contained data on county populations, arrest rates, reported crimes, and county budget allocations to each criminal justice agency. The California Board of Corrections provided jail population statistics (e.g., rated capacities of jails, average daily jail populations). BOC began collecting statistics on jail populations in 1976 and has conducted regular inspections of individual jails every two years since. Using both data sets, I calculated incarceration rates, levels of jail overcrowding, and per prisoner expenditures for 1976 and 1986. The first date represents conditions prior to the onset of jail litigation in most counties; only 3 of the 35 counties under court order (9 percent) were engaged in active litigation prior to 1 January 1976. The second date represents a more active period in jail litigation. During the year 1986, lawsuits were active in 24 of the 35 counties under court order (69 percent); lawsuits in 7 counties (20 percent) had expired prior to 1 January 1986; in 4 counties (11 percent), lawsuits began after 31 December 1986.

## LONGITUDINAL DATA

County correctional expenditures (1963–1988) were obtained from annual reports provided by the California Office of State Controller (1963–1983/84; 1984/85–1988).

## INTERVIEWS

I selected Orange, Santa Clara, and Contra Costa counties for intensive case study: Each county has a large jail population (greater than 500), and each has been under court order for unconstitutional conditions of confinement, including overcrowding. Orange and Santa Clara experienced intrusive, drawn-out court intervention; Contra Costa successfully complied with court orders and averted long-term judicial scrutiny (California Board of Corrections 1988; Kizziah 1984; Welsh and Pontell 1991).

I used a semi-structured "elite interview" method (Dexter 1970; Lofland 1971), with questions based on reviews of jail and prison literature, agency reports, newspapers, and court documents. Interviews focused on perceived causes and effects of jail overcrowding (the problem cited most frequently in complaints), organizational responses, and process and outcomes of litigation, including changes in jail conditions. I posed one set of questions to organizational actors and a separate set to litigants (plaintiffs' or defendants' counsel, judges hearing the case, and defendants named in lawsuits). Interviewees who were both organizational members and defendants in jail lawsuits answered questions from both groups. The two sets of interview questions are presented in Tables A.1 and A.2, respectively.

Sampling of officials was based upon the expertise of key actors, rather than random sampling (see, e.g., Berk and Rossi 1977; Gottfredson and Taylor 1987; UCLA Law Review 1973). In each county I targeted the judge(s) who presided over the jail lawsuit, the legal counsel for plaintiffs and defendants, the district attorney, the public defender, the chief probation officer, members of the board

### TABLE A.1
#### INTERVIEW QUESTIONS: ORGANIZATIONAL PARTICIPANTS

1. What are the major factors that have led to jail overcrowding and/or court orders in your county, and what changes have court orders brought about?

2. In your opinion, have jail overcrowding or court orders resulted in any threat to public safety?

3. What means have been used to reduce overcrowding, and how effective have they been (e.g., early release, alternatives to incarceration)? What problems have surfaced?

4. Do problems in interagency communication contribute to overcrowding and/or court orders?

5. Has public opinion and media coverage of crime influenced incarceration and detention practices? How?

6. Has crime changed in the county over the last few years? Have resources in your branch changed?

7. Have changes in laws and sentencing practices affected jail overcrowding? Which changes have been most significant?

8. How have jail overcrowding and court orders affected policy and decisions at your branch of the criminal justice system?

9. Is building more jails a viable solution *(a)* in the short term? *(b)* in the long term? What else needs to be done, if anything?

## TABLE A.2
### INTERVIEW QUESTIONS: LITIGANTS

1. Was a particular litigation strategy used by either party? How would you describe your (their) general strategy, if any?

2. How were the particular remedies fashioned, and how much participation did (a) the judge, (b) the plaintiffs, and (c) the defendants have? Was this participation adequate?

3. Have court orders achieved their intended effects? Why or why not? Have they reduced overcrowding, or improved general conditions?

4. What problems surfaced in attempting to achieve compliance with court orders? How was compliance monitored by the court?

5. How much difference did the personal or professional characteristics of the participants (judge, defendants, plaintiffs) make in this case? How?

6. Did public opinion about jails or crime influence the process or outcome of this case? How?

7. What other factors, if any, influenced the outcome of this case significantly?

8. In your opinion, have there been any unintended effects of court orders? (E.g., on other agencies? on the community?)

9. Were you satisfied with the outcome of this case? Why or why not?


## TABLE A.3
### RESPONDENTS INTERVIEWED IN THREE COUNTIES

| | County | | | |
|---|---|---|---|---|
| Agency | Orange | Contra Costa | Santa Clara | Total |
| Judges | 5 | 0 | 2 | 7 |
| District attorneys | 4 | 1 | 4 | 9 |
| Public defenders | 2 | 2 | 2 | 6 |
| Legal counsel | 3 | 1 | 1 | 5 |
| Probation | 6 | 2 | 2 | 10 |
| Police | 18 | 2 | 2 | 22 |
| Sheriff or county department of correction | 2 | 2 | 3 | 7 |
| Board of supervisors | 5 | 3 | 2 | 10 |
| Other county executives | 2 | 0 | 2 | 4 |
| Other[a] | 5 | 0 | 1 | 6 |
| TOTAL | 52 | 13 | 21 | 86 |

[a]The category "Other" consists of 1 special master, 1 professional corrections consultant, 1 community service director, 2 court administration officers, and 1 dean of a local law school.

of supervisors, and local police chiefs. I contacted not only the head of each agency, but also knowledgeable informants referred by key people. Orange County was "oversampled" as part of a broader study on jail overcrowding (Welsh et al. 1990; Welsh et al. 1991). I obtained all but two planned interviews: It was impossible to arrange an agreeable interview time with the judge who heard the jail lawsuit in Contra Costa, and defendants' legal counsel in Santa Clara (Office of the County Counsel) refused to be interviewed. A total of 86 interviews were conducted; the breakdowns within each county are shown in Table A.3.

Interviews lasted from 30 to 90 minutes. In all but seven instances, respondents allowed themselves to be tape-recorded. In Orange County, interviews were conducted over the seven months between September 1987 and March 1988. Interviews in Contra Costa were conducted in February 1989. Interviews in Santa Clara were conducted in February and March 1989.

# Notes

## CHAPTER 1

1. For discussion regarding a proposed "severity index" of overcrowding and related definitional problems, see Klofas, Stojkovich, and Kalinich 1992.

## CHAPTER 2

1. Two counties (Alpine and Sierra) have no jails; they contract inmates to contiguous counties.

2. The sheriff's budget is measured separately from the jail budget by the California Bureau of Criminal Statistics (BCS). In 1976, the sheriff was responsible for running county jails in all but two counties (Madera and Napa). The sheriff is often responsible for other functions, such as law enforcement, investigation, and court transfers. Although the sheriff's budget and the jail budget are measured separately, we would expect some overlap between the two, as monies are shifted from one function (e.g., law enforcement, administration) to the other (jail operations). BCS jail figures specifically exclude capital expenditures.

3. The California Supreme Court issued an order to show cause to the Lake County sheriff in 1982 after county jail inmates filed a flurry of habeas corpus petitions complaining of inhumane conditions (Los Angeles Daily Journal 1989). The state public defender's office was appointed to represent the inmates, and retired Alameda County Superior Court Judge Spurgeon Avakian was appointed as a referee to take testimony and make findings. In 1983, a settlement agreement was reached. As part of the agreement, the court was asked to transfer jurisdiction over the case to the Lake County Superior Court. However, then Chief Justice Rose Bird refused, explaining that there was no provision in the state constitution for transferring a case back to a trial court once the Supreme Court had exercised jurisdiction over it. As a result, the justices found themselves saddled with monitoring the case for the next seven years.

## CHAPTER 3

1. *Branson v. Winter,* No. 78807 (Cal. Super. Ct., County of Santa Clara, 1981), "First Amended Petition for Writ of Habeas Corpus," 28 April 1981, p. 10.

2. *Stewart v. Gates,* CV 75 3075 WPG(G) (C.D. Cal. 1975), "Amended Civil Rights Complaint for Injunction, Declaratory Judgement, Damages, and Other Appropriate Relief," 22 October 1975, pp. 7–9.

3. Ibid.

## CHAPTER 4

1. In many jail cases the distinction between "orders" and "settlements" is practically meaningless because other court documents clearly indicate that both litigants agreed to the remedy, but either the judge or the litigants preferred for political reasons that the judge alone sign the order. On the other hand, a signed settlement carries no force without the judge's signature and resolve to enforce it.

2. *In re Ervin Branson et al.,* on Habeas Corpus, No. A021183 (Cal. App. 1 Dist. 1983).

3. *Ervin Branson et al. v. County of Santa Clara, Members of the Board of Supervisors of the County of Santa Clara, Robert Winter, Sheriff; County of Santa Clara, Members of the Board of Supervisors of the County of Santa Clara, Robert Winter, Sheriff v. Superior Court of the State of California in and for the County of Santa Clara, Ervin Branson et al.; People of the State of California, Intervenor; A020323 and A020324* (Cal. App. 1 Dist. 1983).

4. *In re Ervin Branson* et al., on Habeas Corpus, No. A021183 (Cal. App. 1 Dist. 1983).

5. *Ervin Branson et al. v. County of Santa Clara, Members of the Board of Supervisors of the County of Santa Clara, Robert Winter, Sheriff; County of Santa Clara, Members of the Board of Supervisors of the County of Santa Clara, Robert Winter, Sheriff v. Superior Court of the State of California in and for the County of Santa Clara, Ervin Branson et al.; People of the State of California, Intervenor; A020303 and A020324* (Cal. App. 1 Dist. 1983).

## CHAPTER 6

1. For more detailed descriptions of time series equations and transformations, see Welsh 1992b.

2. Two counties (Placer, San Francisco) were discarded because of missing data; two others (Kern, San Joaquin) did not have court orders until 1989.

3. Even though matching is a conservative strategy, varying degrees of impact may inflate or deflate the figures in a small sample. If we drop the highest and lowest figures in each category in Table 32 (Sacramento and Trinity; Lassen and Mariposa), we still find a substantially greater rate of change in counties under court order (89.4 percent) than in counties not under order (46.3 percent).

## CHAPTER 7

1. Spector and Kitsuse (1977) elaborate a useful model for analyzing how specific social issues come to be defined as "problems" and placed on the policy agenda.

# References

Abt Associates. 1980. *American Prisons and Jails,* vol. 1. Washington, D.C.: U.S. Department of Justice.

Adams, Carolyn, David Bartelt, David Elesh, Ira Goldstein, Nancy Kleniewski, and William Yancey. 1991. *Philadelphia: Neighborhoods, Division, and Conflict in a Post-Industrial City.* Philadelphia: Temple University Press.

Advisory Commission on Intergovernmental Relations. 1984. *Jails: Intergovernmental Dimensions of a Local Problem.* Washington, D.C.: Advisory Commission of Intergovernmental Relations.

Aldrich, Howard E. 1979. *Organizations and Environments.* Englewood Cliffs, N.J.: Prentice-Hall.

Allen, Harry E., and Clifford E. Simonsen. 1986. *Corrections in America: An Introduction.* New York: Macmillan.

Alpert, Geoffrey P. 1980. "Prisoners and Their Rights: An Introduction." In Geoffrey P. Alpert, ed., *Legal Rights of Prisoners,* pp. 11–18. Beverly Hills: Sage.

Alpert, Geoffrey P., Ben Crouch, and C. Ronald Huff. 1986. "Prison Reform by Judicial Decree: The Unintended Consequences of Ruiz v. Estelle." In Kenneth C. Haas and Geoffrey P. Alpert, eds., *The Dilemmas of Punishment,* pp. 258–271. Prospect Heights, Ill.: Waveland.

Andrews, Donald A., Ivan Zinger, Robert Hoge, James Bonta, Paul Gendreau, and Francis T. Cullen. 1990. "Does Correctional Treatment Work? A Clinically Relevant and Psychologically Informed Meta-analysis." *Criminology* 28:369–404.

Atherton, Alexine L. 1987. "Journal Retrospective: 1845–1986." *Prison Journal* 67(1):1–37.

Austin, James, and Barry Krisberg. 1982. "The Unmet Promise of Alternatives to Incarceration." *Crime and Delinquency* 28:374–409.

Austin, James, and Aaron David McVey. 1989. *The 1989 NCCD Prison Population Forecast: The Impact of the War on Drugs.* San Francisco: National Council on Crime and Delinquency.

Babcock, William G. 1990. "Litigating Prison Conditions in Philadelphia: Part II." *Prison Journal* 70(2):74–85.

Berk, Richard A., and Peter H. Rossi. 1977. *Prison Reform and State Elites.* Cambridge, Mass.: Ballinger.

Blackmore, John. 1986. "Community Corrections." In Kenneth C. Haas and Geoffrey P. Alpert, eds., *The Dilemmas of Punishment: Readings in Contemporary Corrections,* pp. 412–430. Prospect Heights, Ill.: Waveland.

Blalock, H. M. 1964. *Causal Inferences in Nonexperimental Research.* Chapel Hill: University of North Carolina Press.

Blumstein, Alfred. 1987. "Sentencing and the Prison Crowding Problem." In Stephen D. Gottfredson and Sean McConville, eds., *America's Correctional Crisis: Prison Populations and Public Policy.* Westport, Conn.: Greenwood.

———. 1988. "Prison Populations: A System out of Control?" In Michael Tonry and Norval Morris, eds., *Crime and Justice: A Review of Research,* 10:231–266. Chicago: University of Chicago Press.

Blumstein, Alfred, Jacqueline Cohen, and Harold Miller. 1980. "Demographically Disaggregated Projections of Prison Populations." *Journal of Criminal Justice* 8:1–26.

Brager, George, and Stephen Holloway. 1978. *Changing Human Service Organizations: Politics and Practice.* New York: Free Press.

Brakel, Samuel J. 1979. "Special Masters in Institutional Litigation." *American Bar Foundation Research Journal* 3:543–569.

———. 1986. "Prison Reform Litigation: Has the Revolution Gone Too Far?" *Judicature* 70:5–6, 64–65.

Bronstein, Alvin J. 1980. "Offender Rights Litigation: Historical and Future Developments." In Ira P. Robbins, ed., *Prisoners' Rights Sourcebook,* 2:5–28. New York: Clark Boardman.

Brown, Don W., and Donald W. Crowley. 1979. "The Societal Impact of Law: An Assessment of Research." *Law and Policy Quarterly* 1:253–284.

Bunker, Douglas R., and Marion Wijnberg. 1985. "The Supervisor as a Mediator of Organizational Climate in Public Social Service Organizations." *Administration in Social Work* 9:59–72.

Busher, Walter. 1983. *Jail Overcrowding: Identifying Causes and Planning for Solutions.* Washington, D.C.: Office of Justice Assistance, Research and Statistics.

Byrne, James M., Arthur J. Lurigio, and Joan Petersilia. 1992. *Smart Sentencing: The Emergence of Intermediate Sanctions.* Newbury Park, Calif.: Sage.

California Board of Corrections. 1985. *The State of the Jails in California, Report #2: Prisoner Flow and Release.* Sacramento: State of California.

———. 1988. *Report to the Legislature: Jail Standards and Operations Division—Jail Inspections and Costs of Compliance.* Sacramento: State of California.

California Bureau of Criminal Statistics. 1986. *1985 Criminal Justice Profile* (county profiles). Sacramento: State of California Department of Justice, Division of Law Enforcement, Criminal Identification and Information Branch.

———. 1987. *1986 Criminal Justice Profile* (county profiles). Sacramento: State of California Department of Justice, Division of Law Enforcement, Criminal Identification and Information Branch.

California Office of State Controller. 1963–1983/84. *Annual Report of Financial*

*Transactions Concerning Counties of California.* Sacramento: Office of the State Controller, Division of Local Government Fiscal Affairs.

———. 1984/85–1988. *Counties of California Financial Transactions Annual Report.* Sacramento: Office of the State Controller, Division of Local Government Fiscal Affairs.

Call, Jack E. 1986. "Recent Case Law on Overcrowded Conditions of Confinement: An Assessment of Its Impact on Facility Decisionmaking." In Kenneth C. Haas and Geoffrey P. Alpert, eds., *The Dilemmas of Punishment: Readings in Contemporary Corrections,* pp. 238–257. Prospect Heights, Ill.: Waveland.

Camp, Scott D. 1994. "Assessing the Effects of Organizational Commitment and Job Satisfaction on Turnover: An Event History Approach." *Prison Journal* 74:279–305.

Carroll, Leo, and Mary Beth Doubet. 1983. "U.S. Social Structure and Imprisonment: A Comment." *Criminology* 21:449–456.

Champion, Dean J. 1991. "Jail Inmate Litigation in the 1990s." In Joel A. Thompson and G. Larry Mays, eds., *American Jails: Public Policy Issues,* pp. 197–215. Chicago: Nelson-Hall.

Chan, Janet B. L., and Richard V. Ericson. 1981. *Decarceration and the Economy of Penal Reform.* Toronto: University of Toronto Centre for Criminology.

Chilton, Bradley Stewart, and David C. Nice. 1993. "Triggering Federal Court Intervention in State Prison Reform." *Prison Journal* 73:30–45.

Clear, Todd R., and Patricia M. Harris. 1987. "The Costs of Incarceration." In Stephen D. Gottfredson and Sean McConville, eds., *America's Correctional Crisis,* pp. 37–55. Westport, Conn.: Greenwood.

Cohen, Michael D., James G. March, and Johan P. Olsen. 1972. "A Garbage Can Model of Organizational Choice." *Administrative Science Quarterly* 17:1–25.

Cohen, Stanley. 1972. *Folk Devils and Moral Panics: The Creation of the Mods and Rockers.* New York: St. Martin's.

———. 1979. "The Punitive City: Notes on the Dispersal of Social Control." *Contemporary Crises* 3:339–363.

Coleman, James S. 1957. *Community Conflict.* New York: Free Press.

Collins, William C. 1987. *Collins: Correctional Law 1987.* Olympia, Wash., William C. Collins.

Cook, Thomas D., and Donald T. Campbell. 1979. *Quasi-Experimentation: Design and Analysis for Field Settings.* Boston: Houghton Mifflin.

Cooper, Phillip J. 1988. *Hard Judicial Choices.* New York: Oxford University Press.

Correctional Consultants of California. 1988. *A Report on the Current Conditions of Confinement at Orange County Detention Facilities.* Brea, Calif.: Correctional Consultants of California.

County Administrative Office. 1986. *Systems Approach to Jail Overcrowding in Orange County.* Santa Ana, Calif.: County of Orange.

Crouch, Ben M., and James W. Marquart. 1989. *An Appeal to Justice.* Austin: University of Texas Press.

————. 1990. "Ruiz: Intervention and Emergent Order in Texas Prisons." In John J. DiIulio, Jr., ed., *Courts, Corrections, and the Constitution,* pp. 94–114. New York: Oxford University Press.

Cullen, Francis T., Gregory A. Clark, and John F. Wozniak. 1985. "Explaining the Get Tough Movement: Can the Public Be Blamed? *Federal Probation* 49:16–24.

Cullen, Francis T., Edward J. Latessa, Velmer S. Burton, Jr., and Lucien X. Lombardo. 1993. "The Correctional Orientation of Prison Wardens: Is the Rehabilitative Ideal Supported?" *Criminology* 31:69-92.

Cuvelier, Steven, Shihlung Huang, James W. Marquart, and Velmer S. Burton, Jr. 1992. "Regulating Prison Admissions by Quota: A Descriptive Account of the Texas Allocation Formula." *Prison Journal* 72:99–119.

Daly, Kathleen, Shelly Geballe, and Stanton Wheeler. 1988. "Litigation-Driven Research: A Case Study of Lawyer/Social Scientist Collaboration." *Women's Rights Reporter* 10:221–240.

De Neufville, Judith I., and Stephen E. Barton. 1987. "Myths and the Definition of Policy Problems." *Policy Sciences* 20:181–206.

Dexter, Lewis A. 1970. *Elite and Specialized Interviewing.* Evanston, Ill.: Northwestern University Press.

DiIulio, John J., Jr. 1987. *Governing Prisons: A Comparative Study of Correctional Management.* New York: Free Press.

————, ed. 1990. *Courts, Corrections, and the Constitution.* New York: Oxford University Press.

Doble, John. 1987. *Crime and Punishment: The Public's View.* New York: Prepared by the Public Agenda Foundation for the Edna McConnell Clark Foundation.

Duffee, David. 1989. "Introduction: Special Issue on Instrumental, Human, and Institutional Processes in Criminal Justice Organizations." *Journal of Research in Crime and Delinquency* 26:107–115.

Dunbaugh, Frank M. 1990. "Prospecting for Prospective Relief: The Story of Seeking Compliance with A Federal Court Decree Mandating Humane Conditions of Confinement in the Baltimore City Jail." *Prison Journal* 70:57–73.

Durkheim, Emile. 1947. *The Division of Labour in Society,* Translated by G. G. Simpson. New York: Free Press. (Originally published in 1893.)

Eisenstein, James, and Herbert Jacob. 1977. *Felony Justice: An Organizational Analysis of Criminal Courts.* Boston: Little, Brown.

Ekland-Olson, Sheldon, and Steven J. Martin. 1988. "Organizational Compliance with Court-Ordered Reform." *Law and Society Review* 22:359–383.

————. 1990. "Ruiz: A Struggle over Legitimacy." In John J. DiIulio, Jr., ed., *Courts, Corrections, and the Constitution,* pp. 73–93. New York: Oxford University Press.

Fabian, Sharon L. 1980. "Women Prisoners: Challenge of the Future," In Geoffrey P. Alpert, ed., *Legal Rights of Prisoners*, pp. 171–193. Beverly Hills, Calif.: Sage.

Feeley, Malcolm M. 1973. "Two Models of the Criminal Justice System: An Organizational Perspective." *Law and Society Review* 7:407–425.

———. 1983. *Court Reform on Trial: Why Simple Solutions Fail.* New York: Basic Books.

———. 1989. "The Significance of Prison Conditions Cases: Budgets and Regions." *Law and Society Review* 23:273–282.

Feeley, Malcolm M., and Roger P. Hanson. 1986. "What We Know, Think We Know and Would Like to Know About the Impact of Court Orders on Prison Conditions and Jail Crowding." Presented at the meeting of the Working Group on Jail and Prison Crowding, Committee on Research on Law Enforcement and the Administration of Justice, National Academy of Sciences, Chicago, Ill.

———. 1990. "The Impact of Judicial Intervention on Prisons and Jails: A Framework for Analysis and a Review of the Literature." In John J. DiIulio, ed., *Courts, Corrections, and the Constitution*, pp. 12–46. New York: Oxford University Press.

Feeley, Malcolm M., and Samuel Krislov. 1985. *Constitutional Law.* Boston: Little, Brown.

Felstiner, William F., Richard L. Abel, and Austin Sarat. 1981. "The Emergence of Disputes: Naming, Blaming, Claiming . . . " *Law and Society Review* 15:631–654.

Flynn, Edith E. 1983. "Jails." In Sanford H. Kadish, ed., *Encyclopedia of Crime and Justice*, pp. 915–922. New York: Free Press.

Forehand, Garlie A., and B. von Haller Gilmer. 1964. "Environmental Variation in Studies of Organizational Behavior." *Psychology Bulletin* 62:361–382.

Forst, Martin L. 1977. "To What Extent Should the Criminal Justice System Be a 'System'?" *Crime and Delinquency* 23:403–416.

Frug, Gerald E. 1978. "The Judicial Power of the Purse." *University of Pennsylvania Law Review* 126:715–794.

Fuller, Lon L. 1978. "The Forms and Limits of Adjudication." *Harvard Law Review* 92:353–409.

Galanter, Marc. 1974. "Why the 'Haves' Come Out Ahead: Speculation on the Limits of Legal Change." *Law and Society Review* 9:95–160.

———. 1975. "Afterword: Explaining Litigation." *Law and Society Review* 9:347–368.

Geissinger, Steve. 1990. "Legislators Seek Financial Answers to Counties' Woes." *Orange County Register*, 29 March.

Gettinger, Stephen H. 1984a. *New Generation Jails: An Innovative Approach to an Age-Old Problem.* Prepared under contract from the National Institute of Corrections, U.S. Department of Justice. Washington, D.C.: U.S. Department of Justice, National Institute of Corrections.

———. 1984b. *Assessing Criminal Justice Needs.* Washington, D.C.: U.S. Department of Justice, National Institute of Justice, Research in Brief.

Gibbs, Jack. 1986. "Punishment and Deterrence: Theory, Research, and Penal Policy." In Leon Lipson and Stanton Wheeler, eds., *Law and the Social Sciences,* pp. 319–368. New York: Russell Sage.

Gibbs, John J. 1983. "Problems and Priorities: Perceptions of Jail Custodians and Social Service Providers." *Journal of Criminal Justice* 11:327–338.

Glazer, Nathan. 1975. "Towards an Imperial Judiciary?" *Public Interest* 41:104–123.

———. 1978. "Should Judges Administer Social Services?" *Public Interest* 50:64–80.

Goldfarb, Ronald. 1975. *Jails: The Ultimate Ghetto.* Garden City, N.Y.: Anchor.

Gottfredson, Stephen D., and Ralph B. Taylor. 1987. "Attitudes of Correctional Policymakers and the Public." In Stephen D. Gottfredson and Sean McConville, eds., *America's Correctional Crisis: Prison Populations and Public Policy,* pp. 57–75. Westport, Conn.: Greenwood.

Gottlieb, David J. 1988. "The Legacy of Wolfish and Chapman: Some Thoughts About "Big Prison Case" Litigation in the 1980s." In Ira P. Robbins, ed., *Prisoners and the Law,* pp. 2-3–2-31. New York: Clark Boardman.

Graham, Fred P. 1970. *The Due Process Revolution: The Warren Court's Impact on Criminal Law.* New York: Hayden.

Grieser, Robert C. 1988. *Wardens and State Corrections Commissioners Offer Their Views in National Assessment.* Washington, D.C.: U.S. Department of Justice, Research in Action, NCJ-113584.

Gross, Bertram. 1982. "Reagan's Criminal 'Anti-Crime' Fix." In Alan Gartner, Colin Greer, and Frank Riessman, eds., *What Reagan Is Doing to Us,* pp. 87–108. New York: Harper & Row.

Grossman, Joel B., and Austin Sarat. 1975. "Litigation in the Federal Courts: A Comparative Perspective." *Law and Society Review* 9:321–346.

Gulley, Halbert E., and Dale G. Leathers. 1977. *Communication and Group Process.* New York: Holt, Rinehart and Winston.

Hagan, John. 1989. "Why Is There So Little Criminal Justice Theory? Neglected Macro- and Micro-Level Links Between Organization and Power." *Journal of Research in Crime and Delinquency* 26:116–135.

Hall, Andy. 1985. *Alleviating Jail Overcrowding: A Systems Perspective.* Washington, D.C.: U.S. Department of Justice, National Institute of Justice, Office of Development, Testing, and Dissemination.

———. 1987. *Systemwide Strategies to Alleviate Jail Crowding.* NCJ-94612. Washington, D.C.: U.S. Department of Justice, National Institute of Justice.

Handler, Joel F. 1978. *Social Movements and the Legal System: A Theory of Law Reform and Social Change.* New York: Academic Press.

Hargrove, Erwin C., and John C. Glidewell. 1990. *Impossible Jobs in Public Management.* Lawrence: University Press of Kansas.

Harland, Alan T. 1991. "Jail Crowding and the Process of Criminal Justice Policymaking." *Prison Journal* 71:77–92.

Harland, Alan T., and Philip W. Harris. 1987. "Structuring the Development of Alternatives to Incarceration." In Stephen D. Gottfredson and Sean McConville, eds., *America's Correctional Crisis: Prison Populations and Public Policy*, pp. 179–204. Westport, Conn.: Greenwood.

Harriman, Linda, and Jeffrey Straussman. 1983. "Do Judges Determine Budget Decisions?" *Public Administration Review* 43:343–351.

Harris, M. Kay. 1987. "A Brief for De-escalating Criminal Sanctions." In Stephen D. Gottfredson and Sean McConville, eds., *America's Correctional Crisis: Prison Populations and Public Policy*, pp. 205–220. Westport, Conn.: Greenwood.

Harris, M. Kay, and Dudley P. Spiller, Jr. 1977. *After Decision: Implementation of Judicial Decrees in Correctional Settings*. National Institute of Law Enforcement and Criminal Justice, Law Enforcement Assistance Administration. Washington, D.C.: GPO.

Hawkins, Richard, and Geoffrey P. Alpert. 1989. *American Prison Systems: Punishment and Justice*. Englewood Cliffs, N.J.: Prentice Hall.

Hayes, L. M. 1983. "And Darkness Closes In . . . : A National Study of Jail Suicides." *Criminal Justice and Behavior* 10:461–484.

Heinz, John P., and Peter M. Manikas. 1992. "Networks Among Elites in a Local Criminal Justice System." *Law and Society Review* 26:831–861.

Herman, Susan N. 1988. "Prisoners and Due Process Litigation: An Invitation to the State Courts." In Ira P. Robbins, ed., *Prisoners and the Law*, pp. 5-3–5-28. New York: Clark Boardman.

Horowitz, Donald L. 1977. *The Courts and Social Policy*. Washington, D.C.: Brookings Institute.

Huff, C. Ronald. 1980. "The Discovery of Prisoners' Rights: A Sociological Analysis" In Geoffrey P. Alpert, ed., *Legal Rights of Prisoners*, pp. 47–65. Beverly Hills, Calif.: Sage.

Huff, C. Ronald, and Geoffrey P. Alpert. 1982. "Organizational Compliance with Court-Ordered Reform: The Need for Evaluation Research." In Merry Morash, ed., *Implementing Criminal Justice Policies*, pp. 115–124. Beverly Hills, Calif.: Sage.

Hylton, John H. 1982. "Rhetoric and Reality: A Critical Appraisal of Community Correctional Programs." *Crime and Delinquency* 28–341-373.

Ingraham, Patricia. 1987. "Toward More Systematic Consideration of Policy Design." *Policy Studies Journal* 15:611–628.

Irwin, John, 1985. *The Jail*. Berkeley: University of California Press.

Jackson, Patrick G. 1991. "Competing Ideologies of Jail Confinement." In Joel A. Thompson and G. Larry Mays, eds., *American Jails: Public Policy Issues*, pp. 22–39. Chicago: Nelson-Hall.

Jacobs, James B. 1980. "The Prisoners' Rights Movement and Its Impacts, 1960–80." In Norval Morris and Michael Tonry, eds., *Crime and Justice*, 2:429–470. Chicago: University of Chicago Press.

Jerrell, Jeanette M., and Richard Komisaruk. 1991. "Public Policy Issues in the Delivery of Mental Health Services in a Jail Setting." In Joel A. Thompson and G. Larry Mays, eds., *American Jails: Public Policy Issues,* pp. 100–115. Chicago: Nelson-Hall.

Johnson, Charles A., and Bradley C. Canon. 1984. *Judicial Policies: Implementation and Impact.* Washington, D.C.: CQ Press.

Kalinich, David, Paul Embert, and Jeffrey Senese. 1991. "Mental Health Services for Jail Inmates: Imprecise Standards, Traditional Philosophies, and the Need for Change." In Joel A. Thompson and G. Larry Mays, eds., *American Jails: Public Policy Issues,* pp. 79–99. Chicago: Nelson-Hall.

Kaufman, Gerald. 1985. "The National Prison Overcrowding Project: Policy Analysis and Politics—A New Approach." *Annals of the American Academy of Political and Social Sciences* 478:161–172.

Kaufman, Irving. 1958. "Masters in Federal Courts: Rule 53." *Columbia Law Review* 58:452–469.

Kerle, Kenneth E., and Francis R. Ford. 1982. *The State of Our Nation's Jails.* Washington, D.C.: National Sheriff's Association.

Kessler, Mark. 1990. "Legal Mobilization for Social Reform: Power and the Politics of Agenda Setting," *Law and Society Review,* 24:121–143.

Kidder, Robert L. 1975. "Afterword: Change and Structure in Dispute Processing." *Law and Society Review* 9:385–391.

Kizziah, Carol A. 1984. *The State of the Jails in California, Report #1: Overcrowding in the Jails.* Sacramento, Calif.: Board of Corrections, State of California.

Klofas, John. 1987. "Patterns of Jail Use." *Journal of Criminal Justice* 15:403–412.

———. 1990. "The Jail and the Community." *Justice Quarterly* 7:69–102.

Klofas, John, Stan Stojkovic, and David A. Kalinich. 1992. "The Meaning of Correctional Crowding: Steps Toward an Index of Severity." *Crime and Delinquency* 38:171–188.

Koehler, Cortus T. 1983. *Managing California Counties: Serving People, Solving Problems.* Sacramento: County Supervisors Association of California.

Komarnicki, Mary, and John Doble. 1986. *Crime and Corrections: A Review of Public Opinion Data Since 1975.* Prepared with the support of the Edna McConnell Clark Foundation. New York: Public Agenda Foundation.

Koren, Edward I., John Boston, Elizabeth R. Alexander, and Daniel E. Manville. 1988. "A Primer for Jail Litigators: Some Practical Suggestions for Surviving and Prevailing in Your Lawsuit." In Ira P. Robbins, ed., *Prisoners and the Law,* pp. 17-3–17-94. New York: Clark Boardman.

Landis, J. Richard, and Gary G. Koch. 1977. "The Measurement of Observer Agreement for Categorical Data." *Biometrics* 33:159–174.

Lang, Karen Sorensen. 1988. Santa Clara County Electronic Monitoring Program: Final Evaluation Report. San Jose, Calif.: Quorum. August.

Lieberman, Jethro K. 1981. *The Litigious Society.* New York: Basic Books.

Lofland, John. 1971. *Analyzing Social Settings.* Belmont, Calif.: Wadsworth.

Logan, Charles H. 1993. "Criminal Justice Performance Measures for Prisons." In *Performance Measures for the Criminal Justice System: Discussion Papers from the BJS-Princeton Project,* pp. 19–59. U.S. Department of Justice, Office of Justice Programs, Bureau of Justice Statistics (NCJ-143505). Washington, D.C.: GPO.

Los Angeles Daily Journal. 1989. "Justices End 7-Year Stint as Jail Monitors." 17 October.

Martin, Steve J., and Sheldon Ekland-Olson. 1987. *Texas Prisons: The Walls Came Tumbling Down.* Austin: Texas Monthly Press.

Martinson, Robert. 1974. "What Works? Questions and Answers About Prison Reform." *Public Interest* 35:22–54.

Mattick, Hans W. 1974. "The Contemporary Jails of the United States: An Unknown and Neglected Area of Justice." In Daniel Glaser, ed., *Handbook of Criminology,* pp. 777–848. Chicago: Rand McNally.

Mays, G. Larry, and Frances P. Bernat. 1988. "Jail Reform Litigation: The Issue of Rights and Remedies." *American Journal of Criminal Justice* 12:254–273.

McCarthy, Belinda R. 1990. "A Micro-Level Analysis of Social Structure and Social Control: Interstate Use of Jail and Prison Confinement." *Justice Quarterly* 7:325–340.

McCleary, Richard, and Richard A. Hay, Jr., 1980. *Applied Time Series Analysis for the Social Sciences.* Beverly Hills, Calif.: Sage.

McCoy, Candace. 1986. "The Impact of Section 1983 Litigation on Policymaking in Corrections: A Malpractice Lawsuit by Any Name Would Smell as Sweet." In Kenneth C. Haas and Geoffrey P. Alpert, eds., *The Dilemmas of Punishment,* pp. 224–237. Prospect Heights, Ill.: Waveland.

McDonald, Douglas C. 1989. "The Cost of Corrections: In Search of the Bottom Line." *Research in Corrections* 2(1):1–25.

McShane, Marilyn D., and Frank P. Williams III. 1989. "Running on Empty: Creativity and the Correctional Agenda." *Crime and Delinquency* 35:562–576.

Merton, Robert K. 1968. *Social Theory and Social Structure.* New York: Free Press.

Miethe, Terance D., and Charles A. Moore. 1989. "Sentencing Guidelines: Their Effect in Minnesota." Research in Brief, NCJ-111381. Washington, D.C.: U.S. Department of Justice, Office of Justice Programs, National Institute of Justice.

Millemann, Michael A. 1980. "An Agenda for Prisoner Rights Litigation." In Ira P. Robbins, ed., *Prisoners' Rights Sourcebook,* 2:153–166. New York: Clark Boardman.

Montgomery, Elizabeth. 1980. "Force and Will: An Exploration of the Use of Special Masters to Implement Judicial Decrees." *University of Toledo Law Review* 52:105–123.

Morris, Norval, and Michael Tonry. 1990. *Between Prison and Probation: Intermediate Punishments in a Rational Sentencing System.* New York: Oxford University Press.

Mullen, Joan. 1985. "Prison Crowding and the Evolution of Public Policy." *Annals of the American Academy of Political and Social Science* 478:31–46.

———. 1987. "State Response to Prison Crowding: The Politics of Change." In Stephen D. Gottfredson and Sean McConville, eds., *America's Correctional Crisis: Prison Populations and Public Policy,* pp. 79–109. Westport, Conn.: Greenwood.

Myers, Martha and Susette Talarico. 1987. *The Social Contexts of Criminal Sentencing.* New York: Springer-Verlag.

Nathan, Vincent M. 1979. "The Use of Masters in Institutional Reform Litigation." *University of Toledo Law Review* 10:419–464.

National Council on Crime and Delinquency. 1985. *Marin County Jail Alternatives Study: Final Report.* Prepared by James Austin, Barry Krisberg, and Shirley Melnicoe. San Francisco, Calif.: NCCD.

———. 1988. *Draft: San Francisco Jail Needs Assessment.* San Francisco, Calif.: NCCD.

National Prison Project. 1993. "Status Report: State Prisons and the Courts— January 1, 1993." *National Prison Project Journal* 8(1):3–11.

Needham, John. 1987a. "Overseer Suggests Home Monitor System to Help Ease Jail Crowding." *Los Angeles Times,* 1 March, part II.

———. 1987b. "Supervisors Flooded with Jail Opposition." *Los Angeles Times,* 13 July, part II.

Neely, Richard. 1981. *How Courts Govern America.* New Haven: Yale University Press.

Packer, Herbert L. 1968. *The Limits of the Criminal Sanction.* Stanford, Calif.: Stanford University Press.

Palmer, John W. 1987. *Constitutional Rights of Prisoners.* 3d ed. Cincinnati, Ohio: Anderson.

Palmer, Ted. 1992. *The Re-Emergence of Correctional Intervention.* Newbury Park, Calif.: Sage.

Perlman, Jeffrey A. 1986. "Sheriff Gets OK to Release Inmates Early to Reduce Jail Overcrowding." *Los Angeles Times,* 8 March, part II.

Petersilia, Joan. 1985. *Probation and Felony Offenders.* Washington, D.C.: National Institute of Justice.

———. 1987. *Expanding Options for Criminal Sentencing.* Santa Monica, Calif.: Rand.

———. 1992. "California's Prison Policy: Causes, Costs, and Consequences." *Prison Journal* 72:8–36.

Pontell, Henry N. 1984. *A Capacity to Punish: The Ecology of Crime and Punishment.* Bloomington: Indiana University Press.

Pontell, Henry N., Wayne N. Welsh, Matthew C. Leone, and Patrick Kinkade. 1989. "Prescriptions for Punishment: Official Ideologies and Jail Overcrowding." *American Journal of Criminal Justice* 14(1):43–70.

President's Commission on Law Enforcement and Administration of Justice. 1968. *The Challenge of Crime in a Free Society.* New York: Avon Books.

Quinney, Richard. 1979. *Criminology.* Boston: Little, Brown.

Reiss, Albert. 1971. *The Police and the Public.* New Haven, Conn.: Yale University Press.

Resnick, Judith, and Nancy Shaw. 1980. "Prisoners of Their Sex: Health Problems of Incarcerated Women," In Ira P. Robbins, ed., *Prisoners' Rights Sourcebook,* 2:319–413. New York: Clark Boardman.

Robbins, Ira P., ed. 1987. *Prisoners and the Law.* New York: Clark Boardman.

Rosenberg, Gerald N. 1991. *The Hollow Hope: Can Courts Bring About Social Change?* Chicago: University of Chicago Press.

Rossum, Ralph A. 1978. *The Politics of the Criminal Justice System.* New York: Marcel Dekker.

Rothman, David J. 1973. "Decarcerating Prisoners and Patients." *Civil Liberties Review* 1:8–30.

———. 1980. *Conscience and Convenience: The Asylum and Its Alternatives in Progressive America.* Boston: Little, Brown.

Rusche, Georg, and Otto Kirchheimer. 1939. *Punishment and Social Structure.* New York: Russell and Russell.

Savitz, Leonard D. 1982. "Official Statistics." In Leonard D. Savitz and Norman Johnston, eds., *Contemporary Criminology,* pp. 3–15. New York: John Wiley and Sons.

Scheingold, Stuart. 1984. *The Politics of Law and Order: Street Crime and Public Policy.* New York: Longman.

Schumacher, Michael. 1987. *Supervised Electronic Confinement Pilot Program: Final Report.* Santa Ana, Calif.: Orange County Probation Department.

Schwartz, Barry. 1978. *Psychology of Learning and Behavior.* New York: W. W. Norton.

Scull, Andrew. 1984. *Decarceration: Community Treatment and the Deviant—A Radical Approach.* Englewood Cliffs, N.J.: Prentice Hall.

Selznick, Philip. 1957. *Leadership in Administration.* New York: Harper & Row.

Sherman, Michael, and Gordon Hawkins. 1981. *Imprisonment in America: Choosing the Future.* Chicago: University of Chicago Press.

Shover, Neal, and Werner J. Einstadter. 1988. *Analyzing American Corrections.* Belmont, Calif.: Wadsworth.

Sieber, Sam D. 1981. *Fatal Remedies.* New York: Plenum.

Simon, Jonathan. 1992. Review Essay: " 'The Long Walk Home' to Politics." *Law and Society Review* 26:923–941.

Skogan, Wesley G. 1975. "Measurement Problems in Official and Survey Crime Rates." *Journal of Criminal Justice* 3:17–32.

Skolnick, Jerome. 1966. *Justice Without Trial.* New York: John Wiley.

Skorneck, Carol. 1993. "Anti-Crime Bill is Passed by Senate." *Philadelphia Inquirer,* 20 November.

Skovron, Sandra E., Joseph E. Scott, and Francis T. Cullen. 1988. "Prison

Crowding: Public Attitudes Toward Strategies of Population Control." *Journal of Research in Crime and Delinquency* 25:150–169.

Slater, Philip E. 1976. *The Pursuit of Loneliness: American Culture at the Breaking Point.* Rev. ed. Boston, Mass.: Beacon Press.

Smykla, John O. 1981. *Community-Based Corrections: Principles and Practices.* New York: Macmillan.

Spector, Malcolm, and John I. Kitsuse. 1977. *Constructing Social Problems.* Menlo Park, Calif.: Cummings.

Stogdill, Ralph M. 1974. *Handbook of Leadership.* New York: Free Press.

Sturm, Susan. 1985. "Special Masters Aid in Compliance Efforts." *National Prison Project Journal* 6:9–12.

Susskind, Lawrence, and Jeffrey Cruikshank. 1987. *Breaking the Impasse: Consensual Approaches to Resolving Public Disputes.* New York: Basic Books.

Sutton, John R. 1987. "Doing Time: Dynamics of Imprisonment in the Reformist State." *American Sociological Review* 52:612–630.

Sykes, Gresham M. 1958. *The Society of Captives.* Princeton: Princeton University Press.

Taft, Philip B., Jr. 1983. "Jail Litigation: Winning in Court Is Only Half the Battle." *Corrections Magazine* 9:22–27, 30–31.

Taggart, William A. 1989. "Redefining the Power of the Purse: The Impact of Court-Ordered Prison Reform on State Expenditures for Corrections." *Law and Society Review* 23:241–271.

Thomas, Charles W. 1980. "The Impotence of Correctional Law." In Geoffrey P. Alpert, ed., *Legal Rights of Prisoners,* pp. 243–260. Beverly Hills, Calif.: Sage.

Thomas, Jim, Devin Keeler, and Kathy Harris. 1986. "Issues and Misconceptions in Prisoner Litigation: A Critical View." *Criminology* 24:775–797.

Turner, William B. 1973. "Federal Jurisdiction and Practice in Prisoner Cases." In Michele G. Hermann and Marilyn G. Haft, eds., *Prisoners' Rights Sourcebook,* 1:243–252. New York: Clark Boardman.

UCLA Law Review. 1973. Note: "Judicial Intervention in Corrections: The California Experience—An Empirical Study." *UCLA Law Review* 20:452–580.

University of Illinois Law Forum. 1980. "Preiser v. Rodriguez in Retrospect." In Ira P. Robbins, ed., *Prisoners' Rights Sourcebook,* 2:199–230. New York: Clark Boardman.

U.S. Department of Justice. 1988. *Police Chiefs and Sheriffs Rank Their Criminal Justice Needs.* NCJ-113061. Washington, D.C.: GPO.

———. 1990a. *Justice Expenditures and Employment, 1988.* NCJ-124132. Washington, D.C.: GPO.

———. 1990b. *A Survey of Intermediate Sanctions.* NCJ-124132. Washington, D.C.: GPO.

———. 1991a. *Census of Local Jails, 1988, Volume I: Selected Findings, Methodology, and Summary Tables.* NCJ-127992. Washington, D.C.: Bureau of Justice Statistics, U.S. Department of Justice.

———. 1991b. *Criminal Victimization in the U.S.: 1989.* NCJ-129391. Washington, D.C.: GPO.

———. 1991c. *Criminal Victimization in the U.S.: 1973–88 Trends.* NCJ-129392. Washington, D.C.: GPO.

———. 1992a. *Jail Inmates 1991.* NCJ-134726. Washington, D.C.: GPO.

———. 1992b. *National Update,* vol. 2, no. 1. NCJ–137059. Washington, D.C.: GPO.

———. 1992c. *Prisoners in 1991.* NCJ-134729. Washington, D.C.: GPO.

———. 1993. *Jail Inmates 1992.* NCJ-143284. Washington, D.C.: GPO.

Weick, Karl. 1976. "Educational Organizations as Loosely Coupled Systems." *Administrative Science Quarterly* 21:1–19.

Welsh, Wayne N. 1990. "A Comparative Analysis of Court Orders Against California County Jails: Intervention and Impact." Ph.D. dissertation, University of California, Irvine.

———. 1992a. "The Dynamics of Jail Reform Litigation: A Comparative Analysis of Litigation in California Counties." *Law and Society Review* 26:591–625.

———. 1992b. "Court Orders and County Correctional Expenditures: Power of the Purse?" *Law and Policy* 14:277–311.

———. 1993a. "Changes in Arrest Policies as a Result of Court Orders Against County Jails." *Justice Quarterly* 10:89–120.

———. 1993b. "Ideologies and Incarceration: Legislator Attitudes Toward Jail Overcrowding." *Prison Journal* 73:46–71.

Welsh, Wayne N., Matthew C. Leone, Patrick T. Kinkade, and Henry N. Pontell. 1991. "The Politics of Jail Overcrowding: Public Attitudes and Official Policies." In Joel A. Thompson and G. Larry Mays, eds., *American Jails: Public Policy Issues,* pp. 131–147. Chicago: Nelson-Hall.

Welsh, Wayne N., and Henry N. Pontell. 1991. "Counties in Court: Interorganizational Adaptations to Jail Litigation in California." *Law and Society Review* 25:73–101.

Welsh, Wayne N., Henry N. Pontell, Matthew C. Leone, and Patrick Kinkade. 1990. "Jail Overcrowding: An Analysis of Policy Makers' Perceptions." *Justice Quarterly* 7:341–370.

Wener, Richard, William Frazier, and Jay Farbstein. 1987. "Building Better Jails." *Psychology Today* (June): 40–49.

Wilson, William Julius. 1987. *The Truly Disadvantaged.* Chicago: University of Chicago Press.

Winfree, L. Thomas, Jr., and John D. Wooldredge. 1991. "Exploring Suicides and Deaths by Natural Causes in America's Large Jails: A Panel Study of Institutional Change, 1978 and 1983." In Joel A. Thompson and G. Larry Mays, eds., *American Jails: Public Policy Issues,* pp. 63–78. Chicago: Nelson Hall.

Wohl, Alexander. 1992. "Where There's Smoke: Testing the Boundaries of Prisoner Rights." *ABA Journal* December: 55–56.

Wood, Robert C., ed. 1990. *Remedial Law: When Courts Become Administrators.* Amherst: University of Massachusetts Press.

Wooldredge, John D., and L. Thomas Winfree, Jr. 1992. "An Aggregate-Level Study of Inmate Suicides and Deaths Due to Natural Causes in U.S. Jails." *Journal of Research in Crime and Delinquency* 29:466–479.

Yackle, Larry W. 1989. *Reform and Regret.* New York: Oxford University Press.

Yale Law Journal 1979. Note: " 'Mastering' Intervention in Prisons." *Yale Law Journal* 88:1062–1091.

Zoroya, Gregg. 1988. "Orange Sues to Stop County from Expanding Branch Jail." *Orange County Register,* January.

Zoroya, Gregg, and Barbara A. Serrano. 1988. "Judge Blocks Plan for County Jail in Anaheim." *Orange County Register,* 7 June.

Zupan, Linda L. 1991. *Jails: Reform and the New Generation Philosophy.* Cincinnati, Ohio: Anderson.

# Cases and Statutes

**CASES CITED**

*Balla v. Idaho Board of Corrections*, 656 F. Supp. 1108 (D. Idaho 1987).

*Beck v. County of Santa Clara*, 204 Cal. App. 3d 789, 251 Cal. Rptr. 444 (1988).

*Becker v. County of Merced*, No. 71999 (Cal. Super. Ct., County of Merced, 31 March 1988).

*Bell v. Wolfish*, 441 U.S. 520 (1979).

*Bounds v. Smith*, 430 U.S. 817, 52 L. Ed. 2d 72, 97 S. Ct. 1491 (1977).

*Branson et al. v. Winter et al.*, No. 78807 (Cal. Super. Ct., County of Santa Clara, 21 August 1981).

*Brown v. Board of Education*, 347 U.S. 483 (1954).

*Brown v. Board of Education*, 349 U.S. 294 (1955).

*Casselman et al. v. Graham et al.*, Civil No. S-86-1266 (E.D. Cal., filed 4 August 1987).

*Cherco et al. v. County of Sonoma et al.*, Nos. C-80-0334, C-82-3767 (N.D. Cal., filed 1 July 1982).

*In re Chessman*, 44 Cal. 2d 1; 279 P. 2d 24 (1955).

*Cooper v. Pate*, 378 U.S. 546 (1964).

*Dillard v. Pitchess*, 399 F. Supp. 1225 (C.D. Cal. 1975).

*Estelle v. Gamble*, 429 U.S. 97 (1976).

*Fischer et al. v. Winter et al.*, 564 F. Supp. 281 (N.D. Cal. 1983).

*Fuller et al. v. Tidwell et al.*, Civil No. 87-03026 (C.D. Cal., 23 November 1987).

*Gates v. Collier*, 501 F. 2d 1291 (5th Cir. 1974).

*Golden et al. v. Taylor et al.*, Civil No. S-86-287 (E.D. Cal., 14 March 1986).

*Hedrick et al. v. Grant et al.*, Civil No. S-76-162 (E.D. Cal., filed 12 November 1976).

*In re Hopper et al., In re Bullard, In re Pre-sentenced Inmates*, Nos. 18866-70, 18900, 18936 (Cal. Super. Ct., County of Solano, 31 July 1985).

*Hudler et al. v. Duffy et al.*, No. 404148 (Cal. Super. Ct., County of San Diego, 12 May 1980).

*In re the Inmate Population of Humboldt County Jail*, Nos. 78675, 78670, 77768, 78276, 78686, 81205 (Cal. Super. Ct., County of Humboldt, 23 January 1987).

*Inmates of A, B, and C Tank, Mendocino County Jail v. Mendocino County Sheriff's Office*, No. 7763-C (Cal. Super. Ct., County of Mendocino, 21 January 1983).

251

*In re Inmates of Nevada County Jail,* Nos. 29862, 29892 (Cal. Super. Ct., County of Nevada, 15 June 1983).

*In re Inmates of Riverside County Jail at Indio v. Ben Clark,* Indio No. 33526 (Cal. Super. Ct., County of Riverside, 29 October 1981.)

*Inmates of the Riverside County Jail at Indio v. Clark,* 192 Cal. Rptr. 823 (App. 1983).

*In re Inmates at Riverside County Jail (Doss et al.),* Nos. 151486, 150928, 151686, 151879 (Cal. Super. Ct., County of Riverside, 5 May 1983).

*In re Inmates of Riverside County Jail at Riverside v. Clark,* No. C-169226 (Cal. Super. Ct., County of Riverside, 11 February 1987).

*In re Inmates of Sybil Brand,* No. C-50506 (Cal. Super. Ct., County of Los Angeles, 1 December 1978).

*Inmates of Sybil Brand v. County of Los Angeles,* 181 Cal. Rptr. 599 (Cal. App. 3 Dist. 1982).

*Jahanshahi et al. v. Carpenter et al., Inmates of Santa Barbara County Jail v. Carpenter et al.,* Nos. 156957, 152487, 158862 (Cal. Super. Ct., County of Santa Barbara, 14 November 1985).

*Jones et al. v. Brooks et al.,* No. 84429 (Cal. Super. Ct., County of Butte, 22 February 1985).

*Jones v. Wittenberg, 73 F.R.D. 82, 85 (N.D. Ohio 1976).*

*Kinale et al. v. Dowe et al.,* Civil No. 73-374 (S.D. Cal., filed 29 October 1973).

*Marin County Jail Inmates v. Prandi,* No. 106849 (Cal. Super. Ct., County of Marin, 23 June 1982).

*Mariscal et al. v. Lowe et al., Civil No. S-79-666 (E.D. Cal., filed 16 July 1981).*

*Martino v. Carey, 563 F. Supp. 984 (D. Ore. 1983).*

*Mendoza et al. v. County of Tulare et al.,* No. 91235 (Cal. Super. Ct., County of Tulare, 5 September 1985).

*Meyers et al. v. Jalaty,* No. SP-51213 (Cal. Super. Ct., County of Ventura, 2 June 1983).

*Miller v. Carson,* 401 F. Supp. 835 (M.D. Fla. 1975).

*Miller et al. v. Carpenter et al.,* Nos. 138635, 138720, 139630, 139944, 140032, 140045, 140090 (Cal. Super. Ct., County of Santa Barbara, 28 July 1982).

*Monroe v. Pape,* 365 U.S. 167 (1961).

*In re Morgan, In re Ransbury, and Consolidated Cases,* Nos. 281302-0, 281438-2, 284164-1, 308318-5, 316580-0, 286040-1, 285427-1, 289487-1, 289488-9, 287160-6 (Cal. Super. Ct., County of Fresno, 12 January 1983).

*Muehlberg et al. v. Madera County Dept. of Corrections,* No. 38213 (Cal. Super. Ct., County of Madera, 25 April 1985).

*Offield et al. v. Scott,* No. 46871 (Cal. Super. Ct., County of Placer, 12 May 1977).

*Parsons v. Nunes,* No. 64070 (Cal. Super. Ct., County of Placer, 7 November 1984).

*Pasadena City Board of Education v. Spangler,* 427 U.S. 424 (1976).

*Pell v. Procunier,* 417 U.S. 817, 71 Ohio Op. 2d 195 (1974).

*In re Priest on Habeas Corpus (Consolidated Cases)*, Crim. No. 22427 (Cal. Sup. Ct., filed 20 September 1984).

*Procunier v. Martinez*, 416 U.S. 396, 94 S. Ct. 1800 (1974).

*Pugh v. Locke*, 406 F. Supp. 318 (M.D. Ala. 1976).

*Rhodes v. Chapman*, 452 U.S. 337 (1981).

*Rutherford v. Pitchess [Block]*, 457 F. Supp. 104 (C.D. Cal. 1979).

*Sandoval et al. v. Noren et al.*, No. C-72-2213 (N.D. Cal., filed 26 August 1983).

*Smith et al. v. County of Tehama et al.*, No. 4166 (Cal. Super. Ct., County of Tehama, 23 September, 1986).

*Smith et al. v. Dyer et al.*, Nos. 74184, 63779, 76086, 750121 (Cal. Super. Ct., County of Alameda, 15 August 1983).

*Smith v. Wade*, 75 L. Ed. 2d 632, 103 S. Ct. 1625 (1983).

*In re Smith, In re Gonzales*, Nos. 43450, 44255 (Cal. Super. Ct., County of San Joaquin, 8 May 1989).

*Spain v. Procunier*, 600 F. 2d 189 (9th Cir. 1979).

*Sparks v. Frazier*, Nos. 31293, 31494 (Cal. Super. Ct., County of Madera, 20 July 1984).

*Stewart et al. v. Gates et al.*, 450 F. Supp. 583 (C.D. Cal. 1978).

*Stone et al. v. City and County of San Francisco*, No. C-78-2774 (N.D. Cal., filed 15 July 1982).

*Szynkowski v. Brown, Hall v. Brown*, Nos. 9093, 9155 (Cal. Super. Ct., County of Trinity, 29 May 1986).

*Travis et al. v. Hippard et al.*, No. 51309 (Cal. Super. Ct., County of Napa, 19 August 1988).

*Wilson v. Seiter*, 111 S. Ct. 2321 (1991).

*Wilson et al. v. Superior Court et al. (Branson)*, 240 Cal. Rptr. 131 (Cal. App. 6 Dist. 1987).

*Wolff v. McDonnell*, 418 U.S. 539 (1974).

*Yancey v. Rainey*, No. 29868 (Cal. Super. Ct., County of Contra Costa, 31 March 1985).

*Yeager et al. v. Smith et al.*, No. CV-F-87-493 (E.D. Cal., filed 1 January 1989).


## STATUTES CITED

California Administrative Code, title 15, subchapter 4, sections 1000 et seq. (West 1954 & 1992 Supp.).

California Health and Safety Code (West 1954 & 1992 Supp.).

California Penal Code, pt. 2, title 12 (West 1954 & 1992 Supp.).

Civil Rights Act, 42 USC section 1983 (1970).

# Index

access to courts: Contra Costa County litigation on, 67; effect of attorney selection on violations involving, charged in complaint, 63; and inmate rights, 59; Orange County litigation on, 161; Santa Clara County litigation on, 68; success rates in plaintiffs' obtaining relief sought for complaints involving, 76, 207; violations alleged involving, 62, 63, 205

ACLU. *See* ideologically committed attorneys

administrative segregation: Orange County litigation on, 94, 125; Santa Clara County litigation on, 112; success rates in plaintiffs' obtaining relief sought for, 76; as violation alleged, 205

administrators, of correctional institutions: benefits to, from jail litigation, 153; effect of, on overcrowding and related litigation, 30–32, 36; judges' deferral to expertise of, 10; resistance of, to court-ordered change, 152, 155–157, 186, 198

Alabama, documentation of abuses in, 10

Alameda County, litigation in, 166

Allen, Bruce, 89–93, 121, 122, 133, 134–135, 143, 177–178, 210, 213

American Correctional Association, 215

American Jail Association, 215

Annual Survey of Jails, 22

anticipatory prevention, 158, 217

apathy, public, regarding correctional institutions, 13

Arkansas: documentation of abuses in, 10; judicial intervention and jails in, 157; news media as sensitizing public in, 158

Arneson, Richard, 67, 68, 85–86, 131, 171, 210

arrest rates: impact of court orders on, 185; as triggering factor in jail lawsuits, 41

attorneys: access to, 84; court orders involving communication of, with prisoners, 157; legal aid, 41; negotiations as affected by personal styles of, 137. *See also* counsel, choice of, in jail litigation; ideologically committed attorneys; public defenders

Avakian, Spurgeon, 117, 134, 143, 146–147

bail, remedies ordered in absence of complaint involving, 75. *See also* release on own recognizance (ROR)

*Balla v. Idaho Board of Corrections* (1987), 59

Bancroft, Richard A., 166

bathing facilities. *See* hygiene

bed availability: and double-bunking, 11, 120; Orange County litigation on, 95, 122, 123, 161; Santa Clara County litigation on, 68, 86, 87

*Bell v. Wolfish* (1979), 11, 122

Black Muslims, discrimination against imprisoned, 10, 59

Blumstein, Alfred, 30

body cavity searches, constitutionality of, 11

books, for inmates, 68, 93, 156, 157

*Bounds v. Smith* (1977), 59

*Branson v. Winter* (1981), 68, 69. *See also* Santa Clara County

brutality, and mistreatment of inmates: documentation of, 10; Orange County litigation on, 69; success rates in plaintiffs' obtaining relief sought for, 76

budget constraints. *See* financing and funding

Buffington, John, 131, 169